The Tender Cut

The Tender Cut

Inside the Hidden World of Self-Injury

Patricia A. Adler and Peter Adler

NEW YORK UNIVERSITY PRESS

New York and London

NEW YORK UNIVERSITY PRESS
New York and London
www.nyupress.org

References to Internet websites (URLs) were accurate at the time of writing.
Neither the author nor New York University Press is responsible for URLs
that may have expired or changed since the manuscript was prepared.

Library of Congress Cataloging-in-Publication Data

Adler, Patricia A., 1952–
The tender cut : the rise and transformation of self-injury /
Patricia A. Adler and Peter Adler.
p. ; cm.
Includes bibliographical references and index.
ISBN 978-0-8147-0506-3 (cl : alk. paper) — ISBN 978-0-8147-0507-0
(pb : alk. paper) — ISBN 978-0-8147-0518-6 (e-book)
1. Self-injurious behavior. 2. Adaptability (Psychology) 3. Social isolation.
4. Stress (Psychology) I. Adler, Peter, 1951- II. Title.
[DNLM: 1. Self-Injurious Behavior—psychology. 2. Adaptation, Psychological.
3. Social Environment. 4. Social Isolation—psychology. 5. Stress, Psychological—
psychology. WM 165]
RC569.5.S48A35   2011
362.196'8582—dc22   2010053656

New York University Press books are printed on acid-free paper,
and their binding materials are chosen for strength and durability.
We strive to use environmentally responsible suppliers and materials
to the greatest extent possible in publishing our books.

Manufactured in the United States of America

c 10 9 8 7 6 5 4 3 2 1
p 10 9 8 7 6 5 4 3 2 1

To Mom
Who never hesitates to help,
and who encouraged us to believe that
this book will make a difference.

Contents

Acknowledgments

Some of our previous books have explored topics such as upper-level drug dealers and smugglers, college athletes, our own children and their friends, and employees at Hawaiian resorts. In part, all of these venues were either close to home and/or close to our hearts, and they can be seen as having a fun and playful side. In addition, in all of these previous studies, we have taken in-depth participant-observation roles in conducting the research. Not so here. There was nothing fun or funny about exploring the lives of the self-injurers portrayed in this book. It was, however, compellingly interesting.

We ourselves have never self-injured. Other than being admitted into many of the chat rooms that self-injurers visit, we were not a part of this community. However, no other study of ours has been so intense, so intimate, so intricately entwined in the travails and turmoil of people's lives, and so embedded in both the psychological and sociological aspects of the human condition. What you are about to read may strike you as gruesome, morbid, and depressing but also fascinating, revealing, and important. There are stories of struggle and pain mixed with stories of self-understanding, triumph, and redemption. For admitting us into the most private aspects of their lives, we could not be more thankful to the over one hundred people who poured out their deepest stories and feelings, conjectures and analysis, either face to face, by telephone, or through email, and the literally thousands of people who opened their hearts and lives through email and chat-room conversations. Obviously, without their generosity, openness, and candor, this book could never have been written.

There have been several scholars who have been particularly supportive of this research throughout the past 10 years. People such as David Altheide, Jason Boardman, Dan Cress, William Force, Leslie Irvine, the late John Irwin, Matthew Lust, Carol Rambo, Pepper Schwartz, Phil Vannini, Dennis Waskul, Amy Wilkins, and Hongling Xie gave us feedback, ideas for sources, and intellectual arguments to ponder as we sifted through our data. The faculty in both of our departments at the University of Colorado and the University of Denver were encouraging as we spent a decade working on this longitudinal project. We were fortunate enough to have been invited to present our ideas at two international conferences, in Belgium and France, where European scholars provided feedback and information about the phenomenon of self-injury on the Continent.

Our friends, ever interested in our work, also were encouraging and helpful during these years. Willing to listen to our stories or always asking us about what we were finding out were such people as Sosie Bacon, Tony and Debbie DiRenzo, Heidi Glow, Linda and Bill Jacobsen, Jane Horowitz, Elizabeth Kibbee, Steven and Stephanie Kless, Dana and Steve Newinsky, Regina and Kevin Richter, and Marc Taron. Close friends such as David Cain, Justin Gottschlich, Bob Lombardo, and Kevin Vryan were especially helpful in teaching us about the complexities of cyber space, as it was evolving and developing in the first decade of the twenty-first century. These people continually reminded us that what we were doing would be of interest to a general audience and not just members of the medical, psychological, sociological, or academic communities.

Many of our students, some professors in their own right now, also stuck with us, served as sounding boards to our developing ideas, and saw the potential in the research we were doing. In particular, we would like to thank Amanda Conley, Marc Eaton, Lisa Friedlen, Molly George, Joanna Gregson, Ross Haenfler, Allison Hicks, Jennifer Lois, Patrick O'Brien, Lori Peek, Cooper Schwartz, Katherine Sirles, and Jesse Smith. A special shout-out must go to Katy Irwin, not only a former student but a member of our family, who should be credited with giving us the idea for the title of this book.

We were fortunate to have an army of students at the University of Colorado who assisted us in coding the thousands of emails and postings we received and in transcribing the interviews. The coders were Kevin Bukstein, Nichole Golden, Amanda Hong, Kaela Joseph, Ayla Karlin, Lizzie Lerman, Kristin Nelson, Lindsay Okonowsky, Nick Passanante, Kate Plapinger, Nikki Ross-Zehnder, Seth Schy, and Emily Shapiro. The transcribers were Pamela Barnett, Jeffrey Benn, Elizabeth Combs, Ariel Friedman, Rickey Gates, Peter Kleinberg, Kelsey McVey, Amanda Nicholas, Rachel Orland, Julie Richter, Casey Temanson, Jacobi Wade, and Alexandra Wolf. Professor Larry Boehm at the University of Colorado provided funding for the transcription through the Undergraduate Research Opportunities Program. We are grateful to Karen Conterio and Wendy Lader at SAFE Alternatives, who helped us assemble a national list of therapeutic referrals for people who contacted us for information and interviews.

During our years in academia, we have associated with a score of editors or more, all of them professional, knowledgeable, and a joy with whom to work. In this book, it has been our singular pleasure to work with Ilene Kalish at NYU Press, who is fast becoming one of the visionary editors in sociology. The list that she has put together at NYU Press is impressive, and we are proud to be among her charges. Ever since we first approached Ilene about the book, she has been supportive, patient (beyond belief), and trusting in our abilities to come through with a quality final product. We could not expect more from an editor. In addition, the intrepid Aiden Amos, Ilene's assistant, was always there for us, to answer a question, to provide information, or by the end, just as a friend who wanted to help this book see the light of day. Others at NYU Press, such as Despina Papazoglou Gimbel, Andrew Katz, Mary Beth Jarrad, and Betsy Steve were instrumental in the production, copy-editing, marketing, and publicity for this book. Finally, there were two anonymous reviewers, who provided detailed, critical, and helpful suggestions to an earlier manuscript.

No book is ever completed in a vacuum. Throughout the years, our family has been fascinated and intrigued by the stories we told, bringing their own questions and general cultural knowledge and curiosity to the project. They were enormously helpful in offering and responding to our developing ideas. Now grown, Jori and Brye continue to be a source of inspiration for us. We are also lucky enough to now add another member, BJ Miller, our son-in-law and a palliative care physician, who better than anyone we know understands the vagaries of human suffering and shows compassion every day toward humanity. Our siblings, nieces, and nephews are constant reminders of the goodness in people, as each of them values camaraderie, charity, and hope. Our mother Bea, 90 years young, and father, Ben, 85, teach us that with age comes wisdom and faith, lessons we hope will stay with us for a lifetime.

However, there is one special family member, our mother Pat Heller, a family therapist, and the person to whom this book is dedicated, who constantly reminded us that the work we were doing could make an impact, that there were readers out there who needed to hear what we had to say, and that the importance of this project was to give voice to the silent self-injurers who are out there. She also convinced us that practitioners in her field would be interested in learning more about this behavior and that a sociological approach, one that they heard all too infrequently, offered a critical dimension into understanding this behavior. Mom always kept our heads in the game, our chins up, and pushed us to the finish line.

Portions of earlier versions of this work have appeared in the following publications: Patricia A. Adler and Peter Adler, "Self-Injurers as Loners: The Social Organization of Solitary Deviance," *Deviant Behavior* 26(4) (2005), used by permission of Taylor & Francis; Patricia A. Adler and Peter Adler, "The Demedicalization of Self-Injury: From Psychopathology to Sociological Deviance," *Journal of Contemporary Ethnography* 36(5) (2007), used by permission of Sage Publications; "The Cyber Worlds of Self-Injurers: Deviant Communities, Relationships, and Selves," *Symbolic Interaction* 31(1) (2008), used by permission of the University of California Press. We are grateful to the publishers and copyright holders for permission to reprint this material.

Introduction

Self-injury has existed for nearly all of recorded history. Although it has been defined and regarded in various ways over time, its rise in the 1990s and early 2000s has taken a specific, although contested, form and meaning. We focus in this book on the deliberate, nonsuicidal destruction of one's own body tissue, incorporating practices such as self-cutting, burning, branding, scratching, picking at skin (also called acne mutilation, psychogenic or neurotic excoriation, self-inflicted dermatosis or dermatillomania), reopening wounds, biting, head banging, hair pulling (trichotillomania), hitting (with a hammer or other object), swallowing or embedding objects, breaking bones or teeth, tearing or severely biting cuticles or nails, and chewing the inside of the mouth. Our goal here is to discuss the form of this latest incarnation of self-injury, now often regarded as a typical behavior among adolescents, describing and analyzing it through the voices and from the perspective of those who practice it. We call these people the "practitioners."

Referring to self-injury as "tender" in the title of this book carries with it a distinct purpose, especially since previous treatments have often used harsher words, such as "mutilation," "scarred souls," and "a bright red scream." It may seem oxymoronic to refer to cutting oneself intentionally as *tender*. By this term we intend to convey what the individuals we studied thought about this behavior, which was accepting. Nearly all of these people regarded this behavior as a coping strategy, perhaps one they wished they did not need (and might someday be able to quit), but one that functioned to fill needs for them nevertheless. Several referred to it as a form of "self-therapy," noting that when things were rough and they had nowhere else to turn, a brief interlude helped them to pull themselves together. People felt better after injuring than they had before. Many used terminology to describe it such as "a friend" and "my own special thing." We dedicate ourselves here to representing their perspectives and providing a nonjudgmental voice for their experiences.

The Social Transformation of Self-Injury

The rise of self-injury has been accompanied by a significant transformation in its prevalence and social meaning. The past several centuries saw this behavior regarded as a form of psychological pathology, practiced largely by people, especially young, white, middle-class women, who suffered from mental illness. However, during the 1990s the behavior began to expand, taking on new connotations and converts as it did. In this book we describe how self-injury changed from being the limited and hidden practice of the psychologically disordered to becoming a cult youth phenomenon, then a form of more typical teenage angst, and then the province of a wide swath of socially disempowered individuals in broader age, race, gender, and class groups.

As its practice spread, it became associated with different groups who used it in myriad contexts to express their anguish and disaffection with society. Unconventional youth used it to claim membership and express status in an alternative, hard-core punk subculture that over time morphed into the Goth and later the emo subcultures. Adolescents used it as a mechanism to cope with the traumas typically associated with the dramatic physical and personal changes, shifting social alliances, identity uncertainty, raw nastiness, inarticulateness, insecurity, and general emotional drama associated with the 'tween and teenage years of life. From here it spread to populations who were structurally disadvantaged, for various reasons, and lacked the social power necessary to ameliorate their situations or improve their lives.

In expanding, self-injury took on new social meanings, remaining a behavior practiced by psychologically troubled individuals who used it to soothe their trauma, but it also became a legitimated mode of emotional expression and relief among a much wider population. Society learned, in small circles at first but diffusing concentrically outward, that people who were neither suicidal nor mentally ill were using self-inflicted injury to cope with life's difficulties. The stigma attached to this behavior was regarded initially as shocking, disgusting, and dangerous. It then evolved to becoming considered merely troubled and finally to representing an inarticulate and underappreciated cry for help. By the end of the twenty-first century's first decade, self-injury represented an entrenched and still growing phenomenon that could easily be considered a fad. Although not the expression of a happy or typical life experience, it nonetheless conveyed an allure of daring, dangerousness, risk, desperation, and hope that many people, especially youth, found attractive. As a result, it spread rapidly among populations vulnerable to this mystique, changing from being something that was generally self-invented by individuals in private to a socially learned and contagious behavior.

In this process it became transformed from an essentially psychological disorder into a sociological occurrence. The way people injure their bodies is socially contoured, shaped by various subsets of normative and alternative subcultures. Yet, without wanting to pathologize it, we acknowledge that self-injury falls within the realm of a social problem. There are harms potentially associated with its practice that include social isolation, ostracization, labeling and stigma, infection, scarring, and habituation. As such, a greater understanding of its full dimensions is important from a public health perspective.

Involved for many years with a hidden and demonized practice, self-injurers suffered from society's views of their behavior. For many, isolated or faced with physicians (particularly in emergency rooms) and mental-health professionals largely uninformed, misinformed, or judgmental about what was seen as their self-destructive actions, treatment often made their lives worse instead of better. Yet although they found themselves isolated and powerless, self-injurers have fought to give some legitimacy to what most people see as deviant acts. This has been difficult because self-injury tends to be conducted covertly, secretly, and privately. Only in the early twenty-first century did self-injurers begin to find a common community, and then only in cyber space, where they could communicate, learn from each other, and offer each other knowledge and understanding. One online support group offered this assessment of the definition and extent of self-injury:

> An estimated one percent of American's use physical self-harm as a way of coping with stress; the rate of self-injury in other industrial nations is probably similar. Still, self-injury remains a taboo subject, a behavior that is considered freakish or outlandish and is highly stigmatized by medical professionals and the lay public alike. Self-harm, also called self-injury, self-inflicted violence, or self-mutilation, can be defined as self-inflicted physical harm severe enough to cause tissue damage or leave visible marks that do not fade within a few hours. Acts done for purposes of suicide or for ritual, sexual, or ornamentation purposes are not considered self-injury.[1]

The terminology used to refer to this behavior has gone by the various names listed in the quotation in addition to *deliberate self-harm syndrome* and *self-wounding*. We choose, here, to use the term *self-injury*, although in the original psycho-medical treatments of this topic it was called *self-mutilation*, and the term *self-harm* is popular with many European practitioners and sites. In a politicized field, our decision is based on two factors. First, *self-injury* was the idiom most commonly used by the people we studied in person and online, who noted that terms such as *mutilation* imply, inaccurately, that the goal is self-disfigurement. We also found the idiom *self-injury* the most common in the small collection of inpatient treatment centers that arose during the early twenty-first century focusing specifically on self-injurious behavior;[2] these centers turned people away from words such as *cutting* or *mutilation* because they were too triggering. Following our belief in the importance of language and our commitment to practitioners' views and definitions, we use this term throughout the book.

Self-Injury and the Body

The body plays a central role in self-injurers' means of self-solace and self-expression. This topic begs for an embodied analysis, since people who practice it use their bodies as the vehicle for enacting and relieving their trauma. They write the text of their inner pain on their skin, transforming themselves as they do so. Scholarly focus on the body was largely overlooked until recently, with the specifically embodied nature of culture and society either ignored or assumed to reside within the white, male, heterosexual, patriarchal, able-bodied, adult, first-world, middle-class experience.[3] The body was taken for granted as always present, hence never a subject of analysis. Since the mid-1980s, however, the body and embodiment have become objects of a blossoming critical reflection. Focus has been directed at the social body, the way we as people relate to each other as social beings through our bodies, and how social relationships shape our bodies.

There is not a single strain of embodied theory and research but a host of topics, themes, and issues situated within the various social sciences and grounded in a wide array of theoretical traditions and levels of analysis. Various scholarly approaches to the body exist, ranging from structural (Marxism, feminism) to cultural (Durkheim, cultural studies) to symbolic interactionist (Weber, pragmatism, symbolic interactionism) and psycho-medical (psychoanalytic, biological, medical) perspectives.

One difference in these perspectives involves the tension between viewing the body as object or subject. Perspectives that take bodies as cultural objects look at the way they are molded to conform to external rules and regimens. This involves examining how people's bodies are shaped by the norms of public and private bodily behavior, the regulation of body habits, and the social ownership and control of the body. Objectifying the body looks at the way it is controlled by social training, bifurcating the mind-body relationship but giving primary consideration to the systems of society as they are internalized by people. Bodies, then, are objects shaped by society and culture. Foucault has been especially influential in raising awareness of the way mechanisms of bodily control are influenced by the "panopticon" of institutions such as prisons, schools, hospitals, and social mores, leading people to internalize the omnipresent gaze of society.[4] Society, thus, teaches people to control their bodies-as-objects.

Consideration of the body-as-subject tends to individualize embodiment, focusing on how people create and inhabit their bodies. This approach looks at the basis of bodily understandings in individuals' experiences. Individual concerns are elevated beyond the level of culture and social structure, a perspective that associates this approach with a neoliberal conception of free will and individual rights. The psycho-medical tradition is most strongly associated with this perspective, having a dominating influence on the field, with its focus on the individual's body at the expense of social forces. The body is thus the product of self-creation and self-reconstruction but is viewed through the lens of psycho-medical approaches to the self. Relatedly, the body social may be considered either the prime symbol of the self or the creation of society, something people have versus something they are, individual and personal or common to all of humanity, and either the acting subject or the acted-upon object.[5]

None of these approaches has more intrinsic merit than others; they must all be balanced against each other. We argue that the body and its embodiment must be viewed as reciprocally incorporating all of these dimensions and processes: as nuanced, complex, and multifaceted, subject to the interweaving of subjective experiences, interpersonal interactions, cultural processes, social organization, institutional arrangements, and social structure.[6]

In this book we consider how self-injurers' lives and experiences are shaped through the cultural and structural forces that surround them and, at the same time, how they view and use their bodies, including offering a temporal understanding of how this may change over the course of their self-injurious careers.

Types of Self-Injury

Portraits of individual people and their behavior, although isolated, may coalesce to give a rich sense of the range of practices in which the self-injurers we discuss were involved. In this section we offer some vignettes depicting a variety of self-injurious behaviors. These are not intended to provide a comprehensive landscape of all acts that could be classified under this rubric, but when taken together, they give readers a sense of what to imagine when picturing self-injurious acts.

By far the most common behavior we encountered was *cutting*, and this practice has received the most recognition, in scholarly, medical, and popular outlets. One estimate of the prevalence of various acts, in comparison to each other, suggests the following distribution:[7]

Cutting: 72 percent
Burning: 35 percent
Self-hitting: 30 percent
Interference w/ wound healing: 22 percent
Hair pulling: 10 percent
Bone breaking: 8 percent
Multiple methods: 78 percent (included in above)[8]

Janice, a 22-year-old graduate student from a loving and supportive family, had been raped early in high school and was subsequently plagued in both high school and college by interpersonal issues and fears that men were stalking her. She sometimes felt on shaky ground socially and was rejected by friends for telling stories. She described what became a typical episode of cutting:

I think I was fifteen [in 1994]. It was right after—it was about four months after I was raped. So it was a traumatic time. And I had just a really bad day, huge fight with everyone in my family, miserable day at school. I was thinking nonstop about that event, and I went to take a bath. When I was in the bath, I was shaving my legs, and I cut myself really badly, and it made me feel a lot better and gave me something else to focus on. For some reason, if you're that upset, seeing that you're physically hurt, seeing blood in the water, or whatever, made me feel a lot better.

An online poster noted that sometimes cutting was the only thing that could give her relief:

The release that I get is something that talking about it cannot give me nor anything my parents could have given me. SI is almost like a drug that you want to stop, but are not able to. You know that what you are doing is wrong, but stopping it is not possible until the person is ready to say that I do not want this in my life any longer. Speaking only for myself, I know that things can get really bad and I am not able to deal very well with the emotions of it all and I become overwhelmed and I feel that the only option that I have is to harm myself.

Second in prevalence was *burning*. People innovated in their burning, using all sorts of implements, from matches to grill igniters, chemicals, and a range of creative sources. Erica, with whom we talked when she was an 18-year-old college freshman, had been sexually abused by her older brother when she was seven. Although she claimed that the abuse was not connected to her self-injury, she never revealed it to her family members, who glorified her brother. This made her feel isolated from her parents and siblings and hung over her head. In 1998, when she was 12, she heard about self-injury from a television show, and shortly after that one of her classmates confessed to her that she was cutting. Erica progressed from scratching herself with her fingernails to using a paper clip, through a range of different utensils, before finally settling on an X-Acto knife. Then she added burning. She described the way she used to burn:

Q: When did you try burning?
ERICA: I started burning in, like, probably my sophomore year.
Q: What did you use?
ERICA: Curling iron. That's all I ever used, a curling iron.
Q: How did you do it?
ERICA: I would just literally just hold the curling iron to my skin until I got a big huge blister thing. Have a random scar from it.
Q: Where did you put it on yourself?
ERICA: I have one here [*shows arm*], and then I did some on my legs and some up here [*shows torso*].
Q: And so you'd heat it up, and how long would you hold it on for?
ERICA: I don't know. It depended. Long enough for me to be satisfied with the results.
Q: How did the burn differ from the cut?
ERICA: The burns were way worse after. Way worse. I—like, obviously it doesn't hurt when you're doing it but afterward. No one's going to tell me that theirs don't hurt. There's no way in hell. That you don't wake up in the middle of the night and just not be able to move. The burns were so much worse after.
Q: From blistering?
ERICA: Yeah. And just, like, I don't know. You've obviously had a burn before, the tightness, I don't know. So I didn't burn that much because of that. But I liked it.

When we spoke with Judy, she was a 21-year-old college student in Louisiana majoring in music therapy. She began her injuring when she was 14, partly as the result of her mother's verbal abusiveness and her parents' constant bickering, which ended in a divorce. Afterward, she felt responsible for her two younger brothers and internalized the blame for her family's situation. Although she primarily cut, she experimented with inflicting chemical burns on herself:

> I had put oven cleaner on my skin and left it there for a while, and it gave me a chemical burn. And it kept oozing even though I was putting Neosporin on it and covering it with Band-Aids, but uh, kept oozing. But my counselor was like, "You should go get that checked out." And it turned out I had a second-degree burn, and the doctor said, "You know, if you would have had a third-degree burn, you would have had to get a skin graft."

Third in popularity among our respondents was *branding*. Jane, who was 19 and a sophomore in college when she spoke to us, had been a model student from a typical, intact family throughout her high school career. A cheerleader, she impressed the people in her school and community as being totally happy and stable. Yet when she was dumped by a boyfriend without a good explanation during her junior year of high school, she tried branding:

> JANE: I would take a coin of some sort and heat it up with a lighter or a candle or something like that just so it got really hot, and I would leave it on my wrist and not touch it and just leave it there until it burned to the point where it cooled down so that all of the heat had gone and burned me.
>
> Q: So you used the flat of the coin?
>
> JANE: Yeah. Just stuck it on there and left it on there. Then senior year I did it a couple times, but it wasn't like something I was doing every weekend. It was like every four to five months. So I only think I did it like three times my senior year, twice my junior year. I did it, I can't remember how many times during my freshman year in college. But it was more often, and I would brand myself for longer with hotter kinds of things. It was a different type of burn; it was a more extreme burn than I had been doing before because the first two times you couldn't really see anything, not that much damage. It looked like I hit my arm on a coffee pot or something like that.

Erica, who was abused by her brother, was intrigued by the whole act of self-injury and tried many different forms, one of which was *bone breaking*. Although she realized that these were things other people did not do, she struggled to hang on to an image of herself as "normal" for as long as she could. She described her experience:

ERICA: I broke my hand.

Q: On purpose?

ERICA: Uh huh.

Q: How did you do that?

ERICA: I—you know those big hotel doors that connect two rooms? There's like a door, like metal, huge. I just held my hand like this on it. I just slammed it in there. I got in a big fight with one of my friends, and I was pissed.

Q: And how did that feel?

ERICA: I really liked it actually, to be honest with you. Yeah, it was good, for sure.

Q: And you slammed your left hand in the door or your right?

ERICA: This one, so left. I'm right-handed.

Q: So how long did that put you out of business in your left hand for? You said you broke it?

ERICA: Yeah, I did. A few weeks. I wouldn't go to the doctor because I did it more than once, and I didn't know if they could tell. But my fingers obviously didn't move, so it had to have been broken right here. And I had just gotten rid of the bump thing, calcium thing, like it just went down. So it wouldn't work for a few weeks, like a month. It was so gross. It was disgusting.

Q: And do you have any attraction or get any benefits out of the scars, blisters, or bumps in between your self-injury episodes?

ERICA: Yeah, I guess. Yeah, I mean, as far as cutting, I would try to never get them to heal. I just liked the fact that they were there. I never put Neosporin on them. So I guess so. Burning, you can't do anything about it anyway. And the hand thing wasn't going away.

Breaking one's bones was actually a fairly common injury for boys, who would take out their anger and frustration on themselves by hitting or punching things. Twenty-year-old Billy described his family background as typically middle-class suburban and his family relations as normal, but he acknowledged that he was not a happy kid. He smashed his hand into a tree and broke it when he was 13, then followed this up at 14 with a suicide attempt by swallowing a full bottle of Tylenol. He was hospitalized twice during his high school years and became a regular cutter during this period. Looking back on his tree incident, Billy later characterized it as early self-injurious behavior.

Bone-breaking was also practiced by kids who felt distress at an early age and did not know why they did it or what it meant. This was more common among people who later displayed long-term patterns of depression or who had problematic family situations, such as Molly. From a strict religious family in rural Texas, 20-year-old Molly was raised in a traditional and authoritarian manner. She described her early injurious behaviors:

MOLLY: I was nine when I started beating myself up and breaking bones. It was never an attention thing for me. It was always—I just hurt, and I don't know how to get rid of the pain. I was the oldest. I felt that I wasn't allowed to cry, I wasn't allowed to show emotion. And when I would break down and start crying when I was younger, my dad would walk in my room and go, "If you're going to cry, let me give you a reason to cry." And he'd pull off his belt, and he'd buff me.

Q: And what made you decide to break your bones? Do you remember?

MOLLY: I was standing in the garage doing something, and I was always my dad's tomboy. And I was building something out of wood, and my dad walked into the garage and said, "Use this little-girl hammer; it's lighter." And he made me mad because I was like, "Well what's the difference? We're both people. Why should I have to use a little-girl hammer, and my brother gets to use the big one?" And I was like, "Well, I'll show him that I can use the big-person hammer." And I broke my wrist in three places.

Q: You smashed your wrist with a hammer?

MOLLY: By holding my arm against the work bench and taking the hammer in my right hand and just hitting it repetitively, over and over and over, until it hurt so bad I couldn't do it anymore.

These types of episodes were accompanied throughout her childhood and adolescence by repetitive intentional bicycle accidents that gave her hairline fractures and by running into and punching brick walls with her fists. From there she tried shooting herself with the nail guns her father used in his construction work and eventually graduated to full-fledged cutting.

Less severe than breaking one's bones is self-inflicted *bruising*. Lois grew up in a divorced family in Las Vegas and had lived in some tough neighborhoods.

She eventually joined a Goth subculture and cut, but as a youth she had a history of bruising herself. Slamming her forearm, forehead, calves, or shins into hard objects, her goal was the pain and swelling that resulted. This numbed her emotional feelings when she had no other outlet. Joanna, a 19-year-old college sophomore, had a traumatic childhood because, after her parents divorced, her mother remarried an abuser. He began by verbally humiliating Joanna about her weight and her looks, and he eventually progressed to hitting, punching, and slamming her against walls. Joanna's cutting started at 14 in an attempt to get her mother's help, but her mother brushed it off as "attention-getting." Joanna described another of the ways she self-injured in futile attempts to rescue herself from this desperately unhappy situation:

JOANNA: I used to give myself black eyes.
Q: How did you do that?
JOANNA: I would take my lacrosse stick or a ball and pound constantly.
Q: In your eye socket?
JOANNA: Yeah, it was bizarre.
Q: What did that feel like?
JOANNA: It gave me a headache. I can't explain the black-eye thing as well as
    I can explain the other things. It was just another thing I could do.
Q: How often did you do that?
JOANNA: I did it three times. I got a real purple shiner on my eye.

Less common were people who engaged in episodes of *picking*. One member of an Internet support group described her history of picking:

I'm 48 years old and have been injuring myself since I was about 14. I've been in and out of therapy since I was 17, yet I never told anyone about it. Not until four years ago did I ever tell anyone that since I was a young child, I've been afraid of unfamiliar places and people. I was diagnosed with social phobia then, and I never told anyone about it because I was too embarrassed. Still, the self-injury was the most difficult thing I ever had to disclose. There are people in my life who likely would be quite shocked if they knew. I've been so good at hiding the truth that even my partner of nine years didn't know. I could always explain away injuries because I worked outside a lot. We worked different shifts, and I often could hide injuries until they healed. I'm not a cutter. I've never taken a knife or any other type of blade to my skin. My weapons of choice have been nail clippers, tweezers, needles and my own fingernails. None of my injuries has been life-threatening or serious enough to require medical attention, mostly just ugly. Any flaw on my skin—an insect bite, a scratch, pimple or even a small skin tag—gets clawed at, scratched at, picked at, until I'm bleeding all over my body. Small scratches that would have healed in a couple of days without leaving a scar are picked at until they are gaping wounds, remaining for a month or longer and leaving small scars all over my body. No part of my body is without a scar that shouldn't be there. Nothing that would alarm anyone, though. Nothing that would reveal my secret to the casual observer. And scars that are noticeable enough that someone asks me how I got them, I always have a reasonable explanation.

I'm tired of hiding, and I want it to end. I don't want to die with my own blood under my fingernails. My therapist and I have talked about it only a little bit. We have so many other issues to work on. I've suffered from major depression, PTSD [post-traumatic stress disorder] and social phobia since I was a child, having had my first suicidal thoughts when I was only about 10 years old. I made the first attempt when I was 17. I've also been diagnosed with borderline personality disorder and have had varying types of insomnia since I was a child. I graduated from high school a year late because of that first attempt and eventually went to college on a state mental-disability grant and graduated cum laude. I was a journalist for 16 years and was damn good at my job, but the mental-health issues brought with them an anger that I couldn't control. That anger eventually destroyed my life. I lost my career, my home and my partner.

Related to picking is *scratching* or *clawing*.[9] Lynn, a 36-year-old neuroscientist working for a company that tests pharmaceuticals, began to self-injure two years prior to our interview. Describing herself as severely obsessive-compulsive (OCD), she would scratch at her skin so badly that it became raw and bled:

LYNN: I'm a scratcher. I scratch myself with my fingernails. I started with my wrists and hands, and recently I've moved on to my legs and feet. I've scarred myself severely. It starts by me scratching really hard at a small area, and then it becomes this feedback thing where I get the sensation from it where it's—you know, it's not a hurt sensation, maybe a tingle, and I go through it for a while until it's, you know, to the point where it starts to hurt. I'll sit there, let's say at a meeting, and just start rubbing on my wrist with my other hand, and then I scratch. I might start one and then a couple hours later go back to it, you know, again. Once it's raw, usually the next day, I don't pick at it because that's when it hurts. They're a good half inch by half inch in size so they'll be big enough where I'll get a scab because the skin's tried to join back up. You know, it's wide enough that it will form a scab.

Q: And is that something that you'll pick and prevent from healing, or do you go somewhere else then?

LYNN: I pick at it once it scabs. I mean, not right away. I wait, and then once it gets to a point where it's past the painful part, or I tend to scratch around it, you know, 'cause I still get this good sensation scratching around it.

People made clear distinctions between these types of self-injuries and the homosocial bonding commonly practiced by (usually high-school-aged) boys. Particularly common in athletic or other hypermasculine subcultures, young men engaged in various injurious acts, probably the most common being self-burning, to prove that they were tough and could take the pain. This reinforced their identity and connection to the group. Jason, a 22-year-old college student when he spoke to us, described a history of group injury. It began at the age of nine, when he and his friends inserted mechanical pencils into electrical outlets and held hands to get a big jolt. The one closest to the wall received the strongest shock and the highest status, which progressively diminished as they went down the chain. Then they rotated. When they told kids in school about it, the other boys thought it was cool and lined up to join them. They had to seek ever-stronger electrical generators in their search for a jolt that would reach to the end of the chain. As teenagers, they graduated on to group branding rituals in which they would heat up metal objects, such as keys or bottle caps, and burn them into their flesh. Eventually their parents noticed these marks, but once they explained these acts as masculinity rituals, they were permitted to continue. Ironically, they described these later acts as giving the same kind of release as more traditional self-injury:

It was more like if the time was right, we would do it. If we felt like we needed a pick-me-up, we would self-inflict ourselves. You know, sometimes you have to yell out and let all the emotions out, and I think that's what part of it was when it got to the part where we branded ourselves. It would be a long day, or mad at your parents. I can recall a couple instances where you would be mad at a bad athletic event. So heat up some metal and put a little mark on your body.

History

Based on our research, we propose three significant historical periods that have affected the population, prevalence, social organization, meaning, and practice of self-injury. The behavior of individuals who engaged in this practice during these three periods was socially shaped in different ways.

Ancient and Ritualistic or Hidden

Self-injury can be traced back to ancient civilizations. Many early mentions surround culturally sanctioned rituals and practices dating to the time of Herodotus in the fifth century BC, when martial leaders sliced their flesh prior to battle. Shamans throughout cross-cultural history have painfully dismembered themselves, often in anticipation of attaining religious reconstruction and purification. In the early Christian era, priests and zealots mortified their flesh, modeling themselves on Jesus, seeking to attain salvation. The Catholic Church reinforced some of these extremes of religiosity, canonizing noteworthy self-injurers as saints.[10] Rites of passage in primitive societies often involved body modification, infliction of pain, tooth extraction, and slicing or removal of body parts. Examples of scarification, immolation, dismemberment, flagellation, and other forms of self-mutilation can be seen all the way through the Middle Ages, practiced by religious fanatics, leaders, and their followers.[11]

Self-mutilation has also been chronicled as occurring throughout this time among outcasts and the severely disturbed or mentally ill. Basing their actions on religious inspiration, fears of being sinful, or self-doubt, individuals from biblical times into the recent past have plucked out their eyes, mutilated their genitals, self-aborted, and self-castrated. Records indicate that some mental patients have removed sexual organs because they feared they could not control their sexual urges.[12]

Beginning in the mid-twentieth century, scholarly research from the psychiatric field began to document cases of more specifically focused self-injury. The term *self-mutilation* was introduced by Karl Menninger in 1938, when he documented its growth and classified it as a destructive but nonsuicidal act. Studies from the 1960s to the 1980s then noted the rise of "wrist-cutting syndrome," associating it with unmarried, attractive, intelligent young women.[13] This idea generated more psychiatric interest and broadened the notion into terms such as "delicate self-cutting," "non-fatal self-harm," and "deliberate self-harm," eventually expanding into other variants such as "self-picking" and "plucking."[14]

These psychiatric studies all were based on inpatient treatment populations, and knowledge of the behavior was limited to psychiatric professionals and the populations they served. Tracy, a 31-year-old librarian, described what it was like to be a cutter during the tail end of this period. She self-invented her cutting in the 1980s, during a period of high frustration in her early twenties. Although she found it satisfying to cut herself, she thought she was alone in this act. When she decided to check into a mental hospital in 1990, she was shocked to discover that other people engaged in similar behavior:

> TRACY: It was a relief to be in the hospital, but it was also incredibly frightening. And it—it took a while for me to accept that: "I'm a mental patient." But I also, well, I discovered that a lot of other people were doing the same things that I was. That was really the first time that I encountered other people who had similar scratches, scars.
> Q: How did that make you feel?
> TRACY: Actually, it was very helpful, to realize that this was a coping mechanism, perhaps not a *good* one but a coping mechanism that other people had resorted to.

Burgeoning Awareness

Our interviews and archival searches suggest that sometime during the 1990s public awareness of self-injury began to rise, with depictions of it appearing in books, films, television shows, and other media.[15] Several celebrities publicly admitted that they self-injured, among them Fiona Apple, Drew Barrymore, Brody Dale, Johnny Depp, Richey Edwards, Colin Farrell, Kelly Holmes, Angelina Jolie, Courtney Love, Marilyn Manson, Shirley Manson, Princess Diana, Christina Ricci, Amy Studt, Sid Vicious, Amy Winehouse, and Elizabeth Wurtzel.[16] In 1997, the *New York Times Magazine* ran a cover article on self-injury that grabbed a lot of attention,[17] *Newsweek* and *Time* ran stories on it in 1998,[18] and discussions of it flourished among high school populations. This burgeoning awareness spread fairly rapidly through the segments of the population that were most likely to come into contact with self-injurers: adolescents, young adults, educators, doctors, social workers, and psychologists.

People who cut or burned at this time, still often through self-discovery, acknowledged that their peers were becoming more aware of the existence of self-injury as a phenomenon, although most did not really understand what it meant. Valerie saw a high school friend with cuts on her arm in 1996 and asked her about it. When she heard what her friend reported, she tried it herself. Rumors abounded around her school about a girl who cut herself, but Valerie felt that since others did not really understand the meaning of the act, they could not comprehend why the girl would do something so strange. In fact, it was this ignorance that prompted her to come forward for an interview with us in November 2001:

> Part of the reason, when you mentioned in our sociology class that you were doing a study—the reason I decided to say something to you that I had any experience whatsoever is that a lot of people in class didn't know what it was. And that upset me, because I was like, "What? What were they doing if they all were like, you know, treating it as less than it is?" Everyone was like, "Cutting, what's that?" They didn't—the kids in class, you know, were kind of scoffing at the idea. In high school, a lot of kids didn't know how to label it. They knew, you know, I think a lot of them knew that it was pretty self-inflicted, but none of them knew why you would do that to yourself. They couldn't understand, you know. It took me a while to just get used to the idea of that this is how people control themselves. But even for me at first, while I knew the label, I didn't know the reasoning or the justification.

Young people who were into the punk, hard rock, or heavy metal music scenes were exposed in collective venues to musicians' songs about and displays of self-injury. Gary, another of our earliest interviews in late 2001, was a 24-year-old college junior when we talked. Introduced to injuring by a high school friend, he started out by burning himself in 1991. He discussed his observation of the rising awareness of this phenomenon in the culture:

> GARY: Yeah, when I was in high school, the faculty of the school, they just really had never heard of it. They didn't know what it was.
>
> Q: Right. And when was that?
>
> GARY: That was like '92–'93. By '95 stuff was probably at the break of popular rave culture, I guess you could say, and a lot of the kids who were into raves were conceivably also into cutting. There would be, like, a parallel, because I would say that there's definitely some kind of connection between cutting and drug culture. Not that they're, you know, connected or whatever. I guess it really started to come out with Marilyn Manson. You know, that was a big deal. And he was based on sort of those earlier, you know, punk rockers like Iggy Pop and GG Allin and others. But Marilyn Manson would have to be the epitome of the showy cutting.

Q: And so, when was that?

GARY: That was probably like '96 or so. I would say that that's really the first kind of big media awareness of this that really ever came out. Before that, it was really unknown—I mean, nobody. Just obscure punk rock records was the only place where you would hear about this, and maybe in some studies or some sort of thing. But it was pretty rare. You just never heard about it. So I would say '96: '96 would probably be the year.

Robert confirmed Gary's assessment. Twenty years old when we spoke with him in early 2002, he began cutting when he was 13 or 14, in 1994 or '95. At that time he noted that no one knew about it, and he could hide his behavior easily. Quitting for a few years, he resumed the behavior in 1998 and noted distinctly that by then it had hit public awareness through exposure on such television shows as *The Guardian* and *ER*. Gary explained the way cutting was portrayed in the early days of the punk scene:

The main reason they would do it, in my eyes, was for attention grabbing. Whether that was subconscious or not, that's kind of their purpose for it, basically. Usually it was anything sharp, really: a knife. I've seen weird things: nail files, all kinds of things used. Letter carving, those kinds of things. I've also seen it where it's sort of a different situation where it's like, along with like the punk rock lifestyle. GG Allin was sort of famous for cutting, that sort of thing, on stage, so a lot of punks would do that. It's their style.

Cyber Era and Burgeoning Silent Epidemic

We place the dawn of a third period around 2001–2002, when Websites began to appear on the Internet focused on self-injury (self-mutilation, self-harm), complete with public chat rooms where people could interact with fellow and former self-injurers, those who wished to discourage the practice, and random other visitors. Internet self-injury sites and groups have enabled the development of cyber subcultures and cyber relationships in which communities of self-injurers flourish and grow. At the same time, during this phase the practice of self-injury became widespread among a broader range of people: prisoners, especially juvenile delinquents; fostered or homeless street youth and others who suffer and lack control over themselves; boys and men; people of color; those from lower socioeconomic statuses; members of alternative youth subcultures; youth suffering typical adolescent stress; military personnel; and a growing group of older hard-core users who began the practice to seek relief but settled into a lifetime pattern of chronic self-injury.

It is hard to know if public awareness of self-injury expanded so much after this time because of a genuine growth in the extent of its practice or because the broader public became aware of it as a phenomenon and began to recognize its marks for what they were. Diana, a 44-year-old mother in Sweden living on disability, self-invented her cutting in 1999 at age 36. She voiced the opinion that the practice had grown much more widespread:

> I'm pretty convinced that it has grown; I mean, I know some people who say that it's just been, you know, it's just so much more noticed and talked about today and people have always been doing it and stuff like that, but I am very convinced that it has increased a lot in numbers. It is a part of young people's culture today, when it certainly wasn't when I was young. And I mean, I used to hang out with the punk rockers and stuff. I mean, if it had been a common thing back then, I probably would have heard of it. I can see with my kids it's just a part of life. I mean, they—they have friends who have been cutting; it's just a thing everybody knows about.

At the same time, people began to identify the signs and scars more clearly. Shannon, who started as a high school sophomore, discussed the public recognition of her self-injury. When her sister got married during the summer of 2002, her mother was furious and embarrassed because Shannon's self-injuries showed in her sleeveless bridesmaid dress. The excuses she had commonly offered in the past of getting scratched no longer worked effectively, and it generated a lot of talk around the wedding.

Everyone with whom we spoke acknowledged the rising faddishness of self-injury. Many compared it to the boom in piercing and tattooing in the 1990s. Others related it to the growth of eating disorders. Online posters were very critical of the general growth of this behavior, as one young woman expressed in 2004:

> I remember when I had started cutting, I thought I was the only one who did it. The first time I found out others were was in sixth or seventh grade backstage at a play I was doing and four of us talked about how we were depressed and from there found out we were all cutters. I never talked about my cutting. This year (my freshman year) I walked into school second semester and its everywhere. There was this girl that would get pissed off at a teacher and shove saftey pins into her hands. Or other that would

compare scars and their recent adventures in the middle of out commons area. Its pathetic. I love how a lot of them are so against "posers." Look at them. This would be the last thing I would ever want to pose about. Because we all know cutting makes you cool. Thats why most of us suffer from depression, or anorexia, or are bi polar.

Many of our contacts, in fact, saw self-injury as a "burgeoning epidemic." Ross Droft, a suburban high school health teacher, estimated in 2006 that out of the 3,800 adolescents in his school, 30 percent cut themselves. Hannah, a young woman who had spent 30 days in one of the specialized self-injury clinics, discussed the prevalence in her former high school in 2005:

> Among teenagers, a ridiculous number do it. A *ridiculous* number! And they can talk to each other about it, and they're all so—like I said, in high school I was in that little subculture, the punks and the Goths—and they're all, "We're all fucked up. Look how fucked up I am. I'm more fucked up than you are." Among teenagers it's so rampant. I'd run across people that I'd known for years, and I'd see them in the bathroom with their sleeves pulled up so they could wash their hands, and I'd glance over and see a little mark that I could identify as injuring. And I'd be like, "Oh, God damn. Look at that! Another." I really believe that there are a lot more men who do it than we know about because, God, how masculine, you know?

The breadth of self-injury as a practice extends beyond the stereotypical view of faddish teenagers, however. Cindy, a 19-year-old salesperson in Pennsylvania who had both experience with inpatient hospitalization and an extensive Internet support group background, summed it up in 2005: "I was amazed, but there are a lot of middle-aged people who seem to have perfect jobs and good lives, married with children and everything, and they self-harm. I think it's a very quiet epidemic. It's very hush-hush."

Overview

The population we studied, composed primarily of noninstitutionalized self-injurers living in their natural settings, goes beyond the tip of the iceberg seen by the psycho-medical experts in clinics, hospitals, and treatment centers to shed light onto this larger, hidden population. Ours is the first major academic work to address those individuals at large who practice self-injury alone, in secret, and those who engage in it but congregate into cyber subcultures and cyber communities facilitated by the postmodern technology of the Internet. Many recent works address the explosion of self-injury in the teenage population. We discuss this group but also focus on several more hidden groups: longer-term, middle-aged and older participants who support each other and have ambivalent feelings about stopping, more men and people of color, more disadvantaged populations who lack control over themselves, such as fostered or homeless street youth and incarcerated and military populations.

In chapter 2, we begin by reviewing the literature on self-injury and outlining the demographics of the population that has been proposed. We then present our data, augmented by other sociological and media accounts, which show that the existing psycho-medical views of both the behavior and those who engage in it are extremely limited and no longer accurate.

The rest of the chapters follow a combination of the developmental progression of the behavior and its temporal evolution over history. That is, we begin by looking, in chapter 3, at the ways people got into self-injury and how this was influenced by the era during which they started. We then turn in chapter 4 to the nature of the experience. We consider the act of self-injury from start to finish and present a description of how practitioners feel as they contemplate doing it, begin the act, and feel its sensations. We present some of the diversity of their approaches to finding suitable places to injure themselves and to deciding when they have injured enough and when to bring the episode to a good or bad close.

Chapter 5 takes a more historical perspective, looking at the 1990s and early 2000s, when self-injury started to spread and became more sociological, but before the Internet brought about communities and subcultures of participants. Self-injurers lived in isolation as "loner deviants" then, unlikely to confide in others about it and facing harsh reactions when they did. Chapter 6 moves us into the most recent phase of this behavior by looking at the rise of self-injury on the Internet and the vast array of changes wrought by this development. This chapter, along with chapters 7 and 8, examines in detail some of the sociological dimensions of the cyber subcultures of self-injury. People who chose to look for others like themselves found community online, and it gave them a base on which to build a host of new social meanings, norms, and values. In chapter 6, we examine the way their lives and acts were changed and how finding others affected their behaviors and sense of self. Chapter 7 takes a closer look at the nature of their Internet communities, from the way these are organized to the roles of various types of members and their stratification hierarchies to their effect on their members. In chapter 8, we look at the relationships self-injurers forge with others in cyber space, exploring the nature of their Internet interactions and associations and some of the patterns and issues people encounter in balancing an intimate, inner, secret world with an outer, shielded, face-to-face world. We compare and contrast self-injurers' cyber relationships with those they maintained in the solid world[19] and discuss their feelings about how these relationships influenced both them and their deviant practice.

In chapter 10, we develop the fullest sociological implications of this revolution in self-injury by looking at the effects of its transformation from a hidden, psychological illness to a social phenomenon. We consider how self-injury's spread, understanding, practice, and community have significantly impacted the way it is viewed by society. We discuss the social meanings associated with the philosophy and lifestyle proposed by those who celebrate its practice.

Chapter 11 takes a career analysis of the pathways that self-injurers typically follow as they progress through their experience with this behavior. We consider the different pathways taken by the types of people likely to become involved with it, differentiating between those who have significant psychological problems and those who adopt it because of its trendy, dark, and mysterious connotation of anguish. We offer suggestions on why some people move through the career stages quickly and spin out while others stick with it for longer periods of time. We conclude by looking at how and why people move away from self-injury, what motivates them, how they make the break, the typical patterns of quitting and relapse, and the effects of this practice on their lives after self-injury.

In chapter 12, we add to the empirical knowledge of self-injury by tracing its rise as a contemporary social phenomenon, articulating its different sociohistorical periods. We offer theoretical analyses of the nature and implications of the postmodern cyber communities, relationships, and selves, pondering the relationship between the solid world and the virtual world, as it is experienced by these and other cyber travelers. Finally, we discuss the destigmatization that self-injury has achieved over the course of our study and the moral passage that self-injury has taken thus far and is likely to attain in the future.

For brief biographical descriptions of all the participants quoted in this book, see http://www.nyupress.org/tendercut/.

2

Literature and Population

This book highlights the sociological nature of self-injury in several ways, two of which are profiled in this chapter. First, we discuss the contribution we make to a sociological analysis of the data on self-injury, expanding the understanding of self-injury beyond the way it has traditionally been conceptualized by the psycho-medical establishment with a new, sociological lens. Second, and perhaps more important, we show how the population of self-injurers has spread from a narrow, clinically conceptualized base into the broader reaches of the mainstream. These discussions lay a foundation for the examination of the development of new empirical conceptions and new theoretical analyses that will unfold throughout the rest of this book.

Literature

Sociologists have come to the study of self-injury later than the psycho-medical community did. Yet when the behavior spilled beyond the psychiatric bounds, it took on sociological dimensions that were unaddressed by the clinical definition and framework. We lay out the psycho-medical perspective here, noting its view of self-injurers' characteristics and motivations. Sociological literature addressing this topic has mostly come from a feminist perspective, casting self-injury within the framework of patriarchal exploitation and oppression. Other literature that we examine includes the postmodern perspective, and its conceptions of space and the self as transformed by technology and media, and the empirical literature, which has been geared mostly toward a public audience of self-injurers and treatment professionals.

Psycho-Medical

Most discussions of self-injury derive from within the parameters of the psychological and treatment professions. The canonical bible of the psychiatric field, the *Diagnostic and Statistical Manual of Mental Disorders* (DSM), sponsored in all its ongoing editions (IV-TR in 2000 being the most recent) by the American Psychiatric Association, classifies two main axes of psychological conditions. Severely clinical, biochemical, organic conditions fall into the Axis I category, comprising such problems as schizophrenia, bipolar disorder, depression, gender identity disorder, and others. Axis II disorders are environmentally rather than organically caused, rooted in psychological or situational problems incurred during people's maladaptive childhoods. Self-injury is not listed as a disorder unto itself in any of these editions but, rather, as a symptom of several other disorders, most notably those having to do with impulse control. It is lodged primarily within the "dramatic-emotional" cluster B dimension and is associated as an occasional side effect of borderline personality disorder (BPD: inappropriate anger and impulsive self-harming behavior),[1] antisocial personality disorder (the tendency to be aggressive, to have reckless disregard for personal safety), histrionic personality disorder (a pervasive pattern of excessive emotionality and attention-seeking behavior often enacted through physical appearance), post-traumatic stress disorder (sometimes due to rape or war), various dissociative disorders (including multiple personality disorder), eating disorders,[2] and a range of other conditions such as kleptomania, Addison's disease, depersonalization, substance abuse,[3] alcohol dependence, and assorted depressive disorders.[4]

There are some scholars who believe that self-injury should be clinically classified as a separate impulse-control disorder in its own right. They argue that beyond self-injurers' impulsivity, most of them do not meet the other diagnostic criteria of BPD such as binge eating, substance abuse, unsafe sex, and reckless driving. E. Mansell Pattison and Joel Kahan (1983) were the first to suggest a separate classification, positing it as the deliberate self-harm (DSH) syndrome. They argued that it should be defined as characterized by severe, uncontrollable impulse disorders, major self-mutilation, onset in early adolescence,[5] a low level of lethality, and repetitive episodes over the years, making it a continuing disorder rather than a temporary practice at a dramatic point in life. Armando Favazza published the first major comprehensive and historical study of this behavior in 1987, documenting its existence across a broad array of eras and cultures and classifying a full range of self-injurious behaviors into three forms: major self-mutilation (radical acts such as self-surgeries, auto-castration, eye enucleation, and limb amputation); stereotypic self-mutilation (repetitive or rhythmic acts such as head banging, self-hitting, self-scratching, and self-hair-pulling—often found in autistic or other mentally ill persons); and moderate/superficial self-mutilation (with three distinct subtypes—compulsive, episodic, and repetitive—characterized mostly by skin cutting and burning).

We concern ourselves in this book, as does most of the psycho-medical literature, primarily with the moderate/superficial category, the most prevalent, although some of our subjects displayed more stereotypic behavior. In addition to excluding major and stereotypic self-mutilation, we do not include in our focus Münchausen syndrome, the psychological (somatic, factitious) disorder in which people feign physical or mental illness in order to draw sympathy to themselves or to gain admittance to hospitals or clinics, because it is not the behavior of people seeking, privately, to salve their inner turmoil through a physical vent or release but the deceptive presentation of faked symptoms in order to garner medical attention. Although many people self-injure as part of their desire to decorate their bodies, we also decided to exclude tattooees, piercers, and scarifiers from our project since their primary goal was body decoration, rather than the pain, release, or grounding sought by self-injurers.[6]

Causes

The psychiatric community has outlined specific risk factors characterizing individuals who are likely to self-injure. Specifically, they cite a number of features of people's youth that predict their likelihood of self-injuring. Prominent among the risk factors is childhood sexual abuse or neglect; pathological family relationships; and childhood trauma, neglect, or insecure attachment, especially to the primary caregiver.[7] Some scholars have theorized that self-injury is connected to passivity (especially among girls) and suicidality, while others argue that it is not connected to suicidality.[8] Self-injury has been correlated by psychiatrists with sexual promiscuity, abnormalities in childhood, abnormal menstruation, and genital conflict.[9]

Cognitively, self-injury is thought to be caused by psychological determinants of negative affect (depression, anger, and anxiety) compounded with cognitive biases (hopelessness, low self-esteem).[10] Deprivation, rejection, or loss of love is presupposed to develop into feelings of anger or resentment toward the person responsible and subsequently to be internalized and directed additionally at oneself. This leads people to develop a sense of guilt and worthlessness. Women turn pain and hostility inward, while men externalize their hurt and engage in outwardly destructive behavior. Women tend to be overrepresented in self-harming and eating disorders, while we see more men engaging in substance/alcohol abuse and violent outbursts.[11] In sum, psychiatrists and psychologists locate the root cause of self-injury in childhood experiences that take place within the family, especially within the context of the caregiving relationship.

Effects

Self-injury was considered for many years a suicidal gesture (and is still regarded that way among some nonexperts), with users pathologized and regarded as weak. Most scholars today, however, recognize it as a means by which practitioners seek a temporary form of relief and view self-injurers as capable or resilient.[12] Although the behavior is morbid and often maladaptive, we agree with others that it overwhelmingly represents an attempt at self-help. These behaviors often provide immediate but short-term release from anxiety, depersonalization, racing thoughts, and rapidly fluctuating emotions. Self-injury tends to lead to the lessening of tension, cessation of depersonalization (grounding), euphoria, improved sexual feelings, diminution of anger, satisfaction of self-punishment urges, security, uniqueness, manipulation of others, and relief from feelings of depression, loneliness, loss, and alienation. It provides a sense of control, reconfirms the presence of one's body, dulls feelings, and converts unbearable emotional pain into manageable physical pain.[13] As such, it represents an emotion-regulation strategy and a grounding technique to end dissociative episodes.[14] These effects usually (but not always) last the remainder of the day, with some individuals experiencing relief for several days or even weeks. Many continue to derive benefits after they self-injure by looking at or picking the scabs for as long as they remain.

Feminist

Feminist scholars became interested in self-injury soon after it blossomed onto the public scene because of the large number of women involved with this behavior. Historically, psychology and psychiatry have treated the self in a "disembodied" manner, meaning that it was free of culture, class, race, and gender. The feminist perspective, with its more cultural and structural approach, stands in critical contrast to the dominant medical and psychological explanations for self-injury, which focused on individual pathology. Many feminist scholars have critiqued the notion of a disembodied self as both illogical and dangerous and have challenged the medicalized view of the body as devoid of social context.

Gendered analyses of the female experience emphasize the multifaceted ways that women's lives are embodied. From earliest childhood, women learn that their social capital is significantly measured by their appearance.

Researchers have shown that people are favorably biased toward attractive women;[15] in fact, they specifically note a "halo effect," whereby attractive people are assumed to be smarter, more personable, and preferential to those who look worse.[16] Attractive people enjoy higher chances of economic success and are considered healthier, more competent, and more appealing than those who are less attractive.[17] Women's success in the arena of dating and marriage is often seen as tied to their appearance, as women often trade their looks in the mating market for men's financial prowess as providers.[18] Thus, while all people have a body, women and their representations of self are particularly tied to the body they inhabit.[19]

Performance of the ideal female gender role entails enacting certain disciplinary practices on the body, such as removal of undesirable hair, skin softening and depigmentation, and weight management. Women who are lax in these practices may be harshly judged by the pervasive microdisciplinarians in schools, workplaces, and families,[20] may become defined as deviant, and may be medicalized as pathological.[21] Those who desecrate their bodies in unfeminine ways such as heavy piercing or tattooing may subject themselves to harsh criticism.[22] Yet these behaviors also represent ways that women are able to enact and reenact the self on a daily basis. Feminists suggest that these practices derive from an oppressive misogynist culture, and they deconstruct the scientifically constructed, medicalized meanings of self-injury to examine mechanisms in society that turn self-injurers into the "Other"[23] and foster this behavior.

Some feminists suggest that specific instances of female victimization can lead to self-injury.[24] Sheila Jeffreys offers a more radical approach, arguing that self-injury occurs within the context of patriarchal society and that women who engage in this practice are (sometimes unconsciously) carrying out violence against themselves rooted in their more abstract victimization by "male dominance over despised groups" of society.[25] She considers men who practice this behavior, similarly, victims of patriarchal oppression and likely weak or gay. Radical feminists, Jeffreys argues, politically reject all terms for this behavior except for *self-mutilation,* because they believe that other terms hide the violence and oppression directed against women (and those men) victimized by patriarchal society. She uses *self-mutilation* (and *self-mutilation by proxy*) to describe not only the behaviors discussed in this book but also tattooing, piercing, cosmetic surgery, transsexual surgery, mosh-pit dancing, dieting, and wearing high-heeled shoes. She argues that "self-help" discourse masks the association between self-harm and the gendered nature of male domination of girls and women by positioning the selfharmer (usually female) as fully agentic and not the victim of male (usually sexual) abuse. This discourse masquerades as "false liberation." Many other feminists, while not as radical, agree that the problem is mostly connected to the experiences of women and girls under domination and that many such individualized problems have political, especially patriarchal, explanations.[26]

Yet another way to look at self-injury from a feminist perspective is to view it as an act of personal agency on the part of the subject. Several feminists have critiqued Jeffreys's arguments, alleging that she produces an account of "false consciousness" and that there are more complex ways of understanding the relationship between self and body.[27] In this book we add to this feminist critique of the medical model's disempowerment of self-injurers and explore further the ways that self-injury is influenced by the multiple meanings of structural, cultural, and interactional frameworks and is both practiced and received within a gendered context.

Postmodern

The cyber world represents a new frontier, one that extends what have often been colloquially referred to as the fourth and fifth dimensions: time and space. Just as Murray Melbin (1978) analyzed the night as a temporal frontier, the cyber world is a domain that occurs in a new form of space that is both "out there" and "in here"; it is simultaneously public and social while remaining private and solitary. It is a postmodern form of space, created by technology and populated by disembodied people in a virtual universe that is detached from the physical locations known as *place.* These spaces are fertile locations for the rise of virtual communities, defined by Howard Rheingold as "social aggregations that emerge from the Net when enough people carry on those public discussions long enough, with sufficient human feeling, to form webs of personal relationships in cyberspace" (1993, p. 5). These communities challenge traditional notions of identity and community,[28] with some observers suggesting that cyberspace is radically altering our conceptions of community and the nature of our communities.[29]

This arena offers a fertile ground for an analysis of the self. Postmodern theorists have for some time debunked the linear, logical, unified, and core view of the self as modernist and outdated. This more conventional, or realist, view sees the self as a genuine, real attribute, as reflexive, self-conscious, rational, and therefore autonomous. The modernist self is seen as anchored in stable, mainstream social structures, in social values, in relationships to friends and communities, that is, in permanence. In contrast, postmodernists reject this model as clinging to a modernist view of the real, or autonomous, self and failing to recognize its demise.[30] They consider the self in the postmodern era erased and dismantled, saturated[31] by the many voices of humankind. The postmodern self is flexible or "protean,"[32] fluid, nonlinear, heterogeneous, multiple, and fragmented, a realm of narrative and discourse rather than a permanent, real thing.[33] The quest for self-presentation has replaced the quest for meaning.[34]

The self-concept has become an artifact of Jean Baudrillard's (1983) hyperreality, replaced by the simulacrum, or the self-image. Postmodernists see the self, then, as an illusion, evoked situationally, but adaptive and fragmented, emotionally flat and depthless.[35] Fundamentally eroded, the postmodern self is like the layers of Erving Goffman's onion: devoid of a core, it is decentered[36] and ultimately dissolved.[37] Postmodernists claim that the cyber world has witnessed the ultimate realization of the postmodern self. In this research we consider the way self-injurers conceive and present their selves through the postmodern medium of the Internet, and we assess the impact that the venues through which they interact and the communities and relationships they socially construct there have on these conceptions and presentations.

Empirical

In the twenty-first century there was an explosion of books addressing self-injury. The first and largest body of literature adopted the traditional psycho-medical definition of self-injurers as suffering from psychiatric disorders and was geared primarily toward an applied medical or clinical audience.[38] Few of these works document the full extent of the spread of this behavior. They are limited in their scope by relying for their data on therapeutic clients or inpatient psychiatric populations, thereby missing the much larger numbers of self-injurers who engage in the practice but remain hidden.

A second body of work oriented its presentation toward a popular, or trade, audience.[39] These books took a broader view of self-injurers and often used journalistic interviewing techniques, thus expanding our understanding of how self-injury could occur in a nonpsychotic, noninstitutionalized population. But they lack both a systematic, rigorous method of data gathering and the type of analysis found in academic work.

A third body of literature took people who participated in this behavior as its audience.[40] These books, while grounded in the participants' perspectives, are fundamentally geared toward helping self-injurers control and quit their behavior.

Demographics of Self-Injurers

Just as the discussion of self-injury's characteristics, causes, and effects has been dominated by the psycho-medical model, so too has society's general impression of the population that engages in this behavior. We first review this traditional view of self-injurers' demographics, then contrast this with the demographics of our research population, augmenting that with other sociological and media reports. Our research population includes many who sought help from therapists, hospitals, and specialized clinics. But it also goes beyond those, incorporating individuals who have avoided these venues by managing their ills and behavior either alone or with the support of like-minded others.

The Psycho-Medical Population

In positing the psycho-medical view of self-injurers' demographics, a mix of scholars and clinicians have suggested that the behavior often starts in early adolescence, desisting sometime after adolescence.[41] According to their research, girls have generally been considered more frequent practitioners than boys,[42] with some noting as high a figure in their samples as 82 percent women (which is not that different from our sample).[43] At the same time, others have countered that male practitioners are more numerous or are equal in number to women.[44] Traditionally, like eating disorders, self-injury has been seen as located primarily among an intelligent, middle- or upper-class population[45] that is disproportionately Caucasian.[46] Finally, psychologists have viewed it as a short-term, adolescent phenomenon, although Favazza (1998) suggested that it might persist for a decade or two (typically no more than 10–15 years), with periods of waxing and waning occurring intermittently.

Prevalence estimates have been hard to formulate, with traditional data based primarily on inpatient psychiatric wards and emergency-room admissions. The numbers of self-injurers have been approximated as 20 percent of all adult psychiatric inpatients,[47] with 40 to 80 percent in the more concentrated adolescent population. Emergency-room data are more confusing to isolate, since most self-inflicted injuries consist of poisonings.[48] Psychologists then attempted to extrapolate from these data to the prevalence of self-injury in the general population, offering guesses of between 1 and 4 percent of the at-large population, with up to 20 percent of the adolescent subgroup.[49] Although we lack broad-scale epidemiological data from sociological surveys to help refine these assessments, psychologists have estimated that as many as 4 percent of adults in the general population report a history of self-injury, with approximately 1 percent of this total population engaging in severe self-injury.[50] More recent studies of adolescents have suggested that the North American rates on self-injuring may be as high as 14–15 percent,[51] reaching up to nearly 50 percent in the ninth and tenth grades,[52] with college students at similarly high rates.[53]

The Sociological Population

More recent studies and our own data have found that self-injury is much more widespread. We outline several groups for which it has grown more prevalent and discuss the characteristics of some demographic variables affecting its practice.

Alternative Youth Subcultures

One of these groups is alternative youth subcultures. Several people from our earliest interviews reported that they were part of the 1990s punk music scene, such as Gary and Robert. Others found that they could not make it in junior high or high school with the popular social or athletic crowds and so were drawn into more alternative social groups. Natalie, a 22-year-old college student, reflected back on her friends in junior high school:

> Eighth grade was the point at which I really started getting sociable, identifying with this alternative subculture. It wasn't like I hung out with the freaks and the rejects and, like, the outcasts. I definitely was in the subculture of the stoners and the punks, and we hung out on the bridge, and I started smoking and doing drugs. And, um, at that point I associated with more people who also hurt themselves.

Some of these alternative groups, often considered by teachers as the "wrong crowd," acted out, dressed in black, wore heavy makeup, listened to music such as Marilyn Manson, and identified as Goths. Eighteen-year-old Leith still wore a three-quarter-length black trench coat every day in college, a residual of his high school style. In 2000 he began to hang out with kids who were self-injuring. He found it an accepted behavior within his crowd. Many of them were nihilists who delighted in showing off by burning or cutting themselves. Mandy, another college student, recalled that in high school "the perfect people—the kids who seem to have everything"—could not relate to the problems she was going through and the feelings she was experiencing. She then started hanging out with other people, with whom she could verbalize her emotions more. "The kids who are, like, 'that's cool,' tend to be from the subculture of, like, Goth or freak or what have you, where mutilation is acceptable." Cody, another member of a Goth subculture, mentioned that she learned about self-injury from a friend she made in eighth grade who had gotten into it while in a white-supremacist gang in a mental hospital. Many nonclinical programs, including residential and day ones, have sprung up over the past several years to assist troubled adolescents who engage in self-injury along with other antisocial behavior.

Others self-injured as a form of teenage rebellion, to shock their parents, teachers, or members of the community. Outward rebellion may have represented some part of the motivation for kids to join punk or straight-edge (sXe) scenes. Religious repression also led some to rebel inwardly, such as Maggie, a 25-year-old nurse, who secretly self-injured as a youth when she was completely enclosed by her parents' and the community Elders' strict Mormon beliefs.

Trendy Offshoots
Instead of being drawn to self-injury as a result of disenchantment with society, some youth saw it as a trendy behavior. Vanessa, a 20-year-old college student, noted that she was currently part of a group that engaged in both self-injury and decorative body modification. Lauren, a 21-year-old college student, had a circle of lesbian friends who used self-injury in their rituals, sometimes using it for blood bonding and other times to represent the male phallus.[54] Men often self-injured, as we noted earlier, by burning, shocking, or branding themselves as part of male homosocial bonding rituals.[55] Finally, self-injury could be the province of young, trendy youth who did it to be hip. Cindy, the 19-year-old retail salesperson, recounted how people showed others that they were cool:

> I know there's this one site you can go to—I think it's called bluedragonfly or something like that—where they actually sell self-harm bracelets, and if you have one of these bracelets, you're in the clique or something. You're supposed to wear them on your arms to cover your scars, and the more bracelets you have, the more advanced you are in self-harming. So I guess it's something people can do to be cool.

Typical Adolescent Stress
Beyond these groups, a large group of self-injurers consisted of teenagers suffering no more than typical adolescent stress. Although the psycho-medical literature suggests that people who self-injure come from backgrounds of psychological abuse and neglect, many people with whom we communi-

cated directly or who posted on the Internet had unremarkable youths. Sally, a 22-year-old college student, asserted that she came from a close and happy family. Tracey, an English woman in her early 40s, posted, "I've been self-harming for 12 years. I've got no history of abuse, and my recollections of my childhood are happy, so why do I SI? Who knows?"

Sometimes even small events felt overwhelming to individuals going through the difficulties of adolescence. Mandy, the former Goth, noted, "My stepfather used to make fun of my weight or call me ugly." Rachel, another student, believed that in junior high school her mother liked her sister better than she liked her. When Mark was a teenager he became depressed after his father remarried and the new wife brought in a stepbrother.

Some self-injurers rooted their unhappiness in peer social situations. Rachel, a 23-year-old college student with an intact, happy family, blamed her friends for driving her to self-injure:

> It happened the first time when my group turned against me for some reason. They alienated me for a week straight. They started rumors about me. I didn't go to any activities that week, and I didn't even go to school. I was so sad, it just started. I was crying and so upset and couldn't stop crying, and I just took a coat hanger, and that's how it started.

Others turned to self-injury because they felt they had no friends, describing themselves as isolated and lonely. Alice, an attractive 22-year-old college senior, noted, "I never had very many friends in school. I still don't. I always felt pretty isolated, and I took that to heart, felt that there was something wrong with me. I've always felt like people don't like me, and I don't fit in, and I didn't really know why." Jennie, a 21-year-old college student, rooted her unhappiness leading to self-injury in the problems of a romantic relationship: "I guess I was having a difficult time in general: puberty, school. I had this boyfriend, it wasn't the most healthy relationship, and I wasn't getting along very well with my sister. So I think I blamed myself for everything, and I guess I took it out on myself."

Romantic traumas, while an occasional cause of girls' self-injury, were a more major factor cited by boys for injuring themselves. Breakups, fights, or other forms of rejection turned them inward to cut. Others from typical family backgrounds turned to self-injury due to the usual causes of adolescent angst: school stress, overcommitment in extracurricular activities, or a driving sense of perfectionism. When people failed to meet up to their or their family's expectations, they punished themselves. Sally, the 21-year-old college student, described her turn to self-injury:

It was a rough time for me. I got miserable. I just didn't feel like confiding in my parents. They probably would have been a great resource of help, come to think of it, but I was at that age where I wasn't comfortable talking to my parents about that sort of thing, and I felt no one understood. So my friend told me about her newfound technique, and I tried it as something that may unleash some of my stress. And it kind of was, which reinforced it.

Barbara Kantrowitz and Karen Springen (2005) have suggested that this generation of adolescents faces unique pressures. They are more likely to be from divorced or unstable families, to abuse substances, to have eating disorders, to struggle with depression, and to commit suicide.[56] Some young people who experience all these issues struggle to differentiate themselves from the crowd by suggesting they have "real" problems. Dialogue from the HBO drama *Six Feet Under,* in 2005, suggests that self-injury became a current popular form of expressing "teenage angst":

PATIENT: Maybe I should see your supervisor [*twirling her hair*]. I don't
    know if you're ready for me.
BRENDA (THERAPIST): You might be right. But, um, now that we're
    here . . .
PATIENT: I'm a very complex person.
BRENDA: I'm sure you are.
PATIENT: I keep ending up in hospitals.
BRENDA: Really? Well, tell me about that.
PATIENT: Well. A few times for anorexia. Twice for alcohol poisoning. Once
    I hit an artery. I'm a cutter [*smiles*]. And I keep pulling my hair out
    [*frowns*].
BRENDA: So I see.
PATIENT: It's all this pressure to be normal [*crying*]. And I can't. And
    nobody understands.
BRENDA: I think I do.

Age
The typical profile of self-injurers as teenagers is reinforced by their greater visibility and communication. Youth have more socially accepted venues for expressing their emotions through this behavior because it is openly known. They also flock readily to online sites to discuss their social dramas and alienation. They are very comfortable journaling and blogging about their feelings. Some Internet groups require people to be at least 13 years

old to post, so this signals the age that some forums consider the behavior acceptable.

Yet at the same time, many older people self-injure. Contrary to the literature's depiction of the phenomenon as fundamentally adolescent, roughly half of the "regulars" we encountered on the Internet were over 20, and a quarter were over 30.[57] Dana, a college sophomore, suggested that the age range of the people she encountered in the sites she frequented was "12 to 45 or 50. The most common age range is probably 20 to 25, but there is definitely some extremes."

Many forums were created to cater to the older harming crowd. People over 30 often posted that they felt their needs got lost sometime because the focus, both online and in the solid world, was often directed toward teenagers. For some, this represented the continuation of an old behavior, either steadily or intermittently, into their adulthood. Melissa, a 39-year-old college clerical worker, described the people with whom she interacted on the Web daily:

They just do it and do it for all these years, and it just becomes a part of their life. For example, a woman on one support group, she's self-harmed for over 20 years, and not a single soul knows about it except the people she writes to on the Internet. She's not in therapy, she doesn't go to a doctor or anything, and she just continues to do it.

Another woman posted to the Internet, "hi! My name is Heidi and I am now 26 years old. I have been struggling with SI since I was 10 years old. I did make it to 6 months and a day ago I slipped up. I am trying to get back on track and not be so hard on myself."

Because these older individuals were expected to "grow out of it" yet did not, they felt especially stigmatized and alienated. They sensed the pressure, as one middle-aged woman posted, that they were "supposed to have their lives together by now." Tasha, a 24-year-old first-grade teaching assistant, said, "That's part of why I had a lot of trouble dealing with it and the reality of it, because I felt like I should have outgrown it and was really, you know, embarrassed to think that this was something that I still do."

Other older people (30s and beyond), who began their self-injury more recently, felt that there was no place in the social definition of the behavior to explain people starting it as adults. One man stated that he self-injured for the first time when he was 40, remarking that he was "against the stereotype." He attributed his beginning to self-injure to a midlife crisis. Another man in the older population wrote,

I started seeing a marriage counselor in June 2002. In July of 2003 when my wife asked for the divorce I continued with the counseling. I started to cut in 2004. Since than I have had 2 psychiatrist and 4 counselors. Been hospitalized more than I want to admit to and I I fear I am in a lot of trouble.

People of this age have a much harder time than adolescents finding individuals in the solid world to whom they can talk about their injuring. As a result, the Internet groups serve an important mechanism, helping to normalize a behavior that is uncommon at their age. The groups also offer people the opportunity to escape isolation. Yet at the same time, some younger people found older people's postings frightening. Judy, the 21-year-old music therapy major from Louisiana, noted that the age span of what she saw was unnerving: "They have teenagers and 20-somethings like me and people in their 40s and a few people in their 50s. So actually and that kind of scares me because, wow, the behavior can last that long, and I don't want that."

Gender

Our research supports the greater prevalence of women in the self-injuring population. Of the people we spoke with, 85 percent were women. In 2002, one group reported the results of an informal Internet survey, and the composition of an email support mailing list for self-injurers showed women constituting two-thirds of its population.[58] It is likely, and our subjects confirm, that women are socialized to internalize anger and men to externalize it.

We noted earlier that some men were more likely to flaunt their injuries in obvious, harsh, and showy ways. This may be due to their greater socialization to repress emotion, so that it comes out as anger.[59] Jimmy further remarked on what he saw as the hypermasculine stereotype into which men were supposed to fit: "Just the whole—I play hockey, and I play drums. And I mean, hockey player, I mean, supposed to be an idiot brute." His departure from this role expectation furthered his sense of inadequacy. Cody noted in recollecting about her friend who was drawn into a white-supremacist gang in junior high school, "He was very into self-mutilation, and he liked to burn himself with lighters. I mean, severe burns, some pretty gnarly burns up and down his arms; cut himself a lot." Robert noted in comparing the self-injuries he observed of guys and girls,

Guys I've known have cut deeper and left bigger scars. The ones they made on their arms were very big and thick. The girls' scars that I've seen have been way more delicate. So for guys, I've seen fewer scars, but thicker scars.

The girls usually had thin scars all down their arms. For guys, it gained them status in the alternative subculture.

When we asked Cody about the peer status of her friend who mutilated so seriously and openly, she noted that the crowd he hung with at school was very popular.

This social effect serves as a contrast to older men who self-injured. By the time they were into their 30s and 40s, open self-injury no longer benefited them socially. Women were more likely to see it as a sign of weakness than of strength. Nancy described the older guys she saw on her Websites and chat rooms as "a lot of men whose wives have left them. And they're absolutely lost, and they have begun, like, self-injurious behavior. . . . Most of the men I find really do want to talk. And then me, I know for myself that if I keep them talking, I can't be cutting. So thus my 5 hours became 10 hours."

Social Class/Race

In contrast to the assumption that self-injury is the nearly exclusive behavior of middle- and upper-class people, we heard about a lot of this behavior occurring among other populations. Although computer access and extensive Internet participation may be limited by financial resources, making it more difficult for people of lesser means to gain access to these venues, self-injury has become much more common among people of nonwhite race/ethnicities[60] and those who suffer and lack control over themselves, such as troubled[61] or homeless street youth.[62] Cody spent considerable time during a period when she dropped out of high school hanging out downtown with homeless kids from a range of different ethnicities who were taking hallucinogens and sleeping on the streets. She observed a lot of cutting and scars on people who scratched themselves with their fingernails, knives, pieces of broken plastic, and other implements they picked up on the streets. She noted that the cuts she saw were very deep, especially on young black men, and she felt it reflected the despair and hopelessness these people felt.

Joanna did several stints in mental hospitals for cuts and suicide attempts. While there, she also noted a different class of people:

I heard about it in my high school as rich kids not knowing what to do, or that it was attention driven. But when I went to the hospital and saw these inner-city kids doing it too—I mean, like, loads of black girls—I was like, "Oh wow." . . . I think that's the underlying issue: control. It's feeling like you don't have control, and you want to take over somehow.

Self-injury is reported to be rampant among the incarcerated, in jails and prisons as well as in juvenile detention centers,[63] where people of lower socio-economic status and minority ethnicity are disproportionately prevalent, as well as in the military,[64] where stress is high, personal control is low, and racial/ethnic mixing is common. Soldiers have long performed intentionally self-injurious acts to avoid initial or returning military service. But there has been a "rising trend," beginning with the Iraq war, in which military doctors are finding an uptick in intentional injuries as more American soldiers serve long, repeated combat tours and develop strong feelings of desperation.[65] This is such a common means of military service avoidance that there are specific military statutes that ban this kind of self-injury. But more recently, the American military has had to add additional bans against self-injurious behavior committed in a time of war and located in a hostile "fire pay zone" (abroad, in combat). Typical self-injurious acts committed while on leave or pass may not interfere with soldiers performing their duties, but official military policy states that these acts "prejudice good order and discipline or discredit the armed forces."

Hanna (2000) found that whereas the rate of American emergency-room hospitalizations for self-inflicted injury among whites stood at 56 out of every 100,000 in the population, blacks with self-inflicted injuries were admitted at a rate of 39 per 100,000 people, and the rate for people admitted for self-inflicted injuries who were races other than black or white was 73 out of 100,000. We also found that self-injury has spread to girls in minority, inner-city neighborhoods, especially those placed in the foster-care system. Thus, self-injury, like eating disorders, which were assumed to be located primarily among white, wealthy girls, has increasingly spread to boys, men, people of color, and those from lower socioeconomic statuses over the course of our research. These populations suffer from structural disadvantages in society.

3

Studying Self-Injury

The germ of an idea for this study began in the spring of 1982 in Tulsa, Oklahoma. Peter, shortly into his first teaching job, met with a student in his office who came to tell him about an odd practice of hers: she intentionally cut herself. Intrigued and sympathetic, he listened to her story, looked at the small cuts on her legs that she took great pains to hide, and asked questions, with curiosity, about her motivations and sensations from it.

Over subsequent years we both caught further glimpses of similar behavior. As interested and "cool" professors who taught courses on deviance, popular culture, drugs, and sport, we often found ourselves the adults to whom college students turned as sounding boards. Our next encounters with cutting were rare at first but took on greater frequency during the late 1980s and early 1990s. By the mid-'90s we knew or had heard about enough people who cut themselves intentionally that we felt surrounded by it. Yet during the occasional times when we discussed this behavior with friends or colleagues, we found it fundamentally unknown. Then, in the spring of 1996, a young high-school-aged friend of ours, the daughter of close friends, confided to Peter about her cutting. She had never mentioned it to her parents, but she needed someone to talk to about it. Peter was her college adviser (one of his side avocations), and they had a close relationship. This very detailed, intimate conversation caught our attention. We felt the behavior was calling to us to study it, but we were squarely in the middle of another major research project and did not have the time.

The next few years saw cutting beginning to be revealed to the public, as noted in chapter 1. Only a small body of people seemed to notice it, however. Yet this lack of attention also appeared to us as a sign that the behavior was growing; it had all the earmarks of a burgeoning underground phenomenon, much like the increasingly popular but once highly stigmatized tattoo and piercing scenes we were witnessing at the time. As a result, we began to discuss with each other the prospect of undertaking a major study of this behavior.

We were excited by the idea for several reasons. First, we located it sociologically within the field of deviance, our first love in sociology and one in which we had not written for a while. This felt, for us, like a bit of an academic homecoming, although the behavior had been conceptualized so much within psychology that we were not sure how to bring out its sociological dimensions. Second, we felt that the conversations we might have with people would be deep and that we would have the opportunity to delve into people's lives in ways that would be meaningful to both them and us. This prospect fit our personal and academic profiles as purveyors of in-depth conversations. We also felt that we were uniquely suited to do this research, not because of any personal proclivity toward the behavior itself but because we felt that our backgrounds gave us the emotional empathy to understand what we call attitudinal deviance:[1] people who do not think along normative lines. Although we never self-injured, we have lived our lives slightly outside the mainstream, from our unusual families to our hippie youth, to our moderately unconventional lifestyles as college professors, to our admission of drug use while doing research on dealers and smugglers[2] and our rather liberal parenting style. Our decisions in life, to coauthor, to live and to dress informally, to level the plain between our students and ourselves, and to approach deviance as something interesting and natural rather than something in need of repair, made us feel that we could study this behavior nonjudgmentally. Moreover, the intensity of our personalities made us feel that we could empathize with others who were experiencing such acute feelings that it drove them to cut themselves.

We began seeking research approval from the university's institutional review board (IRB) in 2000. Although we had some difficulty and had to proceed carefully and with limitations, we eventually got permission to do the study.[3]

Face-to-Face Interviews

Armed with these constraints, we began soliciting for interviews in the fall of 2001. We thought it would be extremely difficult to recruit people. We told everyone we knew about our study, we went on radio shows and gave out our email addresses, and we made brief presentations in our and others' classes, asking people for help with our research. Most people had never, even at this time, heard of self-injury. Yet interested parties started to trickle in. With college students readily available, we were not far from what emerged as a demographic center of typical practitioners. Due to the extremely sensitive nature of this topic and the gendered patterning of the people who came forward, after several attempts at dual interviews that proved awkward (in front of a man), we elected to have Patti conduct the large majority of the interviews. These followed a natural history approach and then moved to specific sociological concerns that evolved abductively over the course of the project.[4] Very intense, the interviews often left Patti exhausted after conducting, transcribing, or rereading them.

In addition, Peter would listen to the taped interviews, and Patti had to relive some of the most intense moments for him. She found herself engaging with acute emotional empathy, becoming drawn into people's experiences of pain, sadness, and frustration. It was not unusual for people to become somewhat choked up as they spoke and for Patti to offer to skip to the next question, an offer that was invariably declined. People came to talk. Even though the contact she had with people was fleeting, it was so emotionally powerful that both parties felt an intimate depth connection, and many of the people who were interviewed followed up with email communications to Patti for many years. People noted that they told her things in these interviews that they would never have said to anyone they actually knew or interacted with in their everyday lives, precisely because they would never have to see her again.

At the end of the interview, Patti asked each respondent what made him or her volunteer to come forward. Many, as we saw with Valerie in chapter 1, wanted to educate the public, to find a way to tell people what was going on, that there was a name for this and a syndrome associated with it. Others wanted to direct their attention specifically at others who cut. Jennie, who was 21 when we spoke with her in early 2004, explained the reason she contacted us for the study:

> Yeah, I didn't want to do it at first, because it is a hard thing to talk about, and people aren't used to talking about it; people don't understand it. I guess the reason I am doing it is because I figure you'll write about it in one of your books, and people will learn about it. And maybe people will understand it a little bit more, I guess for people to know that it actually goes on and that it is somewhat common. It isn't just people who are crazy who do it.

Paula, a 38-year-old holistic massage therapist interviewed in 2006, was aiming to educate professionals in the field. She was dealing with a gradual process of coming out of the closet in her own healing journey and thought this could be part of that process for her. But further, she wanted to contribute to a body of research so that counselors and therapists would have a better idea of what was actually happening in the community, rather than strictly in the psychiatric hospitals. She had experienced uneducated and bad treatment in these kinds of places and wanted future patients to have better outcomes. MaryBeth, who in college was still struggling with her self-injury, discussed our research solicitation with her mother, who advised her to do the interview because it might bring her closure.

We also found ourselves on the receiving end of the interviewees' questions. Many asked us how their particular experiences compared with what we knew from our casual conversations, readings, and interviews with others. When in October 2001 we interviewed Dana, who had primarily burned herself in middle school with cigarettes and incense, she noted that she had never spoken about it to anyone in her life. She wanted to know if she was the only person who did this, what kind of other people did it, and why they did it. She was extraordinarily relieved to learn she was not alone.

As knowledge of our interest in this topic spread, people from around the country began to contact us in person, by phone, and by email, worried about friends or family members who self-injured. We dispensed referrals to therapists and treatment facilities, literature recommendations, and our knowledge of the sociological trends and patterns we had observed. We did more media interviews and (later) wrote entries in scholarly encyclopedias.[5] Through these informal and broadcast conversations we became aware of more cases around the country, with the unintentional outcome that the base of our sample broadened further.[6]

Going to the Internet

In addition, due to our own interest, we started searching the Web for relevant sites in 2001. Googling *self-injury, self-mutilation, self-harm,* and all variants of these terms, we found a host of diverse sites. People posted individual blogs, publicly sharing their diaries and reflections. There were Web-sites owned by individuals who told their stories and invited others to join them in posting there. Unofficial sites were created by people who assembled informal facts about self-injury. Some of these asked people to post photos of their cuts, brands, and burns, accompanied, or not, by comments. There were also interactive groups such as bulletin boards, listservs, and newsgroups located on Yahoo, Google, MySpace, and the like. If you wanted to see what others had written, postings were organized by topics or "threads," with someone posting a comment or question and others responding to it. The entire history of these interactions was often archived on the site. For convenience, some sites offered to let people become members, which came with the advantage of delivering postings directly to one's email account, although these could still be accessed by nonmembers who wandered onto the site. During these early years, all the groups and sites we found were open to the public. We joined half a dozen of these or more, specifically mentioning our status as college professors and researchers.

Sometime later in 2002 we asked the IRB for permission to expand the study by using Internet data and joined a growing (and some scholars have argued reluctant)[7] group of Internet ethnographers.[8] We participated in these sites informally, interacting with others, asking questions, and posting opinions. Over the course of the years that we conducted this research we developed deeper cyber relationships with people we met on bulletin boards and in groups, through interviews, through side instant messages (IMs), email conversations, participation in chat rooms, and through friends of these friends, and these dozen or so individuals helped us as we struggled to conceptualize our data, sharing their life stories with us and regularly responding to the sociological questions we posed. This computer-mediated-communication (CMC) offered insight into the subcultures of self-injurers and their naturally occurring conversations, serving as a version of participant-observation.[9] We used these conversations to help us generate questions for our interviews, and when we were accepted into groups as overt researchers, we used them as data. In order to maintain the integrity of the respondents' remarks, all postings are presented here unedited (incorporating their grammatical and typological mistakes as well as Internet and self-injury slang), with the exception of replacing real screen names with pseudonyms.

We then asked the IRB in 2003 to let us use the Web as a vehicle to augment our subject recruitment.[10] Once permission was granted, we applied for permission from sites' list owners to post research solicitations. We uploaded copies of our informed-consent form, therapeutic referrals in major American cities, and the complete range of interview topics to Patti's Website, directing potential participants to view these materials before agreeing to be interviewed. Due to the vulnerable nature of the population, we specifically told people that we were not interested in interviewing minors over the telephone, and we asked people who agreed to talk with us to print, to sign, and to fax or mail us their consent form along with proof of their age. One early solicitation read,

> I am not a self-injurer. I'm a college professor doing research on self-injury and have many young friends who self-injure. I've done over 40 interviews with people who self-cut, burn, brand, hair-pull, and break their bones. I'm

interested in learning more about self-injury. I have one paper that is under review at a scholarly journal that I would be happy to share with you and am working on others. Right now I'm interested in looking at the effect of cyber-subcultures on people's behaviors. I see lots of chats naturally occurring about this topic all the time. I can provide help to people who want to do research in the form of scholarly references. I can also share my findings with people, but I'd rather not do that before I interview you so that I do not overly influence my data. I am not trying to get people on or off of self-injury. I've been asked by one list moderator to be a consultant for him. I'll be happy to answer any of your further questions. I'd ultimately like to solicit some volunteers for telephone interviews. All of this is completely confidential, of course. The purpose of my research is to bring greater understanding to this behavior and to make people who do it feel like they're not so alone or so deviant. My college students who I've interviewed say they want me to publish what they have told me to help others. For information about me, you can follow this link to my Website: http://spot.colorado.edu/~adler/.

People's responses to the posts varied, with some contacting us enthusiastically, others inquiring what an interview would be like and then deciding they did not have the courage to do one, and still others reacting against the idea of research. These posts then got passed around by members of multiple groups, without our knowledge, from one site to another, so that we were contacted by people from completely unfamiliar sites. Finally, as we began to publish articles from our research, self-injurers read them and contacted us directly, asking to be included in our study.

As a result, we shifted the bulk of our data gathering to telephone interviews, although we continued to conduct occasional interviews face to face. The geographic spread of our respondents increased dramatically across the United States and into many countries abroad, including Canada, the United Kingdom, Sweden, Australia, New Zealand, Bulgaria, the Netherlands, and Germany. We also broadened our age span, adding many more older and long-term injurers. This study draws on over 135 in-depth, life-history interviews, conducted in person and on the telephone, constituting what we believe to be the largest sample of qualitative interviews with noninstitutionalized self-injurers ever gathered. Participants ranged in age from 16 to their mid-50s, with many more women than men (85 percent women and 15 percent men), nearly all Caucasian.

Over the course of our research we also collected tens of thousands (in the range of 30,000–40,000) of Internet messages and emails, including those posted publicly and those written to and by us. In 2006 we enlisted the aid of three student coders to help us sort and analyze the emails and postings from the Internet groups. At this time we were working on one paper, and the students helped us find posts and emails pertinent to our specific focus. We repeated this process again in 2008 with ten more student coders, expanding the project greatly. Each student took one set of emails we had collected from a group, board, or chat room and poured through the years of postings we had assembled. We divided the students into groups of five and met with each group biweekly. At each session the students submitted notes and memos about the material they had scanned, and we brainstormed for sociological codes, categories, concepts, trends, and patterns.

We started with an outline for this book composed of chapters and the headings and subheadings within each. As the weeks and the meetings continued, we abductively used the ideas generated there to modify and expand these outlines. After 15 weeks we decided we had enough data for two books, one based solely on the Internet postings. Since that was not our intent, we had to scale back the use of these Internet sources. This book draws primarily from our interview data, supplemented secondarily by the general cultural understandings we drew from participant-observation on the Internet and thirdly on data drawn from the cyber postings of self-injurers.

The Internet Evolves

Over the years that we were actively involved in the self-injury cyber world, it took several twists and turns. The earliest of the sites we discovered probably originated during the late 1990s. At that time, most sites were privately owned and unmonitored. Participants often used the term *self-mutilation,* and it was not uncommon to find graphic details and pictures of injuries. Sites had names such as "bleed me," "ruin your life," "bioetchings," "bleeding to ease the pain," "cut it out," and "gallery of pain." Their main purpose, it appeared, was to offer fellowship to self-harmers so they would know they were not alone. One site designer discussed the purpose of his site:

[This site] started back in 1999 very unlike it is today. First conceived by [the site owner]—it was a discussion site built around the idea of Self-Destruction, in all its forms. I first started with [this site] on the first day— as it was I that was hired to build it. Things started slowly and although not many people came by with the intention of in depth discussion—we soon realised the site was being hit upon by a different sort of person. Our totally free, open and non-judgmental discussion ground became the safe haven for a small pocket of self-harmers who had long searched the internet for somewhere they felt they belonged. It seemed they had found it.

Many of the earliest postings we found on Internet sites, then, were avowedly pro-self-injury:

> I'm new here and [the site owner] says to introduce myself upon joining so here it is. I am extremely sadistic, and my favorite way of hurting someone is to slice them open. I have cut myself before and have had other people do it to me, but I love to get a better view of the flesh just falling open and filling with blood. The only way to do that is to do it on someone else. :). Can't wait to share pix and stories with so many other people interested In the same thing I am.

A response to this post read,

> you're creepy..and i respect that.. alot. i'm a twisted lady, and my killing weapon of choice is a knife because a gun is to easy.
> check out my blog. it's seriously not as angsty as i'd wish, but i like to keep an air of mystery about my dark swell of depression.

People with whom we spoke during the early phases of our research, or who were older and whose experiences dated back to these years, talked about the sites they found back then. Katherine was a 23-year-old college student in Tennessee when we spoke with her in 2005. Her self-injury dated back to 1996, when she was in ninth grade. She talked about her early Internet experiences:

> Q: So you looked it up to find information about it. What'd you see? When was this?
> KATHERINE: Around '99 or 2000. Mostly just a lot of crap that pissed me off about it. Just clichéd stuff like, "You're not alone, there's help." I don't think that it's something that I want help with, or need help with. I think everybody's got their thing. People drink or smoke or whatever. Everybody's got something. Like religion. I just kind of see it that way.
> Q: So did you ever seek out any chat groups?
> KATHERINE: No. Well, actually you can watch other people talking about it. I never said anything about it, but I would read other conversations

that other people were having. And I was just like, "That's not me." So I didn't ever participate in anything.

Q: What kinds of stuff? Were they reinforcing it, stopping it, defining it?

KATHERINE: Reinforcing it. I never saw any conversations about people getting help for it. Like people giving each other tips for covering up or tips for excuses.

Danielle was a 35-year-old Florida housewife and mother of three who was sexually abused by her brother at age seven and had been in and out of treatment facilities, including one specially geared toward self-injury. She described what she found in her early exploration of Internet sites at around this same period:

I went on the site just because I felt that I could help people. There were kids on there, I mean kids, 10–12 years old, that were talking about cutting very graphically. It wasn't helpful to me, but even when I would suggest other alternatives, they were like, "Well, I was never abused. I just like doing that." To me, that doesn't help the cause; this isn't a fashion statement. It was hard for me to relate to those kids because they were doing it for different reasons than I was.

Some of these sites only lasted a short time, disappearing as their owners grew tired of supporting them or moved on. Others were closed down by their host servers if they became too graphic. Yet people sought them out because, as Paula, the 38-year-old massage therapist and scab picker noted, "All these people were needing community around this experience, and what that community is and the purpose it serves and what it looks like is being created now." As sites disappeared, new ones sprang up to take their place. One blogger, Sukee, introduced her Website with the following remarks:

I think a lot of people here on [site name] search for topics they feel strongly about or can relate to, or even something that vaguely interests them. So, I naturally searched for the topic of self-injury, self-mutilation, cutting, or whatever you want to call it. A lot of the blogs I read were very disheartening, uninformed, or quoted from a book. Long story short, I was pretty offended by some of them and wanted to set the record clear . . . on my own personal account.

In response, some sites changed their names. Erica, the young bone-breaker, discussed how her favorite site changed its name:

ERICA: I had heard they were banning pro-ana sites. I figured there had to be pro-cutting sites. So I Googled *pro-self abuse,* and I found ruinyourlife.com. But recently a few months went by, and I hadn't used it, and when I tried to go there, it was gone. So I searched for it, and I found it. It's recoveryourlife.com now.

Q: Did it change the nature of the site?

ERICA: No. It's the exact same. They just wanted to make it sound better. It's still definitely a pro site. It's not why we need to stop. There's also stuff like—it's everything: people who absolutely love cutting to people who have quit.

Other early sites were recovery oriented. One of the largest message boards launched an initial incarnation in 1996. Over time it changed, evolving into its current form around 2001. It offers help to people who recognize that they hurt themselves, although it does not require a commitment to recovery. Diana, the 44-year-old Swedish mother who was unemployed and on disability, was one of the earliest members:

DIANA: I am a regular poster to [board name], you know, since I don't work full-time and I have a lot of time on my hands. But now the board has grown so much. When I joined up in 2001, there was like less than 100 registered members, and now [2007] there's like 10,000. And so it's not like when I first went there: you got to know most of the posters. I sort of hang out with a few people that I know better.

Q: Tell me about the history of the board.

DIANA: Well, when I joined they had just moved to new software, and from what I understand, it all came about from a Web mailing list originally, and then they started to use a Web board. As it has grown, there have always been various subboards, and so you have a lot of different forums now with a different slant so people can sort of choose which areas they want to hang out in. And one main reason I have stuck around on the board is that there are quite a few people there who are not teenagers, who are my age. They have a special subforum for people who are, like, well—we don't have an age limit but people in their 30s, 40s, 50s. And this has been one thing that has been important for me, to be able to connect with people my own age.

At some point during the early to mid-2000s we noticed a privatization movement. Some groups, lists, and boards that had been publicly accessible started closing their access to nonmembers. We did not notice this right away since we had signed up for email delivery, but increasingly new sites we visited asked people to join, and some of the sites we were on debated becoming members only. One list owner asked people to vote by responding to her how they felt about making her list a "members-only community." The next week she posted the results: 15.5 percent said yes; 46.6 percent said no; and 37.9 percent said they would stay either way (the three fixed option choices). Even though the members favored remaining open, she announced her decision to close the list:

> Since more of you don't give a shit either way than anything, I'm going to cater to the "yes" people. Just humor me, alright? We're going to see how much better this works, if it works better at all. I'll be working this week to put all previous posts under 'friends only'. All future posts from the time that I'm done will also be 'friends only'. If we don't like this, it can be changed again. So no pitching a fit saying how you're going to leave because you didn't get your way.

Joining such members-only groups required people to submit their requests to the list owner, who responded by adding them to the list and sending them the rules or policies. We never heard of anyone being denied membership. As groups grew, owners added moderators who helped to approve these requests and responded to posts. Groups and lists also became more specialized and stratified, centering their membership and conversation on certain age groups, issues, orientation toward self-injury, a broad or narrow focus, and their degree of regulation. Paula, the 38-year-old massage therapist, remarked about the rise she saw in sites for older people:

> In the beginning, I definitely felt like I was in the minority. The initial sites were more dominated by younger people, so the older people weren't getting involved at all. And then at some point more and more people were creating sites that were geared towards older folks and issues that they're dealing with: not living with their parents, living with their spouse, living with kids, and whatever they're dealing with. So now there might be more cites online for the isolated, in the closet, older folks that in '99 might not have been as active.

Another change has been the rise and fall of membership levels in cyber support groups. Looking online, we can see that for a moderately typical sample of groups (listed anonymously here), there was a distinct rise and fall of postings. Table 1 offers the message histories of three different groups. This trajectory suggests that postings peaked for several of these forums during the early to middle part of the first decade of the twenty-first century and declined thereafter. Some got off to an earlier start than others (1999, 2000, 2002) and had their greatest usage in the early years (2001, 2003, 2004). No clear evidence of seasonal usage by months was evident. Yet by 2008 the groups' demand seemed to decline, although all three groups are still in existence as of this writing.

In talking to list owners and moderators on the phone, we asked their thoughts about these numbers. Uniformly, they appeared surprised, since they reported seeing new members soliciting for admission regularly, and they felt a continuingly high level of interest. But several early sites (not displayed here) underwent membership declines as the result of contretemps (or what several people called a "snark")[11] that occurred among members, with some (including moderators) driving others away by saying ugly things about them online. One moderator described how a group to which she belonged in an earlier time disbanded: "We used to see more flaming and that kind of stuff. In fact, one of my groups closed because there was so much flaming. We just shut the group down. A huge group, over 1,000, they just shut it down because it got to be ugly." Yet another moderator expressed her feelings that membership was holding or growing:

Q: How many people apply to join?

MODERATOR: Oh, now we're getting a few every day. And when I first started in the group, there were less than 50 of us. And now I think there's over 300. It's been a while since I've been to the membership thing to count. And I think it's getting a little bit too large, and some of us older timer members are starting to say, you know, "We're losing control here." But there are so many groups out there. Maybe with so many, people are spread out more thin between them. Yahoo alone has like a hundred groups that somehow have self-injury tied into them. And then that's not even counting everybody else, you know, MSN and all the other sites with groups. So I don't know how many there actually are out there.

Groups that reacted by instituting regulation often found themselves more successful in holding members. Yet overregulation could leave people feeling unfulfilled, needing additional sites to express themselves. These factors

TABLE 1
Three Groups' Posting Histories

	Jan.	Feb.	Mar.	Apr.	May	June	July	Aug.	Sept.	Oct.	Nov.	Dec.
GROUP 1												
2010	127	78	86	111								
2009	414	333	450	310	12	153	153	655	180	372	119	273
2008	259	274	240	303	233	149	176	203	189	258	203	232
2007	190	196	276	177	280	175	234	333	286	704	300	301
2006	630	822	710	406	395	406	250	252	114	192	165	157
2005	909	1164	1146	1334	2187	1701	1897	858	460	426	398	683
2004	1930	1711	1571	3337	2490	1193	710	1061	1325	1650	932	683
2003	744	569	1024	787	766	657	1103	1085	1377	1208	1616	1658
2002	305	83	96	144	126	144	340	292	759	371	713	826
2001	80	63	70	47	21	55	51	31	39	51	191	315
2000	22	41	92	139	118	75	44	122	97	58	26	60
GROUP 2												
2010	49	42	56	78								
2009	78	155	121	115	20	195	251	142	164	128	100	49
2008	287	458	406	411	494	507	336	283	263	224	195	102
2007	674	629	421	358	487	369	197	257	147	256	166	272
2006	1335	818	601	621	547	471	455	434	474	618	660	333
2005	893	523	655	1180	1269	919	1580	817	696	536	456	636
2004	227	279	143	220	693	550	560	545	280	262	472	1294
2003	360	845	412	293	537	716	480	442	421	338	325	669
2002										64	160	194
GROUP 3												
2010	57	14	2	9								
2009	9	22	4	16	32	69	130	48	22	11	13	16
2008	88	45	31	16	10	88	10	31	48	22	24	14
2007	48	32	13	63	90	16	15	143	166	46	46	64
2006	171	130	86	249	181	332	149	57	79	59	42	45
2005	146	42	92	48	95	65	74	45	64	127	189	105
2004	135	59	67	146	243	128	69	68	127	114	167	130
2003	242	176	144	64	142	122	67	165	52	110	184	108
2002	945	804	170	233	480	253	224	315	379	398	339	255
2001	181	310	843	761	816	312	262	325	459	853	2373	1204
2000	97	126	106	247	250	222	349	174	126	134	73	97
1999							3	32	117	85	142	123

notwithstanding, it appears that self-injury cyber support groups filled an important function in the culture of the phenomenon and attracted significant participation.

Privacy, Access, and Confidentiality

Ethical guidelines pertaining to what is permitted in studying naturally occurring conversation in cyberspace has varied between different scholars, IRBs, and time periods. Some have maintained that researchers may be exempt from obtaining consent for data collected from the public domain, with online newsgroups, Usenet support groups, listservs, Multi-User Dungeons (MUDs), and Internet Relay Chats (IRCs) readily accessible to anyone and, if archived, accessible to the public months or years after messages were posted.[12] Homan (1991) has argued that the ideas surrounding the definition of space as public or private are directly related to the definitions of those who occupy that space, so that the global, democratic nature of virtual spaces suggests that those who use them are fully cognizant of the fact that what they discuss can be read by large numbers of people all over the world.

Paccagnella (1997) agrees, noting that open message boards are freely available to anyone with access to the Internet. Mann and Stewart (2000, p. 46) state that in posting a message there is "implied license to read or even archive the information it contains."[13] Others have suggested that the distinction between public and private on the Internet tends to dissolve because private interactions occur despite public accessibility due to the intimate feeling of Internet communications.[14] They suggest, instead, that researchers should strive (1) to protect the subjects from harm as a result of the research fieldwork and practices, (2) to produce good social science research, and (3) not to unnecessarily perturb the phenomena studied.[15]

We began this research during the era when publicly posted computer-mediated communication was unprotected, and most of the cyber sites we visited or joined were both public and archived. Yet over the course of our study, as sites changed and several privatized, attitudes toward cyber research have shifted and changed. No clear guidelines really exist in any shared, systematic way about using data from Internet groups. As a result, we came to question our initial assumptions and, barring an effective, practical way of obtaining informed consent from members of a fluid and shifting community, we ultimately chose to follow the guidelines of the latter approach. As a result, we have excluded enormous amounts of our Internet data from presentation here (especially descriptions and analyses of particular groups, their dynamics, their composition, and identifiable member postings) and have restricted ourselves to incorporating data from publicly accessible/ archived sites and groups (or those that were public when we accessed them) and from individuals whose identities we believe would be difficult to discern. In this way we have striven to attain a balance that respects both the privacy and integrity of self-injurers and the value of understanding social scientific trends and patterns as they pertain to this world.

4

Becoming a Self-Injurer

In this chapter we begin our exploration of the details of self-injury. As we noted in chapter 1, some of the chapters are tied to historical periods, with earlier times preceding later ones. This chapter examines people's entry into self-injurious behavior in the earlier years of our study. We begin by looking at some of the types of factors that led people to self-injure, then we move to a consideration of the pathways that they followed into the behavior, and then we look at some of the typical patterns of progression that most people followed.

Motivations

In discussing some of the reasons why people become self-injurers, we noted in chapter 2 that the psycho-medical literature has suggested a profile of self-injurers as coming from backgrounds of severe trauma such as physical or sexual abuse and possibly chemical imbalance or mental illness. It is clear from the way people presented themselves that some portion of self-injurers had psychological problems ranging at the more extreme end from clinical or diagnosed conditions (depression, bipolar, anxiety disorders) to milder states of general malaise (they felt sad or bad). Aside from the occasional individual curious about how it felt to self-injure (often drawn into it because of a close friend who engaged in it), most people who cut, burned, or otherwise injured themselves did it because they were in some sort of emotional distress.

Some self-injurers fit the clinical profile and suffered from serious mental illness. Many of these sought the help of psychiatric professionals, checking into hospitals and inpatient treatment centers. For example, Marnie, a 51-year-old former bank teller, told us that she suffered from dissociative identity disorder (DID, multiple personality syndrome) and had struggled throughout her life to deal with the "alters" who sometimes took over her body. She had huge gaps in her life that she could not remember, dating all the way back to high school, and she sometimes communicated with her alters, who tried to teach her things to fill in the gaps. Her recollection of anything prior to age 18 was completely gone, and by the time the life that she could recall began, she had already lost touch with her parents, siblings, and whatever traumatic events caused her severe dissociation.

Although Marnie's story was the most severe we heard, many of the people who participated in our research took psychiatric medications and had been diagnosed with a variety of conditions, mostly involving anxiety and depression. It is important to remember, however, that the incidence of psychological diagnoses for all sorts of conditions and the percentage of the people taking psychoactive medications increased dramatically during the 1990s and the early twenty-first century, so that people with conditions that might have earlier been regarded as falling within the "normal" range became regarded as diagnosable and treatable.[1]

At the same time, a lesser degree of suffering appeared adequate to drive people to seek the relief self-injury offered. In the middle range, many people we interviewed had damaging life experiences such as rape or domestic violence but fell short of mental illness. Adam, 22, a nontraditional college freshman, sported dreadlocks and grunge-style clothing. His father had died when he was very young, and his mother remarried a harsh disciplinarian. His stepfather "reformed" him with severe verbal abuse that frequently escalated into belt whippings followed by banishment into his room. Grounded, isolated, and alone, he turned to self-injury to transfer the pain in his head and his heart to a physical manifestation. Katy, a 20-year-old college student and elementary education major, was raised by very religious parents who eventually became pastors. Because her parents spent so much time with their religious study groups, they often left her alone with a neighbor boy, who molested her over a period of four years. She was later date-raped at age 17. Although she told her parents about the latter episode a year after it happened, she could never summon the personal resources to speak to them about the repeated molestation.

Many self-injurers, however, were driven to this behavior by nothing more serious than the minor stresses typically associated with normal adolescence. Chelsea, a 19-year-old college student, in reflecting back on the first time she cut herself at age 15, had a hard time remembering the impetus. She said, "I just remember, like, I—I wasn't happy or something, and I wanted to see what it would feel like." She could pinpoint no real trauma that led to her feelings of unhappiness. Rachel, who was 23 when we spoke with her, began injuring herself in high school as the result of trouble with her friends. She described how this began:

RACHEL: The first time my group turned against me for some reason. They alienated me for a week straight, they started rumors about me. I didn't go to any activities that week, and I didn't even go to school. So I was so sad, it just started. I was crying and so upset and couldn't stop crying, and I just took a coat hanger, and that's how it started.

Q: Talk to me a little bit more about the first time. You sat there with a coat hanger,

RACHEL: It felt so much better to sit there and scratch myself than to have my heart broke and crying. It eased me, it made me feel better. I was taking it out on my arm as opposed to crying. I felt like I was accomplishing something rather than sitting there crying and being upset for no reason.

People cited upsets with their friends, romantic relationships, and family members as having led them to self-injury. Mike was a scruffy-looking college student who always wore a stocking cap. He started cutting and burning himself between the ages of 12 and 14. When he was in high school Mike's girlfriend broke up with him, leaving him devastated. He reflected, "Yeah, I thought every relationship was the end of the world. I kept getting further and further depressed, and I just needed something to where I could vent and rage without having any outward signs so that anybody could tell anything was wrong." He turned to cutting to assuage his feelings of sadness. Others cited family problems, such as Tamara's feeling that her father liked her sister better than her, Amy's conviction that neither of her parents liked her, or Joyce's sadness at not getting along with her sister and brother.

Some people chose self-injury as a mode of rebellion. Amy, a 19-year-old hospital worker and part-time community college student, reflected back on the onset of her burning at the age of 14: "I was just depressed, and it was just a way of feeling something. At that time I was into the honors classes, and I was a goody two-shoes. So I just determined to be all-out bad. I started smoking and doing a whole bunch of other stuff. Burning was one of my rebellious types of acts."

Whether it was loneliness, insecurity, depression, anxiety, alienation, or rebellion, self-injury provided a form of comfort that assisted these young people during a stressful period of their lives.

Onset

The nature and mode of individuals' initial entry into this deviance could often be connected to the period of time in which they started to self-injure.

Self-Inventing

Our research suggests that people who engaged in this practice prior to 1996, before it emerged into public awareness, invented it on their own. Alice, a 22-year-old waitress, reflected on the way her cutting began:

> ALICE: And I don't really know why I started to do it. For some reason it just was something that I think I just did almost accidentally for the very first time I did it. I was probably 12 or 13 [in 1992] and for some odd reason got some sense of relief out of it.
> Q: How, accidentally, did you happen to do it?
> ALICE: I think I was just messing around with a sharp knife and just happened to inflict it, maybe just even out of curiosity, on one of my own fingers. For some reason, I don't know what it was—maybe the adrenaline you get out of it—if you're feeling down, it provides a sense of relief for you or something.

Curiously, Alice's brother had a group of friends who burned and branded themselves with keys, bottle caps, and other items, so she was aware of self-injurious behavior. But she rejected the connection between their behavior and her own. She considered their group behavior a "manly, male, masculine thing" that socially solidified them, whereas her behavior isolated her from others. And while she noted that the guys got a sense of pride out of it, she considered her injurious acts "more about pain and being unhappy and sort of self-loathing."

Robin, who contacted us through an Internet posting when she was 33, had worked in law and business. She had a tendency as a young child to hurt herself, although she did not understand the meaning of these acts. She explained:

> ROBIN: I hit myself. I—I don't know, I hit my face a lot. I didn't understand what was really wrong with it; I didn't understand that it was something odd. I know it made everyone else really angry; I was in trouble for it all the time. It was some really stupid things like stapling myself, my fingers, and I don't know, stupid things only a kid would think of to do, I guess. Because I was probably eight when I started cutting.
> Q: Uh huh, and what did you think about it when you were eight, nine, ten?
> ROBIN: You know, I didn't even really think about it. It was just something I did. I didn't think about it until later, like, "Oh, my God, why did I do that to myself?"

q: So once you started doing it, what did you think?

ROBIN: I guess that it was something private because I already had experience through hitting myself that it was something wrong, that it was something I thought I liked it, but I didn't understand why. I had no clue as to why.

Judy, the Louisiana college student majoring in music therapy, found herself extremely upset one day when she was young and did not have the emotional resources to deal with her feelings. Taking some tweezers, she ran them across her skin and immediately noticed a release of all her tension, anxiety, stress, and frustration. She described this moment as "the beginning of the end, the end of the beginning."

Marissa, a 43-year-old wife and mother when we spoke, had worked in a large state university as a secretary for a while but became so depressed that she retreated to her home and eventually to her bedroom, from which she rarely emerged. A depressed shut-in living on disability, she spent hours on the Internet talking to people all over the globe. She described the day in the 1970s that she was whittling a stick with a knife and accidentally cut herself. Immediately dissociating, which she noted as "fairly easy during this difficult period" in her life, she spaced out and enjoyed a "nice endorphin rush." This convinced her to try it again.

Hearing about It

People who began to self-injure after 1996 had generally heard of it before.

Through the Media

As reports about the existence and nature of self-injury began filtering out to the public through magazines and television, some people became curious to experiment with it.[2] Ellen, a 19-year-old college student, read about self-injury in *Seventeen* magazine in 1996 when she was 12. Her reaction to the story was, "Ooh, I want to try that." Crystal, a graduate student, reflected, "I probably read about it in one of those teen magazines. I'm sure I got a lot of my bad ideas from those." Anya was a rebel who hung out in the Goth scene in junior high. At age 13 she saw an episode of the television show *7th Heaven* that took a heavy-handed moralistic tone against some teens who were portrayed as self-mutilating with razor blades. Angered by the show's tone, Anya got annoyed; she noted, "When I got pissed off, I wanted to do what they were telling them not to do. That's what I hate about the media."

Dana, a college sophomore, struggled as a child with her moods, although at the time she did not understand why. She was later diagnosed as depressive. Although she remembered having heard about self-injury on *Dateline* and through articles in teen magazines as early as 1996 or '97, it was not until five years later that she finally understood what these people were talking about. After feeling particularly bad one day, she reflected back on a magazine story she had read of someone's recovery that described her pathway to feeling better. Ironically, the part that stuck with her was the description of the anguish the author had previously undergone and the relief the cutting provided. This influenced her to do it herself:

> I was like, "Other people have done it; I'll try it. Maybe I'll feel better." And like, "I'll know what these people are talking about, because whenever I've heard these stories, these people have sounded like me, and so, maybe if I try something like them, it will feel better." I'd completely ignore the last part of the story, where they'd be like, "Oh, I've recovered," you know, the happy ending. I wasn't concerned with how they are feeling now and how they fixed it.

Several respondents noted that they improved or perfected their techniques from exposure to self-injury in the media. Janice, the graduate student from the supportive family whose rape led to her social problems, saw a documentary on the Learning Channel that discussed the way people cut themselves. She discussed her reaction to the show:

> It was a horrible reaction, and it's actually—I saw that there were better ways to do it, basically, besides a razor in the shower. I was like, "An X-Acto knife! Oh, yeah, that would work way better." It showed this girl as being—she was this totally pretty, popular girl who did that, and I understand now that it was supposed to be like, you know, people who are pretty and popular aren't always perfect, and they have problems, but she didn't really have any severe consequences. She didn't die, no one she knew died, no one she knew stopped liking her. I mean, she cut herself, she went to therapy, and stopped. That to me didn't seem like a very bad consequence, and she got to do that and get rid of her feelings that way, and no one really bothered her about it.

Lois, the Goth who started out by bruising herself, made her first cuts at age 14. Although she grew up in such an isolated environment that she had not previously heard of cutting, she figured it might be less of a blunt pain than the bruising. Her first efforts involved using a broken razor to cut the inside of her thigh. Despite the sting she felt and disliked, she kept thinking about cutting and wanting to do it again. On her second try, her leg became infected. But then she saw the film *Girl Interrupted,* in which one of the characters cuts a massive amount into her thigh. This taught her that it was something people did, made her feel more comfortable trying it again, and gave her ideas on how to cut without bringing on infection.

For others, the attention brought to self-injury through these media gave them a general cultural awareness of the phenomenon. Scott had seen it in the movies and other places, but had never thought about it personally. These earlier revelations never fascinated him or resonated with him until several years later, when he decided to try it. For many like Scott, early exposure brought no immediate action but facilitated their decision to do it at a later date, since they knew it was "out there."

From Others

Less common in the 1990s, but growing in frequency over time, was hearing about self-injury face to face. Some people learned about it in institutional settings. Joanna, who tried to show her mother her pain by blackening her eyes, heard about it at school, in health class. One day her teacher taught a section on it, saying that it was "about stress and emotional problems and how people take out their problems." She had not really paid attention at the time to what was covered there because she did not think it could help with her emotional problems. But later, when her stepfather's abusiveness became more onerous, she tried it and found it a viable outlet: "Like, when blood starts to flow, it's like your emotions are finally flowing out." As in Scott's case, she unconsciously banked this awareness for use in the future. People are often attracted by the allure and intrigue of deviant activities, whether they assess the behavior as positive or not, and may be drawn to various forms of deviance despite potential, recognizable drawbacks.

As we mentioned in chapter 1, other institutional locations where people learned directly about self-injury included psychiatric wards. Carla, the 16-year-old who had just been released from her second hospitalization, saw people there who cut and burned themselves. The first time she did not think anything of it. After she was released, though, and found herself getting depressed again, she thought, "Oh, maybe I'll try it; they said it felt good, and it was a release of stress." It then became part of her coping repertoire. Paula, the 38-year-old scab-picking massage therapist, also got her first exposure to self-injury in the hospital in the early 1980s. Committed following a suicide attempt, she became exposed to a huge community of people who were deeply troubled and self-destructive. She learned skills such as how to make a razor out of a cigarette filter. Yet upon her release, there was still no knowledge of the behavior in the general population, as the culture of self-mutilation was "very, very on the fringes." She did not realize that it was something anyone else did until 1999 or 2000, when she described it as "finally becoming mainstream."

As time progressed, junior high or high school kids began, occasionally at first, to learn about self-injury from their friends, similar to the way many newcomers often begin their initial involvements in deviant subcultures. Aaron discovered when he was 15 that his girlfriend was cutting herself. Trying to protect her, he took the knife away and told her to stop. But then, curious, he gave it a try to see what it felt like firsthand: "That's kind of cliché, but I just kind of did it because I wanted to know why people did it and see what it was about." Yet, lacking the angst that brought most self-injurers to this behavior, all he got were some scars and a lot of pain. He offers an interesting example of a "failed cutter."

Jimmy, from Alaska, was intrigued by the jokes people made about self-injury, but because of the terrible sadness he felt, he gave it a try to see if it would help. Hannah, the 19-year-old college student, learned about it from a "cool guy." In eighth grade (in 1999) she was in a "pretty cool teen club," and a boy she liked showed her his scars. Prompted by her positive response, he told her how he got them, and she was impressed. That night she tried it for the first time and liked the results. In school the next day, she was happy when the boy treated her as cool for doing it. He told her more about his scars and how to manage them. This became a special bond between them, and she felt accepted. Gwen had a friend who told her about how she burned herself with a candle, so she went home and tried it that night.

Progression

Some people who tried self-injury held themselves to very strict limits; they carefully measured and controlled their acts by the amount and frequency of the damage. It was more common, however, for people who liked it to progress between their initial acts and subsequent ones.

During early incidents, people were often hesitant and unsure about what they were doing and how they felt about their self-injury. Many had no clear purpose because they were not really sure why they were cutting or burning themselves. Others were so freaked out that they turned away from it for a while, such as Lisa, a 19-year-old college student from a difficult family situation. She had always had a poor relationship with her father that involved a lot of criticism and yelling. After a particularly awful telephone argument, she threw down a glass and deliberately cut herself while cleaning up the pieces. Although she got an immediate sense of relief, she was frightened by what she had done and avoided it for several months. Alice, the 22-year-old waitress, was fearful about cutting into her body, an unknown terrain:

At first you're sort of—I was more careful because it does hurt to a degree; you only do it to a certain level. But as you do it more and more, you get more used to that feeling and more comfortable with doing that to yourself. I think I was able to cut deeper and with sharper and larger objects.

Tracy, the 31-year-old librarian, was afraid in the beginning that she would not be able to stop. But she became more comfortable over time as she realized that she could stop, and then it did not bother her as much. Lisa took a hiatus, but when things got worse again, she remembered that the cut had made her feel better, so she tried it again.

As people returned to their injury, they tended to escalate it in frequency and intensity. Alice noted, "Maybe I even needed more of an intense cut to make myself feel better." Her depression got worse, and the sadder she felt, the worse she cut. Over time, she noted, the cuts "just kept getting more severe and deeper, and the scars got bigger." Sam was a 23-year-old student with a muscular physique and a rich, blond head of hair. Although he looked every bit the self-assured athlete, he struggled with inner demons. As a child he bit his fingernails until they bled, and he turned one of his cheeks inside out to display it, showing how he had chomped it into a raw wound. His history with therapy and psychopharmacological drug treatment went back to his 'tweens. Sam also noted his tendency to cut bigger, deeper, and more visibly over the course of his cutting career. Each time he felt bad, he reasoned to himself that the prior effort had not been adequately successful in making him feel better, so a more "aggressive" approach was needed. The scars he displayed were red and "angry."

Anya, who reacted against the television treatment of self-mutilation, shifted her focus from looking at the blood to feeling the pain. She liked to test herself to see how much more pain she could take without getting "whiney." Amy was a 19-year-old college student who first hurt herself when she was 14. At that time, in middle school, she thought of self-injury as something depressed teenagers did. One day when she felt depressed, she looked around for some way to injure herself. Finding a screw and a lighter, she heated up the screw and applied it to her skin until it cooled. The resulting raised blister drew enough negative attention from friends that she reacted rebelliously, determined to do it again. She discussed the progression of her burning:

Q: Do you feel like your burning evolved or changed over your course of your involvement with it?

AMY: What I did was try and hold it as long as I could, and there were times when I could hold it longer than other times. Then I would try to breathe through it as much as I could, which is why some of the scars are more predominant than others.

Q: Did your ability to hang in there get longer? Did that fluctuate?

AMY: I think it got longer.

Q: Why do you think that is?

AMY: When you stub your toe once, it hurts, but when you do it a lot, you get used to the pain. You get used to it, and your body doesn't scream out as loud to tell you that it hurts.

Some people who became highly active self-injurers noted that they experienced cravings to cut that they considered psychologically addictive. As they cut more and more, it became harder to stop because they wanted to do it so badly. When they were unable to cut for two or three days, they would get nervous and edgy, which sometimes led to fights with friends and family members.

People often evolved in their use of implements. Just as Janice had discovered the X-Acto knife by watching The Learning Channel, Karen, a 19-year-old student with a history of depression, escalated from hitting herself with a ruler to scratching herself with a butter knife, to cutting herself with a Swiss army knife. Similarly, Carla, the 16-year-old with the history of suicide attempts and hospitalizations, evolved to sharper instruments; she started by using a paper clip to scratch herself, moved to using broken CDs, and then graduated to using pen knives, X-Acto knives, razors, and kitchen knives. Rachel began injuring herself with the inside of a picture frame or anything that had an edge, such as fingernail clippers, coat hangers, or scissors, and finally moved to knives. And Wendy moved beyond breaking glasses to buying straight-edged razors and X-Acto-knife blades. This progression from items teenagers commonly had to implements that they had to purchase for the purpose of their cutting accompanied their growing involvement in self-injury.

Other changes people made as they progressed in their injury moved the location of their cuts and burns to other body parts. The most common starting place was the inside of the arms: the left arm for right-handed people, and vice versa. This was easy to access and easy to see. Many people stayed with their inner arms, repeatedly cutting over old wounds or around them. But if their damage got worse, it got harder to hide in this highly visible place, and so they looked for new cutting ground. The legs offered the next most fertile terrain, especially the upper thighs, which could be hidden in shorts. Kelli, who had been sexually assaulted as a young woman and suffered from clinical depression and eating disorders, moved from her hand to her hips and later to her lower legs when she ran out of space. Finding new and satisfying locations posed a continuous challenge. Others used more visible locations such as their outer arms and their chests. Jessie, who at 22 was living in Germany and teaching a special-needs child, even tried the bottoms of her feet when she ran out of space on her upper arms and her thighs. This gave her the added benefit of enabling her to push her feet hard into the ground for relief when she was younger and at school and could not cut or burn at the moment. Lois, the 18-year-old active Goth, cut all over her body, including her torso and breasts. She noticed that some areas had thicker skin, such as the stomach and ribs, and some cut more easily than others. When she ran out of space, she went back over old, healed wounds and reopened them.

Quite a few people who obtained satisfaction from cutting gave other forms of self-injury a try to see what it would do for them, especially if they began to feel less relief from cutting. Adam, the dreadlocked nontraditional student whose stepfather had beaten him with a belt, explained what made him switch and try burning:

I think I was just doing it for so long that it lost its effectiveness. I just got into a routine, and as I got older, you have more stressful things because freshman year there's—it's freshman year: you really don't have a lot of responsibility, you don't have as serious of a life, where, you know, my sister got out, I was trying to get ready for college, and I would just have more issues to deal with in life, and so—no pun intended—but wasn't cutting it anymore. So I decided to try something new. And I think doing that was definitely more intense because there's sounds and smells and stuff, and it's a lot more of an intense way to deal with the issue.

Many self-injurers did not enjoy the burning experience as well as Adam did. Jimmy was a 19-year-old college student in Alaska. When several problems with family members occurred nearly simultaneously during high school, he made a failed suicide attempt, but it led him to discover cutting. From there he escalated his self-injury until he finally tried burning. Burning gave him a sharp pain that brought the relief he sought, but it left him tired, worn out, and then timid. However, his burn got infected and oozed afterward, and he had to clean it out himself. He dealt with it, but it took a long time. During this period he returned to the knife. Riikka, an 18-year-old Dutch premedical student with a history of abuse, found the results of cutting and burning different but both satisfying, and so she interchanged her use of these techniques. If she just felt sad, she cut herself; if she was angry, she burned herself. Jessie, the German special-needs teacher, described an act of burning in detail:

JESSIE: Burning sometimes takes longer just because it takes longer to burn the skin and all that, especially areas that are already scarred. It just doesn't burn as quickly, so normally that can take 20 or 30 minutes.

Q: Do you keep the flame at it continuously or go back and forth on it?

JESSIE: Well, I tend to move back and forth over a small area for a prolonged period of time.

Q: With a lighter?

JESSIE: They're like lighters: the ones you use for charcoal grills and that kinda thing, the ones that have like the gun-thing trigger on it.

Q: And so what happens to your flesh over this period of time?

JESSIE: Um, normally it just starts getting really hot and really red, and then normally a while afterwards is when it starts to puss or blister. But it normally just ends really red when I finish.

Q: Uh huh, and pussing and blistering is when you stop?

JESSIE: No. No. That normally happens about an hour after I stopped. It takes a while before that occurs.

Q: And do these blacken or redden, or what do they look like afterward?

JESSIE: Normally they're still red on the bottom and then have the blisters on top that are—tend to be a little bit pussy, but that's it.

Becoming a self-injurer was thus the entry to a voyage or career of deviance. Joel Best and David Luckenbill (1982) have articulated four modes by which people often enter deviance. Some people moved onto this path via the *defensive* mode, because it looked like the least bad option from among a variety of even worse choices. Kim's father had left the family because he was an alcoholic and a drug addict, and she described her mother as a "psychotic" psychotherapist who thinks she knows everything, is horrible, and ends up "doing things that aren't so great, thinking they're going to be fine." Unhappy in her new family, Kim described herself as "desperate, about as desperate as a person could be." It was in this context that she turned to self-injury as a way of coping with her problems. She explained: "I wasn't trying to hurt myself in any way. I wasn't trying to hurt myself in a way that people would know. I was just trying to get out of a situation I didn't see a way out of." It was not something she liked, but she could think of nothing better.

Others became self-injurers via a *conscious decision,* because it seemed like a reasonable option. Many of these were people who had heard something about self-injury from the media, school, or friends. They learned from what they saw or heard and decided on the basis of large or small bits of knowledge that something about it appealed to them. In pain and looking for relief, young and willing to experiment or rebel or curious and thinking it might benefit them, they intentionally launched into something new.

Third, people *drifted* into self-injury without necessarily realizing it, almost by accident. These were likely to be people who started doing things such as scraping themselves, intentionally falling down or falling into things, or hurting themselves as youngsters, when they had no awareness that these were precursors of more deliberate self-injurious behavior. People who banged themselves like Molly, bruised themselves like Lois, or blackened their eyes like Joanna followed this mode of entry, becoming self-injurers without ever realizing that they had drawn a line in the sand separating their abstinence from their practice of this behavior. Finally, a smaller group was *sponsored* into self-injury by friends who inducted them into this secret way of venting or bonding, such as we saw with Hannah and the cool guy.

Self-injurers thus moved into this behavior for many different reasons. These ranged from severe, organic problems to experienced trauma, to the normal stresses of everyday life. Participants initiated the behavior differently, depending on the era in history and their social context, and they held themselves to minimum involvement or progressed through stages of greater immersion in accordance with their curiosity, their degree of anguish, and their self-control. Yet, like other people who have strayed from the norm, they followed typical patterns of beginning their deviant behavior.

5

The Phenomenology of the Cut

Many scholarly portraits of self-injury are analytical, detached, and impersonal. They objectify and externalize an act that is, at its essence, about feelings. Yet at its core, self-injury is about the pain that drives people and the feelings of relief that they get from it. Comprehending self-injury requires a close, densely textured examination of how this act is carried out, felt, and interpreted by the people who perform it. It requires particular attention to the accompanying range of emotions. Clearly there are different sensations people experience from self-injuring, just as there are different reasons why they do it, so this cannot simply be reduced to a single formula. But the act of self-injury, its preparation, its practice, and its aftermath are experiences that are powerfully important to its practitioners.

Sociologists have written about the relationship between consciousness, the body, and nature. Their quest has been to capture what occurs phenomenally in experience by giving close, descriptive analyses of the deep, inner essence of people's perceptions, interpretations, and understandings of their lifeworlds. This chapter takes a phenomenological approach to looking at the existential sensations of self-injury.

Many people told us that when they reflected on their acts, it felt as if they were replaying a short movie in their minds. In this chapter we use their voices to present the most immediate thoughts and sensations that they reported when they reflected about their experiences of self-injury.

Impetus for the Act

People were prompted to self-injure by a variety of motivations. The greatest number used self-injury as a mechanism to help them deal with life situations that were too intense to handle other ways. Although injuring themselves did not solve their problems, it enabled them to get through difficult periods by a means that they found, at least temporarily, acceptable.

Overwhelming Emotions

People who deliberately inflicted damage on their bodies often did so in response to acute feelings that overwhelmed them, from the most acute physical and psychological victimization to the more mundane stresses associated with typical adolescence and later life.

Stress/Frustration

For many people self-injury started with a range of different emotions, whether they were feeling down in general or were triggered by something in particular. Life events stressed them out so that they felt overwhelmed. Some people tried to process their feelings in other ways, avoiding cutting or burning. But when other solutions did not work, they finally resorted to self-injury. Molly, the 20-year-old girl from the religious family who as a child had smashed her hand with a hammer and intentionally fallen off her bicycle, had a life history full of frustrations and disappointments. Diagnosed in the late 1990s by her elementary school teachers as having attention-deficit/hyperactivity disorder (ADHD), she was physically isolated in her classroom in a cardboard box that had an opening in the front so that she could see no one except for the teacher. Left back in school twice, she found herself at age 10 in a classroom of eight-year-olds, upset and ashamed. Beaten by her dad when they discovered her self-injuries, she was withdrawn from school after seventh grade and homeschooled. At home, her family paid little attention to her, and she never learned the rudiments of math, science, writing, or history. Throughout this period, her father continued to "buff" her with his belt. At one point she described her boyfriend counting 25 raised welt marks on her back. Moving in and out of the house as she made escape attempts that failed, she spoke to us on the phone when she was 20 years old. Her parents had taken a cruise vacation and brought her two siblings but left her behind, alone in the house with her dog. She described what might typically lead her to a cutting incident:

MOLLY: I guess frustration and hurting from stuff from when I was little all the way up to now and not knowing how to cope with anything. I get scared; I cut. I start hurting, and I can't cry; I cut.

Q: Between the time when you start feeling like you might want to cut and when you actually do your cutting, do days pass by? Hours? Do you always do it that same day?

MOLLY: Sometimes it's seconds. I get that feeling of "I hurt so bad," and I know the only thing that can get rid of it is when I cut, but I don't want to cut. Eventually I break down and go, "You know what? Cutting is the only thing that likes me right now. And it's not killin' me yet and definitely not killing me as bad as being anorexic is. And it's my way out. Nobody has to know. It's just between me and the box cutter or the X-Acto knife or the scissors."

Anger

A common feeling triggering self-injury was anger, especially when it built up into explosions of rage. Barb, a 19-year-old college student from a loving family, started picking at her skin with pins and scraping herself against concrete walls in elementary school. She progressed to using razors in sixth grade, a technique she invented for a behavior she thought was all her own. Diagnosed with depression in seventh grade, she was put on a cocktail of antidepressants and sent to a therapist. She described frequent episodes of anger in which she would sit crying, with tears in her eyes, while clenching her fists and trying to manage her feelings. Eventually the only way she could end these episodes was to cut. Bonnie, a 33-year-old bankruptcy coordinator for a student loan service, with a history of sexual abuse, experienced explosions of rage. A 15-year relationship with a man who raped her left her feeling ashamed and dirty. She often had flashbacks to her past hurts that left her with built-up energy and anger that she could not control. Another person, posting to an online support group, described her anger:

> I don't know about most people, but I know I have a lot of anger. Sometimes I believe the anger is what drives me to SI. I was raised where we weren't permitted to ever talk about bad or upsetting things, so the anger built and with it came the SI. Today I struggle with a rage I cannot control, usually against myself.

For young women, anger often turned to self destruction. Lisa, the 19-year-old college student who had struggled with the terrible relationship with her father, suggested that girls feel conformist pressures to a greater extent than boys do.[1] We asked her why she thought self-injury was so much more common with women than with men, and she responded, "With guys, I think it's because there's a broader spectrum of what's acceptable for guys from parents and from just society in general. And for girls, there's just a narrow perspective of what's acceptable." This difference constructed self-injury, to her, as a gendered behavior.

Many young women felt that it was not all right for them to be outwardly angry. Some were raised with parents who yelled at and scared them, so they compensated for that feeling by internalizing their anger. Connie, a 19-year-old college student, had a lot of familial conflict, becoming more stressed when her parents divorced. She often got jumpy and excited, noting, "This was the only thing that would calm me down when I was just so angry. And I wanted to punch walls and stuff like that, but I didn't want to be so loud about it. So it was taking anger out on myself." Others feared the reaction of those who made them angry if they showed their feelings. Penelope, a 20-year-old college student and graphic designer, noted, "Like with my dad, I feel, like, all my anger at him, but I can't take it out on him 'cause he'll kick me out of the house, so I just take it out on myself instead."

Vanessa lived with both her parents in high school, but then they divorced, and her father got custody. Her relationship with her father was tumultuous, a bond she described as more like brother-sister than parent-child. Dragged around to parties when her parents were still growing up or left at home to fend for herself, she often found herself angry at them, especially her father. But rather than hitting or breaking something that might have more severe consequences, she used a knife her father had brought back as a gift from a trip to Europe to cut, telling herself, "I'm going to use this, because he gave this to me, and I want this scar to be like, 'This is what he did to you. Don't ever let him do it to you again.'" In this way, injuring herself became a symbolic substitute for externalizing the wound he inflicted on her.

Lisa, the 19-year-old college student who fought so badly with her father, further suggested that directing her anger inward helped her hide her troubles and maintain a "normal" appearance:

Q: Why do you think you went inward toward self-destruction?
LISA: I don't know. Probably because I didn't want people to know. I didn't want to ruin my future because I wanted to show people that I could be okay, eventually, but I wasn't at the time.
Q: So when you say it was a means of control, was it a way of dealing with the problems that you were having and bringing them under control so that you could go into the world and live your life?
LISA: Go out and still have everyone think that I was fine and I was normal and I was okay, even though I wasn't.

Shannon, an 18-year-old college student, experienced a short period of cutting, burning, and branding after her parents divorced. She went through a "problem-child phase," using self-injury to vent when she was angry. She explained her logic about it this way: "It's like directing your anger in a different way, I guess—like making it all mine and not being angry at anybody else, maybe." Darcy, a 19-year-old college student from a divorced family who started cutting during high school, found herself drawn to self-injury during times when she was really angry or frustrated. Like many other women, she held in her anger toward others.

> When I'm really angry with somebody else—I don't like to be upset with other people, and I don't like to act out upset on other people. So if I'm really upset with what somebody else has done, I'll tell them about it, but it's not to the extent I'd like to. So then I cut myself, and I'm not upset anymore.

Feeling Acutely Bad

Brianna was the "good girl" all through high school, from a family marked by parental discord, an alcoholic brother, and her father's suicide. She excelled at school and maintained a slim appearance by overexercising and controlling her weight. But one day she got so stressed that she made an unsuccessful suicide attempt using Advil. She suggested that high school represents a tough time, for boys as well as for girls, because teenagers are trying to figure out who they are and are experiencing a lot of rejection and social pain. Alice, the 22-year-old waitress, got into self-injury by accidentally messing around with a sharp knife when she was 12 and discovering that the cut she made gave her a sense of relief. After that, she found herself doing it whenever she felt bad or depressed. A cutting episode could be triggered by a particularly hurtful event. She described a time when she felt rejected by everyone around her:

> It was supposed to be my birthday party, although it was really my brother's friends, and nobody was talking to me and nobody was spending any time with me and nobody really cared where I was or what I was doing. And some girl just snapped at me or told me to go away or shut up or something, and that brought it on pretty quickly. I went straight into the bathroom and gave myself a pretty nasty cut. In fact, that was this one right here [*pointing to the one she unsuccessfully tried to have surgically ameliorated*]. It was one of the worst ones that I'd done so far because I was just feeling really hated and lonely. And so I think that feeling really down about yourself and then having somebody say something really mean to you or treat you badly, that just sort of sends you spiraling into an even worse depression than you already are in. 'Cause I generally feel kind of rejected and

isolated from people. And then if someone actually says something kind of mean to me or puts me down, it makes me feel that much worse.

Release

When people self-injured because they felt frustrated, stressed, or angry they usually experienced a sensation of release, such that their pent-up feelings of anxiety dissipated. Dana, the college student who first tried self-injury after reading about it in a magazine, was diagnosed as predisposed to depression and had never spoken to anyone about her self-injury prior to our interview. She said the emotional hurt she experienced was so overwhelming that it often made her cry and feel angry at the same time. When she cut, it let those feelings out. An online poster noted that sometimes injuring was the only thing that could make her feel better:

> The release that I get is something that talking about it cannot give me nor anything my parents could have given me. SI is almost like a drug that you want to stop, but are not able to. You know that what you are doing is wrong, but stopping it is not possible until the person is ready to say that I do not want this in my life any longer. Speaking only for myself, I know that things can get really bad and I am not able to deal very well with the emotions of it all and I become overwhelmed and I feel that the only option that I have is to harm myself.

Jane, a college student, came from a well-adjusted happy family and had been a cheerleader in high school. However, she went through some of the common, painful stresses associated with adolescence. For her, these produced episodes of acute emotional anxiety that precipitated burning or branding incidents:

> I think that when I was doing it, like the process of doing it was so—I was not even there. I don't even remember actually taking out the coin, heating it up, and leaving it on my arm. I remember it, but I don't feel anything from that part. It was just this intense emotion of anxiety and panic and pressure and frustration, and all of a sudden it was a release. So that space before I was doing it, before the pain started, was not even there. It was more like this crazy buildup to all this sudden release. It was like my brain was on automatic for what I was doing, and then I did it, and it was like I was reorganized and I could breathe again because I wasn't so physically strained from the emotions building up, and I could think again and focus on other things.

The Phenomenology of the Cut | 71

Like Jane, Kyra, a 31-year-old Bulgarian former car-rental agent, noted the desperate feeling she got when she felt the need for a self-injury episode coming on. She fought off the feeling for as long as she could, but the need would grow and become insistent. She described the feeling as a "ricochet" that occurred in her head. "I imagine my scar, and it starts ricocheting in my head. It can take months or weeks, but the ricochet will grow faster and faster and faster until there is a moment where I either die or cut myself or go mad. There is a moment when I can't stand it anymore, this ricochet, and I have to do something to relieve the pressure." Paula, the 38-year-old scab-picking massage therapist, said that she became desperate for the release to feel numbed. She described this feeling as a "pain-endorphin-rush cycle," in which she developed such a pain in her head that she had to just hold on until she could self-injure in order to bring about the endorphin rush (what pharmacologists might describe as a "dopamine rush")[2] that would bring relief. After that she described her condition as "in a completely zoned-out, numbed, emotionally numbed, you know, zoned-out state." For 20-year-old Vanessa, the college student whose parents were young when they had her, just making the decision to cut brought her the onset of release, calming her down and creating a state of focus so that she could injure herself. Once she was done, she could exhale a great sigh and move into a deeper calm.

Grounding

Another related impetus for self-injury came from people's need for grounding. Several people described self-injury as the only thing that would settle them down when they were emotionally overwhelmed. One online poster noted, "I feel better afterwards and have a clearer picture of things. I don't really know what drives me to cut. I get panic attacks and the only way to stop them is to cut. Sometimes I don't even think I am really myself when I cut. Its like something takes over and makes me do it." Sam, the 23-year-old blond college student who chomped his cheek and cut more deeply, echoed this sense of being out of control prior to cutting and being restored to solid ground afterward. Uncomfortable with heightened states of feeling, he described himself as the type of person who suppresses as many emotions as possible. Yet unfortunately, he sometimes found himself in the grip of emotions that were painfully too much for him:

> When I feel that way, oftentimes I get lost in it. There is no reprieve, there is nothing outside of it; I am completely gone to hyperfeeling. I get into a state of heightened emotional stress to the point where I am pretty much

inoperable, to the point where I can't even function or focus. My thoughts are racing too fast to control; I can't follow them. A lot of times it feels like I'm losing a battle of my own psyche: one side is basically yelling at me; the other side is trying to cope with it. Sometimes it's even been in front of a mirror. And through that process eventually I bring myself to cutting, and I become human again.

For Sam, this grounded him and brought him back to a sense of reality. The physical pain jolted his mind out of its emotional trauma, giving him a sense that there was something beyond the feelings that engulfed him, enabling him to focus on other things.

(Ir)rationales

Some people developed logical rationales that justified their self-injury. Rather than understanding their drive to injure by citing overwhelming emotion or pain, they had accounts that made sense of their actions to themselves (and occasionally to others) in more measured fashion. These were not necessarily intended to legitimate or neutralize their acts but, rather, to clarify their purpose and meaning.

Show Inside Feelings on Outside

One of the goals expressed by some self-injurers was to convey the emotional pain they were experiencing. Emotional trauma was interior and invisible, and most people were acutely aware of the dangers of expressing their emotional vulnerability. Physical injuries were more concrete, and others could see and accept them better. Self-injuring thus gave them a physical pain that could stand for and take the focus away from their emotional pain. Janice, whose rape led her to imagine men stalking her, knew that in high school discussing emotional trauma might not be well received, whereas external cuts were understandable as rationally painful. She said,

I feel like shit, and now other people can see that. And so if I want to be upset, I can say, "See, look—I'm hurt." No one sees if you're hurt on the inside, but if you have a cut on you, you can say, "That hurts. That's why I'm upset." It was kind of just a way to make me seem more rational to other people, so if I'm upset, I can say it's because I'm physically hurt, not because of anything else.

For Dana, the college sophomore with the tendency toward depression, it was almost more satisfying to focus on physical pain than on inner pain. Inflicting wounds on herself hurt, but it gave her an adrenaline rush and something she could treat with a Band-Aid. Then, she could focus on the physical pain rather than the emotional pain, because the emotional pain was worse. Adam, the dreadlocked 22-year-old freshman whose stepfather had beaten him with a belt, went beyond this idea to suggest that inflicting pain on himself helped lift the burden of his emotional pain. After being "reformed" for relatively minor infractions and sent to his room, he would ruminate there and feel miserable for hours. His first episode of self-injury came accidentally, although he was aware of the phenomenon, through a brush with a kitchen knife. But then he discovered that injuring himself helped him deal with the tortured anguish fostered by his stepfather-jailor. Alone in his room, he learned to shift his perspective from being grounded and in trouble to a focus on self-injury. He used a variety of implements for this purpose, such as kitchen knives, pocket knives, staples, or other rough objects. When people noticed his cuts, he brushed them off as biking or athletic accidents. "I guess the pain in my heart and my head just kind of transferred over to the physical pain so it wasn't so heavy on me," he noted.

Lisa, who was so unhappy living with her father after her parents divorced that she smashed a glass and self-injured with it, tried unsuccessfully to get placed in her mother's custody with her younger brother. But her father clung to her, she thought, to spite her mother. She acknowledged her difficulty articulating her feelings of frustration and unhappiness to people, common at her age, and looked to her self-injury to express these feelings. She suggested, "I think the reason that I first did it was just that my mom would never recognize how my dad was treating me, even though she knew. She just felt like there was nothing that she could do about it. So this was a way for me to show that it did affect me, I guess." Lisa looked to her self-injury almost as a cry for help. This echoes the remark Princess Diana made to journalist Martin Bashir in a November 1995 television interview for BBC's *Panorama*, in which she admitted to self-injuring her arms and legs: "You have so much pain inside yourself that you try and hurt yourself on the outside because you want help."[3]

Control

A second rationale that people often gave to explain their self-injury involved the desire to feel a sense of control over themselves. Katy, who at 20 was a member of two MySpace and one Facebook self-injury support groups, described some of the things she saw people writing: "Um, they write that they were feeling alone and that they were feeling numb and they were feeling out of control." Janice, the graduate student whose rape led to problems, explained how self-injuring helped her overcome this feeling of helplessness:

> You feel like your life's under control because you can control, you know, when you bleed, and you might as well be able to control everything else. To me it seems like other people don't think they can control when they bleed. They think that it just happens when they accidentally get hurt or something bad happens, and so I guess sometimes—this is . . . this is completely egotistical and horrible—I feel like I'm smarter than everyone else because I can control that and I realize that I can, and other people don't realize that they can control that.

Dana, the college sophomore with the history of depression, cast this rationale in terms of controlling versus being controlled by her emotions. By injuring herself, she felt that she could control where her hurt was going to be, how much pressure she could put on the knife, and how much she wanted to cut herself. In this way she controlled the pain, as opposed to having it consume her. Tracy, the 31-year-old librarian, felt more comfortable with pain that she inflicted on herself because she could control it. By cutting herself, she moved her physical pain into the forefront and sidelined the emotional pain of her life. Lois, the 18-year-old college student who belonged to a Goth subculture and dressed in highly vampiric style, echoed this sentiment, noting that by seizing control over her cutting she felt stronger, more empowered. Paula, the 38-year-old holistic massage therapist, echoed this sentiment:

> There was the pain-endorphin-release cycle; there was this redemption cycle; there was this huge piece around control. It's kind of like, life is out of control, the people around me are out of control, everything, my emotions are out of control, everything is out of control. But my body, and this part of my body that I am now going to dominate, is in my control, in a sense. There was definitely a sense of taking something that was uncontainable and putting it into a paradigm that had a boundary, and it had rules, and this is how it worked, and you were the ruler of it.

Many people whose lives felt out of control used self-injury to challenge this feeling. Some viewed this strategy as being gendered, since women and girls often found themselves in disempowered situations.

Not surprisingly, many of the people who used self-injury to boost their feelings of control over their lives were also involved with eating disorders, the most famous of whom was Princess Diana, who struggled for many years with bulimia.[4] People searching for ways to bring control into their lives often turned to controlling their food intake and their bodies.[5] This connection of self-injury to eating disorders was especially prevalent among women, whose gender-role socialization emphasizes the importance of their appearance. Tracy, the 31-year-old librarian, discussed the connection between anorexia and self-injury, noting, "They're both attempts to physically manifest emotional or psychological stresses and problems. At least for me, I always felt like there were these things that I couldn't control that no one could see, and it was helpful to me to make them physical." Tasha, a 24-year-old first-grade teaching assistant, recalled that she had developed an eating disorder at age 13. When she discovered self-injury at 14, however, she gave up her anorexia for cutting. Connecting the two, she mused, "I'm sure it was a control issue; I gave up one aspect of control and took on another."

Another similarity between self-injury and eating disorders is the feeling of release they both generate. Katy, the 20-year-old college student with the MySpace support groups, remarked that she learned about eating disorders from a news magazine show on television. Hearing a girl on screen say that when she ate a lot and threw it up, it felt like a sweet release, she thought, "Well, I need that. I can't get it anymore." Lisa, the college student who lived and struggled with her father, spoke directly about the similar effects of self-injury and eating disorders: "It's the same feeling of relief and release when you, like—when I cut myself or when I would throw up, I just felt so much better." Purging, then, may raise dopamine levels.

Punish/Hurt Self

A third rationale people gave for their self-injury involved their need or appreciation for hurting themselves. Like the prior two rationales, this is clearly a gendered reaction to the female social role. For myriad reasons, women felt the need to punish or hurt themselves. Karen, a 21-year-old college student, believed she needed to punish herself for being so awful. Once she had administered the punishment, she felt better about whatever she had done wrong. Naysa, the 20-year-old college student who had learned about self-injury in health class, felt that if she didn't punish herself, no one was going to do it for her. When she felt nervous and shaky, as if she were going to go crazy or blow up, she punished herself by injuring to make herself feel better. Linda, a 40-year-old former medical transcriptionist, now on disability, felt inadequate because her sexually abusive husband claimed she was not satisfying him sexually. She discussed how she turned her anger at him and at herself into punishment:

> Because my motivation for injuring is pretty much a self-punishing motivation. There's a lot of other ones that people have, but that one is more mine. I just always would feel like I deserved to be punished, and I would kind of wait and be afraid that God was going to do it. And then I thought, "Well, maybe I could do it first." Then also I was sort of tied up in the whole idea that punishment and love could equal each other. I was kind of taught that parents, if they loved their children, would punish them when they did something wrong. So I would put the two of those together, and I just got to where I would just have so much guilt that I couldn't deal with the guilt anymore. Injuring would make the guilt go away for a while, and so that's what I would basically do, just do it until the guilt would go away.

To punish herself she chose spanking, the approach that terrified her the most as a child. Using various household implements such as a wooden spoon, a spatula, a wooden meat tenderizer, or an extension cord, she smacked herself on the buttocks. She picked these implements because she thought they would really hurt.

One Internet poster went even further to claim that she liked to hurt herself. She realized in therapy that she got more animated, relaxed, enthusiastic, and happy when she cut herself, particularly if there was a lot of blood involved. Yet at the same time, she was ashamed that this was the case.

Emotional Blockage

The final type of motivation providing impetus for self-injury involved people's inability to connect with or feel their emotions. This represents the opposite problem from feeling emotionally overwhelmed. Some people reacted to traumatic or difficult life circumstances or experiences with *dissociation,* a psychological defense mechanism in which specific, anxiety-provoking thoughts, emotions, or physical sensations are separated from the rest of the psyche. Marissa, the 43-year-old former university secretary, depressed and on disability, indicated that her cutting was prompted by a lack of emotion. She described herself as often feeling completely blank, dissociated. Self-injury brought her out of her trancelike state and helped her reconnect with her feelings, while at the same time being supported by what she called a "nice endorphin rush."

Others with emotional blockage talked about their sense of numbness and their desire or even need to feel something. Penelope was a 20-year-old college student and graphic designer who spent a lot of time in an online forum. She did not like her sense of feeling disconnected from the world. Because she spent so much of her life feeling numb, she was drawn to the intense feeling she got from self-injury. Judy, the music therapy major in Louisiana with a moderately severe history of self-injury, said her impetus to injure came from her desire for feeling: "I wanted to be able to feel because I swung from depression to complete numbness. It's better to feel pain then nothing, and when I asked my friends if they had ever felt like they couldn't feel anything, they would say, 'What are you talking about?' So I felt weird." Gwen, a 20-year-old college student with extensive experience in a variety of self-injury Internet venues, looked to cutting to help release her feelings. Hating her near-constant sense of numbness, she sought the rush of emotions that cutting would trigger: "I'd do it to make myself cry. And there were a couple of episodes like that where I hadn't cried or like really felt anything for a while, and I just wanted—I felt like, I don't know, I felt like there were bottled-up emotions in me, and I just wanted to get them out, and so that's when I turned to cutting." She found this experience almost addictive.

Timing of the Act

Another consideration is the time when people chose to self-injure. Individuals varied in selecting a time over the course of the day and over the course of the year.

Time of the Day

Sometimes people felt such a strong urge to self-injure that they had to do it whenever and wherever they were. Stressful situations at either work or school or painful encounters with friends, as Alice described when she was hurt by the remarks of someone at her birthday party, could lead to the need for immediate release. In these cases people either ducked into makeshift privacy alcoves or tried to conceal their actions in various ways.

But if their urges were not that overwhelming, most people indicated a preference for injuring themselves in the evening. Many factors elevated the evening hours as the most prominent. One of these was the buildup of frustration and bad feelings that people experienced over the course of the day. People became progressively more frustrated and angry over the day or just stopped to reflect on their daily frustrations in the evening. Dana noted that she usually woke up feeling good but that this feeling gradually dissipated. By evening she often felt herself "back on [her] ass" and then looked to cutting for help. Jane, the college student from the model family and cheerleader background, felt tired by the end of the day, which exacerbated her anxiety levels, leading her to feel frustrated and wanting to cut. Wendy, a 24-year-old graduate research assistant from a happy family background, started burning herself when she was 13 or 14 years old. An overachiever and perfectionist, she used it to punish herself when she did not meet her high standards. After a long and busy day she found the quiet of the night the worst time, because she started processing the events of the day, and they generated a loop of frustration in her mind. Adam, beaten by his stepfather and sent to his room, often found himself there, reflecting on his emotions. Letting down the "happy face" that he acted out in school, the pain of his life asserted itself. By the evening, his other coping mechanisms had failed or were no longer effective.

A second reason people often chose the night to self-injure was for the privacy and opportunity it offered. Many people, especially adolescents, spent a lot of time alone in their rooms after middle and high school. They knew the behavior patterns of other family members and could predict when they could cut or burn undisturbed. Closing themselves in their room or locking themselves in their bathroom, they could be uninterrupted or unnoticed.

Lois, the Goth-dressing college student, noted that in high school she had a lot of trouble sleeping, as did some others. Thus, aside from the privacy Lois found at night, she preferred the evening hours for cutting because it helped her to fall asleep after the act. Liz, a 25-year-old animal trainer and longtime cutter who grew up on a horse-breeding farm in Kentucky, noted that she often had trouble falling asleep unless she cut. Hannah, the college student who went to both the psych ward and the specialized self-injury clinic, got into scratching or cutting herself in high school and rapidly escalated her involvement. She described it as a regular practice:

Yeah, it became a routine thing. After a little while it was every single night right before I would go to bed. I'd read for a while, and then I'd injure, and then I'd go to bed. Most of the time it was when I was upset, but then it just became so routine that I just did it every night regardless of what I was feeling. It was just part of what I did.

Time of the Year

People's likelihood of self-injuring often followed seasonal patterns. Common times of the year emerged as rough periods for different groups of people. Most people cited the winter as their heaviest time of involvement, when they experienced setbacks. Several said this was exacerbated by seasonal affective disorder (SAD). Barb, the college student who started by scraping herself against concrete as a child, noted her tendency to get depressed in the winter and to injure more. In the spring, as she cheered up, her self-injury diminished. Several people posted online about their need for different, stronger meds in the winter due to their SAD.

The winter holiday season was most acutely painful. Portrayals of happy families in the media led individuals whose lives did not fit these storybook images to feel sad and lonely. While others coped with this disappointment by drinking, self-injurers often went "to the razor." One person posted on the Internet, "I have to say that holidays are difficult for some people because they are under the illusion that this should be a happy time when in reality they remind people of how much they are missing in their lives. This is the reason that people struggle at this time of year." Holidays were additionally stressful because they brought more family interaction, increasing drama, judgments, and fights, which could be triggering. People experienced stress from holiday shopping, with one online poster noting that finding money for gifts was more than many people could manage. She questioned, "Do they think that buying gifts for people serves to keep other people thinking they are okay? Does it keep them thinking that they are okay if they keep buying gifts every year?"

Summer could offer dangerous waters for others. With school out and people on vacation, those who did not have as many friends often felt lonely. One person noted online, "I have a tendency to struggle in the summer because there is life brewing and people having fun and it points out to me that i am missing out on it. Feel how you feel, don't let the commercials tell you how they think you should feel." Summer clothing threatened to expose the injuries they had been successfully concealing all winter, especially when activities such as swimming or athletic endeavors were involved, when attire that covered their body was inappropriate.

Rounding out the year, some students reported being able to go without self-injuring over the summer but relapsed when they got back to school. Over the summer they were released from the pressure cooker of the school social scene and could be by themselves and do their own thing. Going back to school meant subjecting themselves to the pain and tyranny of the cliques. School also brought academic pressures and the end of vacation and freedom.

Location of the Act

Part of the phenomenology of self-injury involves the geography of the act, whether the location of people's bodies in space or the location of the space on their bodies.

Location in the World

People's finding a secure location to self-injure where no one would find or interrupt them in the act was critical. Many people preferred to hurt themselves in special places. For the majority this place was home, because it offered privacy and seclusion. Also the feelings of isolation and solitude that often preceded acts of self-injury were more likely to occur when people were alone. Many chose rooms in their homes and tailored these environments to create optimal surroundings. Cindy, the 19-year-old retail salesperson, noted that she always preferred a dark location where she could sit down quietly. Ingrid, a 24-year-old engineering student in Germany, set the stage for her acts in high school by telling everyone else in the house that she was going to bed. Then she turned on instrumental music, which she found soothing. She dimmed the lamps in the room and cut herself by the light of her computer screen or a candle.

Naysa, who learned about self-injury in middle school health class, had a room that was in the basement where her parents rarely ventured. After school, she would seclude herself in her bathroom for injuring, and she never did it anywhere else. Kim, who learned about self-injury at age 14 from a member of her therapy counseling group, used to injure in the bathtub. She chose that setting because, "You're already warm, and you feel a lot more relaxed, and you can actually go to sleep."

People who could not make it home had to injure themselves away from their optimal places. When they were desperate, they found satellite locations at work or school where they could do what they had to do, and then they tried to return to these places when emergency needs arose again. They selected these places for safety, predictability, and impregnability. Bonnie, the 33-year-old bankruptcy coordinator, remarked, "When I was at work, I would go to the same bathroom stall, same time. I usually started out methodically planning and escalated into a frenzy-rage-type cutting." Danielle, a 35-year-old mother of three, also sought refuge in a bathroom stall, where no one knew what she was doing. She described this location as very calming because it felt as if she were in a tunnel by herself.

Location on the Body

Since the great majority of people hid their self-injury from their friends and family members, they needed to find discreet physical locations on themselves to do the damage. As noted earlier, most started with their forearms, the closest and most available part of their bodies. This spot had the advantage of being accessible and visible to them, while being relatively easy to conceal from others.

Men and women tended to choose different locations on their body and different ways of self-injuring. Women usually cut in hidden places such as their inner arms, inner thighs, stomach, and legs, in descending order of frequency. Moderate injurers often did not need to go beyond these prime locations. They made few injuries and small ones, sometimes waiting for old ones to heal before making new ones. They hid their injuries, even from loved ones, often for years, as one online poster noted: "My husband (duh) recently found out (I'm great at hiding it sure, but he DEFINITELY saw the scars). I think he was just sort of ostriching the issue until finally he caught me in the act."

Ashamed of their behavior, most people strove to keep the damage they caused minimal, avoiding decorative inclinations. Mark, a frequent male poster, asked, "When you folks cut, do you cut patterns into your skin, or just make random slices? I'm a pattern maker myself. Call it tattooing, if you will." He was answered by Justine, another frequent poster, who noted, "Just make a line or two or three, I'm not really into it but when necessary it's only a few and I don't need to bring blood, just the act makes me feel better. I'm sure there are lots of others who make patterns but I never have."

This exchange illustrates men's and women's different styles. In contrast to women who hid their cuts, men (like Sam, who chomped his cheek) tended to cut deeper, showier, and in more visible, outward-facing locations such as their chests and upper arms. According to their own accounts and the women who described them, men's self-injuries were often more severe. Kim, who attended group therapy for her injuring in high school, said,

The guys were just worse with it. The guys were very angry, about the world, their parents, the way people treated them. They left permanent, bad scars. They had bandages constantly. They would do the backs of their legs and their wrists. One kid I think cut his sides. I flipped out: I know this is bad; these are permanent. Me and my girlfriend kind of knew it was like a passing thing, so we were more careful. The guys were just more aggressive with it.

The Kit

The implements people used for their injurious acts varied greatly. We found differences between those who thought about it in advance, prepared for it, and were systematic in their approach and those who did not, and there were also differences in how they handled it afterward.

Some people, especially in their early stages, used unsystematic methods, grabbing whatever items were at hand. Kitchen knives and other household utensils were popular, as they were readily available. Crystal, a 22-year-old college student who had a brief, three-month foray into cutting at the end of high school, reacted to tension or fights with her mother by grabbing something sharp from the kitchen or punching her hand into glass windows or mirrors. When Alice, with the unhappy birthday party, could not find something that would injure herself easily, she fell back on any tool at all, even if it was not sharp. She described the results of her cuts with nail clippers and a variety of implements with dull hard surfaces as "pretty gruesome."

People more commonly exercised a systematic preparation in approaching their injury. Some were planned, but not sterile, in the items they used. Eileen, a frequent online poster, kept a Tupperware container in a kitchen drawer in her apartment half filled with broken beer-bottle pieces, packets of razor blades, broken pottery, and used X-Acto knives. She admitted that she spent every waking minute thinking about bleeding, getting caught, someone finding her container, or someone removing her hooded sweatshirt and seeing her self-destruction. Liz, the animal trainer, kept a kit with her implements, although she did not particularly keep them clean.

Mandy, the college freshman who rejected the appeals of her casual friend and got into self-injury through an alternative crowd, picked out the dirtiest of her mother's towels and used it every time, along with blades she had broken out from disposable razors, to cut herself and staunch the bleeding. She eschewed washing these things off because she thought that would be unsanitary, so she just kept cleaning up the drips with the same old ratty towel. Similarly, Rachel just let her cuts bleed out, without washing, licking, or putting ointment on them, and Barb blotted up excess blood with a paper towel but never bothered to treat or to bandage her wounds.

People who got beyond simple, early involvement with self-injury more commonly developed a panoply of sterile techniques that they used. Tips for self-injury hygiene can easily be found on Internet Websites. Anya, who began cutting herself at 13 with a piece of glass, started out cleaning herself by licking her cuts but found that they got infected and left worse scars if she did not use rubbing alcohol. Janice prepared for her cutting as if it were surgery. She adapted the implements and techniques she learned from watching documentaries about self-injury and medicine on the Learning Channel:

> I would sit down and do it; like someone would sit down and prepare to do homework, I would prepare to do it. I'd have my Band-Aids and my paper towels and my Neosporin, and I'd put a new blade on my X-Acto knife, and it was like preparing for surgery. I'd pick where I was going to do it, where it seemed like things had scarred the least before and people would not notice, and I'd make sure no one else was at home, and I'd make anywhere from, like, five to twenty cuts at a time.

Many people were ritualistic when preparing themselves and their equipment for injuring, followed by similar aftercare. For some, these rituals could be as satisfying as their injurious acts. Ingrid, the 21-year-old German engineering student, assembled her kit that included vitamin E oil for previous scars, sterile gauze, antibiotics, surgical tape, scissors, and other general stuff, making sure she had everything in her room before she started so she would not have to leave.

Danielle, the 35-year-old housewife and mother of three, carried her kit around with her wherever she went in case she was out and needed to cut. Katy, the 20-year-old elementary education major in the MySpace support groups, had a particular ritual by which she prepared for and cleaned up after her injury. She closed the blinds in her room and turned off the overhead light, turned on the lamp next to her bed, and rolled up her sleeves or put on a "wife-beater" tank top. She sterilized her tools with rubbing alcohol and cleaned herself with hydrogen peroxide. She opened each package of sterilized gauze and alcohol wipes in a particular order and then prepared to cut. When she was finished, she completely resterilized her cut, resterilized her tools, sealed them in Ziplocs, and put them away in a special box with individual compartments. She took her used implements and put them inside a Ziploc bag, put that bag inside a garbage bag, and then disposed of it in the trash. Lisa, the college student with the bad family situation, saw an irony in the way she hurt herself and then turned around and fixed herself up. She attributed this behavior to learning sterile and medical techniques from her mother, a nurse.

Performing the Act

Turning to the act of self-injury itself, people followed emotional patterns of enactment.

Preparation

In preparing to self-injure, people turned their attention inward. Jessie, the special-needs educator from Germany, liked the fact that she spent the time during the act of self-injury paying attention to herself and not worrying about her parents or life in general. Tracy, the 31-year-old librarian, admitted that she was starting to think of her self-injury as a rather narcissistic way of dealing with her problems.

For some, self-injury came out as a quick, desperation act. It was hurried or rushed when it was precipitated by a sudden crisis or an overwhelming urge. Lois, the Goth college student, described a pattern in high school in which a dramatic social situation induced her to cut:

LOIS: I'd introduce myself, and all of a sudden they're all, "Oh, you're the girl that slept with Emily's boyfriend!" And all of a sudden everyone knew. And I had a very public job: I worked in a theater that everyone went to. And people I just didn't want to face anymore, I had to. So during my breaks, I would just cut myself. I got very sloppy doing it, but it was, like, on my lunch breaks, going into the bathroom, I would cut my ribs because I knew I didn't have to cover those as quickly and just let them bleed, and we had very dark red uniforms, so it was very convenient.

Q: Not even a Band-Aid?

LOIS: No, I just let them bleed until they crusted, and that took about a half an hour, and that was my lunch break.

In contrast, some people dragged the act out slowly, trying to savor the experience. Molly, the 20-year-old who was homeschooled by her religious family, figured that if she was going to have that feeling, it might as well last as long as she could make it because of the "I'm free factor."

People prepared for the act emotionally as well. Adam, sitting on his bed in his room, would dwell on his day, amplifying his feelings of woe. Brianna, the family's good child, kept a journal in which she summoned her emotions. Matt, who had a rough time in high school with family conflict, played sad songs to get him in the mood, a common approach. Others used music to muffle sounds of tears if they were crying, so that people in the house did not hear them.

Focus

During the act itself, people would also feel very emotional. Lois, the Goth college student, lay in bed and thought until she got depressed. Then her emotions welled up inside until she was on the verge of crying. Holding herself at this precipitous state, she would reach over to the cube by her bedside where she kept her razors, stretch out whatever skin she was cutting that evening, and slash. Brianna differentiated between maintenance and highly emotional cuts:

> Sometimes I would cut just for maintenance, and I would have this dull resonating feeling that I just needed to get off my chest. In that case I wouldn't cry. It was just kind of like, "I need to get this done, and I just need to suck this up and get this out." But if something specific happened or I just got done fighting with somebody, then I guess it was this immediate crying right after the incident and crying through the cutting.

Hannah, who learned to self-injure from a cool guy but got into it so much that she landed in the hospital, sometimes took a specific thought and injured to it. Cody, who was also hospitalized during high school, said that she sometimes worked herself up to a panic attack, trying to fight off the urge to cut. In the aftermath of the attack, she would find herself shaky and sweaty. Others attained a feeling of dissociation, moving into a trancelike state.

Quite a few people found immense satisfaction in focusing on the blood they generated. A young man on the Internet wrote, "As the blood drains out of me so does just a little of the anger, pain, and the feeling that no one knows or cares how much I am hurting inside." Mark, a frequent Internet poster, wrote that when he saw the blood and felt the burn, he remembered that he was still there. Some people, like Wendy, started off focusing on the pain but became redirected toward wanting and needing the blood. Molly, the homeschooled shut-in, felt like her blood was her friend. "My own blood isn't going to look back in my face and say, 'You're stupid. Why are you doing this? You're worthless.'" She felt like her blood freed her. Lois, the Goth, judged the extent of the cutting she needed by how much she bled. If the first few cuts bled heavily, she felt satisfied and would just let it bleed for a while. If they did not, she would cut more.

Darcy, who came from a family that divorced badly and remarried poorly during her high school years, thought that her blood had a fantastic color. She noted, "I usually wash it and then let it bleed, because if you get it wet, it bleeds more compared to just letting it bleed. Then it scabs over quickly. You know how lipstick bleeds into the lines on your face? Blood does that too, and that's pretty cool." Sukee blogged on her Website about how important the blood was to her cutting ritual:

> After a while, I couldn't cause enough blood with a pin. I know, it sounds sick, but the blood was a big factor. I tried pieces of glass, but they were jagged and didn't cut smoothly. I tried breaking open a shaving razor, but the blade was too thin and couldn't be manipulated easily. Then, I found a box blade . . . and my weapon of choice. I bought a few straight razors and really started to hurt myself. I am sure a few times I needed stitches, but of course I wouldn't go for help. I would lay on my bed in tears and drag the blade across my skin, sometimes fast and sometimes slow, until the blood ran down my leg and pooled on my mattress. My poor twin bed is still covered in blood stains.

Effects

People compared the feeling of release from self-injury as almost a high, akin to the endorphin release associated with exercising or doing drugs. Janice noted, "It—it's like a total rush. It's like a high. It's almost like doing a drug. It gives you a total adrenaline rush which makes you feel better, no matter what." Brooke, a 21-year-old college senior who started injuring when she was 15 because of the trauma of her family relationships, described the feeling of her blood pressure going up, her heart rate going faster, and getting flushed. Although she felt no pain from the cut, she did feel the sting, and that brought her down. At the same time she felt emotionally intensified and depressed, angry, and scared, all at the same time. Sometimes she cried during cutting episodes, as all these feelings were released in a huge rush. Then it was over, and she felt emotionally spent. Katherine, a 23-year-old college student with a history of depression and suicide attempts, enjoyed the experience and often tried to drag it out as long as she could. However, although she felt good during her injuring, as soon as she stopped she started to feel guilty about it. This change in feeling may be due to the cessation of rising dopamine levels, once the cutting ended.[6] These kinds of mixed emotions were not uncommon.

Some people described even more intense sensations from their injuring. One woman posted on the Internet, "Don't encourage anyone to do this but tonight I cut and that crap felt like an orgasm." Katy, the elementary education major in the MySpace support groups, echoed this sentiment. She noted, "I don't wanna compare it to this, but it was sort of like orgasmic, if that makes any sense at all. Like you would do it until you could finally feel it and feel the release."

Endings

One topic we always raised with the people we interviewed was how they knew an episode of self-injury had come to an end, how much was enough. Answers to this question fell into two categories: by the amount of damage they did or by the feelings they attained.

The Amount of the Damage

People who focused on the amount of damage looked at different dimensions of their actions, with some making an actual "cut count" and others assessing the extent of their harm. Leith, the stylish 18-year-old college student who wore the black trench coat and cap, described arbitrarily picking a number and making that many cuts. Nine was a favorite of his for numerological reasons, but he suggested that he might one day decide to go as far as 100. Ingrid, the German engineering student, usually cut in a series of five lines, then stopped to assess if she needed more. If she was not satisfied, she cut five more times and then another five, three series.

Beyond simple counting, some people looked at the amount of harm they had done. Lois, the Goth college student, cut until she was satisfied with the bleeding pattern. Lynn, the 36-year-old obsessive-compulsive neuroscientist, scratched at her skin until it became raw and bled. Once the bleeding came, she would feel that it was enough. But to get to this point she usually had to tear off the whole first layer of skin to the point where it got raw. Then she stopped.

Adam, the beaten and grounded student, watched what he was doing, and as he saw the layers of skin being scraped away and the area covered with his blood, he eventually came to the conclusion that there was not much more he could cut away "without taking off a limb or something." Marnie, a

51-year-old former bank teller with dissociative identity disorder (DID, multiple personality syndrome), pondered recent episodes of cutting and burning that had drawn to a close. She noted that about two weeks prior she had "cut through the muscle, and that seemed to be enough at the time." Her burning episodes caused greater damage because she sprayed herself with oven cleaner or lighter fluid and then lit it with a match. Oddly detached, she watched this process unfold and made a calculation at the end whether it was enough. Often she did this three or four times in succession, respraying and burning herself, adding each layer of oven cleaner atop the last. She did not stop until the skin turned black.

The Feeling

For those who looked to some feeling rather than the amount of cuts or damage, one indicator that prompted stopping was feeling the pain. Self-injurers differed in reporting what kinds of sensations they experienced from their acts, but those who generally felt no pain looked at its rise as a point of satisfaction. One online poster described how she shifted from rage to pain:

> Have you ever felt kinda high when cutting ? I mean it's happened to me already. But tonight as I just cut like 30 mins ago I was in rage, really! I wouldn't stop :(I would cut and cut and cut (not too deep don't worry) and feel the rage getting stronger before I started to feel that well known and welcome pain and the rage slowly went away. Then I sat on my bed, back and head against the wall and shut my eyes and felt the pain so much this time. It felt a bit like a high. I was smiling and just feeling relieved, empty in my head.

Cindy, the 19-year-old retail salesperson, said that while her mind was often blank during a cutting episode, like an out-of-body experience, the pain that would eventually come "kinda wakes you up." That would suggest to her that she should probably stop. Liz, the animal trainer, similarly described the pain that finally arrived as a jolt that made her look down and realize, "Oh, crap, I've been cutting for a really long time."

Feeling better also prompted some people to stop. Katy, in the online MySpace groups, noted that sometimes she cut for different reasons and that the feeling that prompted her to stop varied with these reasons:

> It all depended on why I was cutting. If I was angry or I was feeling too much, if I needed to calm down, if I needed to control it, if I needed to feel,

I'd stop when I felt something. If I was sad, I'd go until I felt that almost euphoric sensation. It all depended on the reason why and how much of that emotion I had.

Cody went through an emotional cycle each time of cry, cut, panic, and subside. Liz often felt relaxed and good after cutting. Sometimes when she cut with her boyfriend, they would have sex afterward. Diana, the 44-year-old Swede on disability, said she cut until exhaustion, "'Til I feel like I don't have the energy to go on anymore."

Sometimes people who got the positive feelings they sought from injuring experienced negative sensations afterward. Ellen, the college student who heard about self-injury from a teen magazine, said that eventually a mechanism in her brain kicked in and told her she should not be doing this, discouraging her from going any further. Bonnie, the 33-year-old bankruptcy coordinator, said that she felt physically sick afterward, sometimes for days. Her therapist, she said, called this a "hangover effect."

Bad Endings

People knew that there was a risk associated with self-injurious behavior, and most stopped short of bringing on unintended negative consequences. However, bad things could result from their actions, and these fell into interpersonal and medical realms.

Interpersonally, one risk people always took with this hidden, deviant behavior was being discovered. A young woman posted to an online list that she feared having cut too deeply and was looking for advice. Her greatest worry was that as a result of needing assistance, family members would find out her secret. She wrote, "I am going to try to find a help line.... I dont know any numbers to any... but am scared of that too... I will have to use a cell phone or something huh... so they dont trace me?" She asked the other support-group members to advise her on how to get help without being identified.

Others feared that their friends might drop them if they discovered their self-injury. They worried that the taint of mental illness, emotional unbalance, or being a drain on others' personal resources would drive people away. Kim, who began injuring at 14 and had bad family troubles, heard one day from a male friend that her boyfriend had dropped her:

He said Dan knew about it, and I was like, "How the hell did he know?" And he was like, "I don't know, but he knew and he asked me about it, and that's why he broke up with you." My entire hope for the male sex is gone. He didn't even talk to me about it; he just heard about it, got scared, and went away. I think that's how most people would react if they knew about it and weren't doing it themselves and didn't have much information about it. That was my biggest fear: people find out, and they judge.

In the medical category, people sometimes wound up with bad endings from the way they self-injured. We saw earlier that Jimmy, the Alaskan college student, got infected from his burns, which tended to bleed, seep, and ooze.

Another bad medical outcome involved landing in the emergency room. People who cut too deeply found themselves in situations in which their cuts would not close and heal up on their own. We asked people how deeply they needed to cut for a wound to become problematic, and they usually considered half an inch deep the safe limit. When they could not stop the bleeding, they either took themselves to the emergency room or asked a friend to help. Danielle, the 35-year-old housewife and mother of three, lost consciousness for a few minutes after one injury session, and her neighbor, who came to the house, found her and took her to the hospital. Lindsey, a 32-year-old former nurse's aide, was found by the police a few times in mangled states and taken to the hospital in an ambulance. After she got charged for the expensive ambulance rides, she realized that a cab would be a better way to get to the hospital in the future.

Stories abounded on the Web about people's bad experiences in emergency rooms with self-injurious wounds. Some reported that they got blacklisted and turned away from their local hospitals. Others were left untreated for hours, never examined. It was routine for self-injurers to be stitched up by medical students rather than doctors or nurses and handled in a degrading manner. Marissa, the 43-year-old former university secretary, said that people condescended to her horribly in the emergency room, letting her know she was a waste of their time. They preferred to tend to people who had "true accidents." They then proceeded to stitch her up without anesthesia, telling her, "You should be used to the pain."

In contrast to these horror stories, people outside the United States seemed to get treated well in emergency rooms. In Sweden, Diana said that she had to get stitched up on numerous occasions and found the emergency-room doctors nicer than the psychiatric doctors. In the Netherlands, Riikka said that mental health care was quite good, and she mentioned a study reporting that 1 out of 20 people harmed themselves, so it was common for nurses in first-aid departments to have this kind of specialized training. This training affected their attitudes toward self-injurers, she thought. A Canadian online poster reported receiving extraspecial care:

> I am well known at two ER's because in a year I went about 100 times, between a few different ER's but two I went to the most. I know the one hospital that I go to, you are seen by a doctor within 30 minutes or you get a free $20 giftcard to Wal-Mart and they have never had me waiting for more than 30 minutes so that has been cool. I don't always get in and out but I am always in a room seen by a doctor within 30 minutes.

A worse ending was being involuntarily committed to the psych ward of a hospital. Policies governing medical treatment and insurance changed during the late 1990s and early 2000s, with fewer beds available and norms for the length of inpatient hospitalization decreasing dramatically. Many people wrote about the tendency before 2005 or so to commit adults and adolescents into psych wards for a month or longer, and several older people we interviewed described treatments of this length. This has become much rarer, however, with stays often ranging from a week to a month at most.

Sometimes bad endings could come just from people noticing the self-injury, not even from a particularly bad episode. Judy, the 25-year-old music major from Louisiana, was reported in high school to the school counselor by a classmate who noticed her recent cuts. When Judy admitted to the counselor that these were self-inflicted, the counselor called her mother, who suggested sending Judy to a therapist. At Judy's first appointment, the therapist called the hospital and arranged to have her involuntarily admitted. She was terrified.

Danielle, the housewife and mother, described how her parents drove down to Tallahassee, picked her up from college, and brought her to a hospital psych ward, where she spent 35 days. She never went back to college. She described her experience this way: "Really, really bad. I was cutting all the time in there. There were people in there that I could see their illness, which was horrifying for me."

Others got help in inpatient hospital settings. They received advice on how to deal with their problems, on how to resist self-injury. Susan, who at 53 had been in and out of several psych wards, sometimes inflicted extra cuts on herself as she was on her way to the hospital because she was afraid that she might be rejected, as others had been, for not having serious enough problems. It was more common, however, for people to find the help in general psych wards inappropriate and, after they learned the ropes, to end up lying to the hospital staff in order to get out of there. Lindsey, the 32-year-old for-mer nurse's aide, commented on the ironic contradiction of hospitalization:

> It was really funny. The psychiatrist asked me, the last time, he said, "Are you planning to hurt yourself while you're in here?" And I said, "No, I don't usually plan these things." He said, "That's good because if you did, we'd kick you out." It was like, okay, you hurt yourself, get put in, you hurt yourself, get kicked out.

For many, this cycle tended to repeat itself.

Self-injurious episodes were highly emotional from start to finish, illus-trating the intensity of the experience. When people felt bad, they burned with desire to injure. In the midst of the self-injury they soared through a range of feelings. Their endings were filled with guilt, dissociation, relief, and worry. In all, self-injury offered them a profoundly moving series of physical and emotional sensations that they came to crave nearly as critically as the act itself.

6

Loners in the Social World

During the early years of self-injury's rise, in the 1990s and early 2000s, people who self-injured were often isolated from other self-injurers. The behavior was either unknown by much of the public or misunderstood. As a result, practitioners had little or no interaction with others like themselves. This chapter focuses on this period and describes the way self-injuring was affected by the social and historical context of that time.

Sociological categories exist that describe individuals who have similar kinds of relationships and associations with other deviants as self-injurers. Although these analytical types may not fit self-injurers perfectly, they shed insight into some of the underlying dynamics of self-injurers' lives and worlds at the same time as they modify our scholarly conceptions about the social organization of deviance.

Joel Best and David Luckenbill (1982) articulated five types of deviant associations, two of which pertain to our population. *Loners* are defined as people who lack associations with other deviants such as themselves. They do not hang around with fellow deviants, nor do they discuss their deviance with others. This relative isolation requires loner deviants to move into their norm violations on their own, without the knowledge, social support, practical guidance, or reinforcement from others that comes with membership in a deviant subculture. Of all forms of deviants, loners are characterized as those most entrenched in the normative, mainstream culture and are likely, then, to view their deviant acts through the value system of conventionality. Self-injurers, like other deviants such as embezzlers,[1] rapists,[2] physician and pharmacist drug addicts,[3] paranoids,[4] suicides,[5] sexual asphyxiates,[6] and bulimics and anorexics,[7] fit primarily into this category, especially in their solid-world, face-to-face lives and associations.

Colleagues are people who *do* know and socialize with other deviants such as themselves and may even perform their deviant acts in the company of these others. Having other deviants as friends or acquaintances, they gain the benefits of membership in a deviant subculture, such as the diffusion of information to others, social support and camaraderie, and justifications and rationalizations for their deviance. However, colleagues often carry out their deviance alone, without the coparticipation of other deviants who are like them. For instance, colleagues may have victims, as do violent individuals,[8] pool hustlers,[9] and those who make obscene phone calls,[10] or have customers, as do prostitutes,[11] but they must be able to violate norms without the assistance of other, fellow, deviants. Further examples of deviants who organize as colleagues include homeless people,[12] illicit drug users,[13] stutterers,[14] the mentally ill,[15] transvestites[16] and the depressed.[17] While we just suggested that most deviants in the face-to-face solid world operate as loners, in the cyber world, in contrast, they freely associate with others and have access to online acquaintances, friends, communities, and subcultures. They therefore represent an interesting fusion of these two categories.

During the earlier years of our research, nearly all self-injurers functioned as loners, isolated from others, unsure of what they were, and subject to the tyranny of the psycho-medical establishment and its definitions of them as suicidal, mentally ill, and/or dangerous. In this chapter, we depict the early years of the self-injury phenomenon and discuss features of self-injurers' behavior and associations with others. This discussion lays the groundwork for the changes that came later (in the mid- to late 2000s), which we discuss more fully in the next chapter.

Features of Loner Deviance

During the 1990s and the early 2000s, the nascent years of this burgeoning phenomenon, self-injurers exhibited a variety of patterns in the way they structured their acts and organized themselves socially. On their own, as loners, they had to find the deviance, decide to engage in it, and figure out how to do it themselves. They carried out their acts individually, even if they picked up bits of information from other people and places.

Formulating Deviant Ideology

During these years self-injurers were on their own in formulating the meanings and sets of rationalizations legitimating their deviance. They often drew on their respectable training and experiences, not only to develop their techniques but for legitimating their behavior as well. We see this in the rationalizations of convicted rapists, another group of loner deviants;[18] perpetrators commonly denied the violent and forced nature of their acts and suggested instead that their victims precipitated or desired the incidents. Rapists drew on cultural myths, learned hypermasculinity, and their sense of righteous masculine entitlement, all elements of the dominant culture, to justify their behavior. However, in contrast, self-injurers had a much more difficult time providing social meanings and legitimacy to their acts, which were often, especially initially, unclear and undefined.

Early Rationales

Especially near the beginning of self-injury's dramatic rise, novice self-injurers were likely to regard their behavior through the lens of conventional society. Their loner status made them particularly seek the legitimacy and conformity to the norms and values of mainstream society. Alice, the 22-year-old waitress, reflected that she used to think of her cutting as weird:

> I guess just the way that I thought about it was, at first, I was glad that I was able to do it because it made me feel better. Unfortunately it created so much drama and emotionally awkward situations with other people. If they happened to notice what I was doing, which over time more and more people were noticing, it was creating problems in my life. So I guess just the first way that I interpreted it then was it was just my weird way of dealing with my problems. And that I would do it for as long as it did make me feel better.

Others thought about their early experiences with self-injury as bad. Barb, who self-invented her injury as a child by progressing from scraping to burning herself with incense and then to cutting, revealed her normative perspective in acknowledging, "I know it's a bad thing, and you're not supposed to, and most normal people don't. But I like it." For her self-injury represented an "escape," an easy way out of a tough situation.

Over time, these self-injurers individually worked out a view of their deviance as acceptable and solidified their attitudes toward it. Some justified it as all right since it was concealed. Anya, the rebellious Goth, celebrated her cutting as her own private secret, something people kept to themselves. Maggie, raised in a strict Mormon household, used her cutting as a way of adding hidden excitement to her repressed life that kept her from openly challenging family members and church elders.[19] Amy, who decided in her second year of high school that she had been a "goody two-shoes" all her life, wanted to be bad. She figured that it would be normal to balance the scales a little bit.

Some people convinced themselves that their self-injury was a self-protective mechanism, rationalizing that it successfully kept them from doing much worse things. Like shoplifters' "justification by comparison,"[20] they noted that they went through periods of sadness, depression, or self-destruction and that self-injury was somehow a comparatively positive outlet for them. Lisa, whose horrible fight with her father led her to smash a glass, thought initially that her cuts were suicidal moves and that she was just really inept at trying to kill herself. Both 16-year-old Carla, hospitalized twice, and 21-year-old Karen, who cut herself with a Swiss army knife, had made earlier suicide attempts. Karen said, "When I'm cutting, I'm not intentionally wanting to end my life." Both felt that in turning to self-injury they had made significant positive progress.

Others rationalized self-injury as having benefits. Lisa, whose relationship with her father was problematic throughout high school, noted,

> It wasn't illegal. It was affordable. And I could—I could go back to what-ever it was that I needed to do in my life. I could go back to studying or go to work. It doesn't hurt others, it's not addictive, and it didn't cause me permanent damage. All in all, I think I could have done a lot worse.

Maggie, the rebellious Mormon, concluded that her experiences with self-injury were comparable to the calmness people got from a drug-induced or a spiritual experience, yet she could achieve this herself without those crutches. As loners, these people developed and kept their thoughts to themselves.

Social Isolation

Reinforcing these loner deviance tendencies, self-injurers considered their acts personal, not to be shared with others. Like many sexual asphyxiates, self-injurers derived satisfaction from the focus and concentration of being alone while they were engaged in their deviance. It was all about them; the company of others would cause them to lose their complete self-focus in the act, detracting from the experience.

During episodes of self-injury, people tuned out the world and focused exclusively on themselves. Dana, the depressed college student noted, "When I hurt like that, I get really self-involved. I get my blinders on. I'm all about me, and don't disturb me." Mandy, who got into self-injury through an alterna-tive crowd, described her feeling when she cut as insulating: "I'm a part of the world, and I'm in the world, but no matter how close to somebody I get, there's like a thick, or thin—but there's just like a glass wall that I can see through, but I can't touch anybody through it, and nobody can touch me through it either."

This feeling of wanting to separate themselves from others was so intense that Kim, who first heard about self-injury from a patient of her therapist mother at age 14, noted that if someone was cutting him- or herself in her house, even though she also did it, she would be uncomfortable. It was her thing, she said, and she wanted to be alone and in control. Barb, the Swiss-army-knife cutter, in describing why she would not want to share her self-injury with others, explained what she was like during a cutting episode: "I liked being alone; I didn't want people to bother me. I didn't even know people did it socially. I just like being alone by myself. When I'm depressed, I just want people to leave me alone. That's probably why I did the cutting by myself. I didn't like other people around me seeing me do that." Maggie suggested that just as people would not want to masturbate in public, self-injury was similar. It was not a polite subject to do or to talk about with others, and everybody has things that they just do not let others in on, even those to whom they are close. To Maggie and most other self-injurers, it was the most personal thing they did, and they protected the boundaries around it fiercely.

A common reason people self-injured was loneliness and depression. Yet ironically, while they self-injured to avert such feelings, this behavior could exacerbate these conditions. Beth noted that because no one knew about her cutting, she felt apart from her friends. "It's not that no one cared; it's just that no one knew, and I didn't want them to know, so it just made it worse. I just felt completely alone in a bad way." Feelings of loneliness and social isolation were common for many in high school because people's relationships, identities, and ability to understand themselves and peers were particularly challenging at this age.[21]

Social isolation was often exacerbated when self-injurers stayed away from situations in which their scars would be noticeable. Alice, the 22-year-old waitress, noted that she withdrew from friends and social activities to hide her scars:

> Sometimes I would just—I would not go with my friends to a hot tub at a hotel or something. We were all having a good time, but when they went down, I would stay up in the room by myself. And then I'd end up in tears up there because I was so frustrated with myself and with the fact that I have to live with that.

Janice flunked gym class in high school, and endured the ignorant jeers of her classmates, because putting on the shorts required to participate in physical-education activities would have revealed her scars.

Without a deviant subculture to help them legitimate their acts, early self-injurers, like other loner deviants, had feelings of disapproval and embarrassment about their behavior. Like physician drug addicts, they felt shame about their self-destructive behavior. Yet just as their need for social isolation led to behaviors that exacerbated it, their self-injury often caused the feelings of shame that preceded these acts. Several people discussed the way their shame or fear that others would judge them negatively led them to be highly secretive. One male posted a note on a self-injury Website discussing the nature of this shame:

> You might feel alone in your self-injurious activities. This may be due to the fact that you previously did not know anyone else intentionally hurt themselves. Self-injury is a behavior that's rarely discussed in society and has not been exposed by the media; and for these reasons you might have felt alone. You may feel different or "crazy" or abnormal. You may feel shame about your self-injury because you have not yet realized that there are other people who also hurt themselves.

Self-injurers' fears of revealing their behavior to others increased their feelings of shame and isolation, continuing the cycle of self-injury.

Practical Issues

Especially during this early period, self-injurers, as loners, were largely on their own in coping with the practical problems posed by their deviance. One issue involved the decision about how and where to self-injure. Connie, the 19-year-old college student who got angry and had nowhere else to take out her anger, noted that she had never felt any pain from her early, shallow incisions on her arm. She attributed her lack of physical pain to overwhelming emotional distress at the time.[22] But later, when the cuts became more significant, she guessed that it did not hurt because she had become accustomed to cutting her arm. Eventually she became concerned about the visibility of these scars, especially when she was anticipating parental visits or trips to the beach. She wanted to try cutting other parts of her body, but without anyone to consult about it, she feared strong pain. She deprived herself of the relief of cutting prior to her parental visits and trips to the beach. Fearful and frustrated, Connie experienced a typical loner dilemma.

Many practical problems were related to scar management. As previously noted, early self-injurers were able to dismiss this problem as inconsequential because the behavior was not widely known. Even "lame" excuses such as animal scratches, barbwire fences, and motorcycle accidents were accepted without close questioning. Relatively low chances of being suspected and labeled as deviant may also have facilitated or enabled conventional people to enter deviance unsuspected. Alice, with the unhappy birthday party, talked about the kind of carte blanche she had as a 12- and 13-year-old to cut, back in 1993, without being challenged. "I don't think that many people thought about it when they saw cuts: 'What if that's self-inflicted?' They pretty much believed what you'd tell them."

Those who self-injured after the practice emerged and knowledge about it spread received different reactions. Peers, used to hearing about people in their school who self-injured, became moderately inured to the shock of it. When confronted with stories about classmates' scars, they shrugged and dismissed them as copycat moves or cries for help. Yet outside the adolescent world, the behavior was slower to find such nonchalance. More-dedicated self-injurers whose parents became aware of their involvement were watched very carefully and often quizzed about their scars. People searched out more-hidden body locations such as their stomachs and the inside of their thighs. Like tattooees,[23] self-injurers worried about how this behavior, critically important to them now, might affect their future lives, as did Dana, who worried about her scars. These practical problems led many people to think about diminishing their self-injury.

Sharing Knowledge with Others

Self-injurers were torn between the classic loner posture of not confiding in friends and family members about their deviance and making select revelations. Best and Luckenbill (1982) hypothesized that some loners would reveal their behavior to select nonparticipants who could both assist them and help them keep it secret. In contrast to sexual asphyxiates, who sometimes recruited others' help, particularly as they matured in the behavior, self-injurers sought much less of this type of support.

Many reported being treated as having a mental disorder and sent to therapists or psychiatric hospitals when their deviance was revealed. When parents found out (which happened to around one-third of the people we studied), they were often uncomfortable in discussing the problem, dropping the topic after initial awkward conversations. This situation was exacerbated by the weak or bad relationships many self-injurers had with their parents. A common reaction for parents was to send the child to a psychiatrist. Many self-injurers reported refusing to discuss their self-injury with therapists.

Even as late as 2004, Connie was fearful of being considered deviant or odd and stated that she expected to keep her self-injury in the closet forever because the outside world considered it "self-mutilation."

Others were shunned as contagious, burdensome, and potentially mentally ill or suicidal, especially during these early years. Mandy reported the typically expected negative reaction in learning of another's self-injury. Even though she later became a cutter herself, she was disconcerted when she was first approached for help by a casual friend in 1997. She felt overwhelmed and imposed on when a classmate came by one day and pulled up her sleeve, revealing what she had done:

MANDY: It made me really uncomfortable at first, and, like, I mean, we were friends to where we, like, hung out, but it was never anything more than an acquaintance. She didn't really have any other friends, and I enjoyed her company, kind of a thing. It was just in the middle of the field on the way to the buses; it was right there.

Q: Why do you think she showed you?

MANDY: I think a lot of it was, in retrospect, that she just wanted somebody to know so that she wasn't, like, alone anymore, kind of. Because she felt—that was kind of the overall theme of her life, that she felt really alone and didn't have any friends or family or anything that she could really count on or felt cared for her. So I think that was a big thing, just to be like, "Here it is." In a way, I feel like I failed her, because she's living in a halfway house now with a drug dealer and has a baby and that kind of stuff. But I only hear that from mutual friends, so . . .

Q: So what did you take away from that encounter?

MANDY: Just that she had more problems than I could help her deal with, and that's all I thought about at the time was, like, "This is getting a little too deep for me. I'm 14, 13 years old. I don't really want . . ." It scared me, I think, more than anything, because I didn't want to be the person she depended on because I didn't feel ready for that. I still wouldn't, even if she came to me today and said that she needed something. I would be like, "I'm sorry."

Many friends, confronted with this knowledge and feeling too young to handle it themselves, disclosed information about others' self-injury to their parents or their friends' parents.

Janice expressed a similar sentiment of not wanting others to rely on her even when she was in college. She discussed what happened when her friend, who knew she self-injured as well, cut herself deeply in their bathroom one day when visiting her from out of town and then came out to show her, leaving Janice to call the ambulance and clean up all the blood:

> Actually, I am still really, really pissed off at her about that. Really pissed off, because she did it while I was there, and she knew that I had my own problems. And I feel like she purposely put her problems on me, because I had no choice but to bring her to the hospital. I'm not upset that I did— she's my friend, I'm glad I could help her, but . . .

Even though Janice was a cutter herself and had relied on the help of her friends, she felt that this uninvited incursion into her emotional terrain, exacerbated as it was by the bloody mess her friend made, was a violation of their relational bounds.

Eventually many self-injurers did succumb to the desire to unburden themselves. Although most people met with bad reactions, some encountered tacit acceptance, even by people who did not understand their behavior. Noki, an Asian American, discussed an experience she had with a friend in junior high who "therapeutically"[24] disclosed her cutting in 1994, to help lessen the impact of the potential stigma and to make herself feel better by letting others know about her secret:

> We went to her house after that, and we were sitting on her couch. And she said her pills were wearing off, and she was starting to feel uneasy. And I asked her if I should leave because she thought—maybe she thought I was thinking bad of her. And she said that no, somehow I was okay. She knew that I had experienced being bullied also because of my race, and she said that somehow she felt close to me and that I would understand her. I didn't judge her because she was cutting, and I told her that. And she had a kind of really high emotional outburst, and she started crying and said she wanted to stop cutting and also the pills because she couldn't stop. And she said that this was the first time she had told anybody except for her therapist. And I wasn't sure what I was supposed to do, so I just sat there and looked at her and waited until she stopped crying. After that, her mom came home, so she pretended that nothing happened, and I went home. Two days later, I got a letter from her, and she said that that was the first time that she had ever talked to anybody and that she does feel a lot better that she actually did, that she was able to tell somebody who was close to her what kind of problems she had.

Noki held her friend's secret and was supportive, of both her cutting and her desire to stop.

Normative Socialization and Strain

In self-injurers' appeals to others to help support their abstinence, they revealed their views on cutting, burning, and branding as negative, even though they chose to do it. As loners, their acts represented a contradiction to their normative socialization. Lacking a deviant subculture, they were socialized by society, not by fellow deviants, yet they chose this nonnormative path. Like people with eating disorders, self-injurers pursued their behavior to enhance their social conformity. Whereas anorexics and bulimics starved and purged themselves to look better (in their eyes), self-injurers did it to feel better.

Beth displayed her normative perspective when she spoke of feeling ashamed about her behavior: "Oh, yeah. I was ashamed of myself because it's disgusting and it's not normal, which is okay, but it's just bad to do, I think, to yourself, especially if it's because someone else is hurting you or some other reason. I think that's sick, too." Dana reported being frustrated with herself because she had pinned great hopes on the belief that when she got out of high school and went away to college to a new environment, she would be able to leave her cutting behind. She mentioned that she often heard of college referred to as the "magic button" that would fix her life, and many people we interviewed did note this effect. But for Dana, it did not work out that way. She made it through the first year of college without any remission, but during her sophomore year she became unhappy and once again slipped back into her old habit. This made her reassess her definition of cutting as rooted in her "I-hate-high-school story" and connect it to herself more deeply. This was a crushing disappointment, as she had to acknowledge, "My problems actually followed me here, which was really hard, because I realized that I couldn't blame it on high school anymore. You know? Wherever you go, there you are, and it's me." This gave her a "whole sinking feeling" of shame and disappointment.

Many loners choose deviance, then, not because they want to contradict their socialization but because they face situations in which respectable courses of action are unattractive. Although this might not be the case with sexual asphyxia, an activity that practitioners intentionally pursue as a pleasurable, albeit deviant pastime, it certainly describes the actions of many pharmacist and physician drug addicts and embezzlers.

Self-injurers faced a strain between their desires and their ability to attain those desires that often led them into internal struggles. Dana talked about her struggle:

It's not—and I'm not, like—and I never really argue with myself, like, "I really want to cut myself, but I shouldn't," you know? If I really want to, I do, because it's not all the time, so when it does, I just do it because I'm desperate to feel better. So it's never like—I never—I'm never at war with how I should deal with it, like, "Oh, I really want to do it. Where's the knife?" And my other side being like, "Dana, don't do that." It's always, like, one or the other. If I have the urge, I will.

Yet for others, there was a clearer tug between choices. Sam, the big, good-looking blond who chomped his cheek, had been unhappy for a while and had often contemplated suicide. Although his therapist had prescribed an antianxiety medication for him to take, he knew that if he took too much he could hurt himself. Consequently he asked his roommate to hold his pills and only release four at a time. But one time the roommate left the entire bottle out on the counter. Having a particularly bad day, Sam described the dissonance that he often experienced between competing desires for suicide and abstinence:

I had a little argument inside my head about whether to take them. I didn't think I could keep going. And finally I couldn't handle it anymore. I had to do something, so I choose to inflict physical pain because it was the only thing I could think of at the time that would take my mind off of what was going on inside my head. So I cut myself here under my arm.

Sam resolved his dilemma the same way we saw Karen and Carla do earlier, through compromise. Instead of killing himself or doing nothing, he opted to self-injure.[25] Once he had made this choice, he found himself at this cross-roads again, from time to time. When he found himself holding a bunch of pills in his hand, staring at them for 20 minutes, he described his response: "I get to a point where I'm willing to make the cut, but I'm not willing to die. It's kind of a strange thing; I don't understand it myself. Suicide is the ultimate idea, and then the cut seems to be—making the cut, then leaving—seems to make it bearable."

Yet once loners have opted for deviance, they encounter a structural strain between their actions and their normative expectations. Like Sam, some self-injurers resolved this dilemma by forging adaptations that integrated elements from normative and deviant arenas. Beth, who wanted to challenge her "good-girl" image, stopped short of rebelling openly by not getting into drugs or a punk scene or letting her grades deteriorate. Like tattoos deliberately located on concealable parts of the body, Beth's cuts offered her the perfect combination of secret rebellion and superficial conformity.

Whereas Sam compromised for a lesser deviance than he was considering, Dan often found himself bouncing back and forth between competing desires. He gave in to the urge to self-injure and then renounced it, only to pick it back up again:

> Q: Would you say you're still in an active cutting phase of your life?
>
> DAN: I don't think I can answer that question. I hope not. I don't like it. It seems to work at the time, but the next day I look at it and I think I'm stupid for doing that. It hurts, it's unpleasant, and I'm embarrassed and ashamed. Then a few months with that feeling, then something might happen, and I'll get depressed again and do it again.

This reversal of attitudes between accepting and renouncing self-injury was a common situation and usually left practitioners feeling awful. Connie, who was afraid to try new places to cut herself because she feared it would hurt, discussed how she wanted to cut herself so badly but then felt regretful immediately afterward:

> When I'm really upset, I just go do it. I grab my razor or whatever sharp thing there is and just do it. And as soon as I see whatever, either my scratch or my blood or anything, it's just like, "Ahh, I'm okay." And then, literally, it turns around after my relief, and I'm like, "Oh, my God, I'm totally nuts! Why am I doing this?" I know it's not okay. I know it's not healthy. And I automatically feel remorseful for this behavior. Because I don't look at myself and think I'm crazy. But, then, how come I need to do this or feel I need to do this to relieve stress or tension in my life?

For Connie, just seeing her scars was usually enough to assuage her desire to cut again until they had completely healed.

Self-injurers, in postures that are typical for loners, dealt with a lot of guilt over their behavior. Wrestling with their desires, worrying about their appearance to others, feeling overwhelmed by strong emotions, they often lost control over their ability to fulfill their normative expectations. They sometimes regarded themselves as weak, as people who could not hold on to their determination to be normal. One girl posted to an Internet site, "I am a failure. I hate me. I hate, hate, hate me. And this is where I am still at: the extreme guilt."

Instability

Without the support of fellow deviants, loners often find themselves and their behavior more unstable, unable to be sustained over extended periods of time. Although self-injurers generally eschewed the company or support of others, they sometimes wistfully contrasted themselves to other deviants, even fellow loners who seemed less alone. In 2001, Ellen compared self-injury to eating disorders:

> Women hear it all the time, not so much with cutting but with bulimia. You hear about it all the time happening and percentages and how many women are bulimic and how many women are anorexic. So therefore, you don't necessarily find a common bond with other people but more like, you know, you know that other people do it. You know that you're not weird doing it. It's not like that with cutters.

Mike, who cut after tragic romantic breakups, noted that he thought that if people knew others who cut, it would have a greater likelihood of supporting the behavior. Although he did not envision people engaging in the act together, he imagined that they might share their tales about what they did. Men, in particular, might be encouraged to try to outdo one another, in a natural masculine competition. He asserted that this would encourage people to focus on the "wrong" aspects of self-injury. Loners, then, even pondered how their lives would be different if they were socially organized as deviant colleagues.

Self-injurers could occasionally have collegial attributes, thus blurring the typological lines slightly, even during the early years and in the solid world. But without fellow deviants to share their perspectives and reaffirm the meaning of their deviance, self-injurers were more likely to try quitting their behavior. Rachel noted that if she had not been the only self-injurer she knew, she might have done it more frequently and for a longer period of time. Kim had been around some self-injurers in one school, but when she moved to another school, she found it easier to quit, once she was away from them. She described her attitude at her new school as healthier. Instead of withdrawing and feeling alienated, she went to football games and studied for tests. She abandoned her "I don't care" mentality and found new friends who liked her and thought she was a good person. Without the friends who judged her and reinforced her deviant identity, she launched a new persona as a normal high school student.

These early years thus laid the foundation for self-injurious behavior as, with a few exceptions, a solidly loner deviant undertaking.

7

Colleagues in the Cyber World

As we noted in the preceding chapter, most of the people we encountered in our early face-to-face interviews worked hard to hide their self-injury and felt the sting of social condemnation and shame. It was only by 2003 or 2004 (and later for many) that the opportunity to meet and talk to other self-injurers online presented itself. As information on this topic began to appear on the Internet, we expected to encounter more subjects who had ventured into the self-injury cyber world, especially since the people we interviewed, as college students, had computer access and literacy. The majority of our face-to-face interviewees, however, even into 2007 and 2008, chose not to, remaining isolated.

When we expanded the focus and recruitment pool for our research into cyber venues, we found people's experiences vastly different. Self-injurers who ventured online joined people engaged in a host of hidden behaviors who could not or would not congregate in the solid world, to form together into highly social groups and subcultures.

In this chapter we describe the ways that self-injurers' lives were dramatically changed by their cyber communication, compared to solid-world isolates. Yet it is important to remember that at the same time two important trends were also occurring: many people were choosing *not* to seek out other self-injurers on the Web, and the extremely large majority of people who did seek and find other self-injurers in cyberspace continued to remain as closeted about their self-injury in their daily solid-world lives as they had before. Ironically, while they were cyber colleagues, they remained deviant loners in their solid-world settings.

Going to the Internet

Beginning in the early 2000s, people began using the Internet as a self-injury resource for several reasons. Some gathered knowledge for class papers or scholarly research. Others sought information to help their friends, children, or partners. A few went to preach to or condemn self-injurers. Most felt confused and alone, unable to find solid-world counterparts,[1] and sought help for themselves. Paula, the 38-year-old holistic massage therapist who had picked open wounds for years, described the frustration that led her to search the Web:

> Sometimes the picking episodes would be like three or four hours long, and when I would use the needle, this wasn't a hugely bloody thing, but it was a little bloody. And I'd be in a position like this [*leaning the top of her head down and forward toward the mirror, but with her eyes peeking up*], in kind of a grimace, because you can't be in a position like this for three hours without being really physically just pshhh. And you know, I'm emotionally disconnected, so there'd be this sort of like insane look in my eyes. And I'm looking in the mirror, and I'm not really seeing my reflection because I'm focusing on this. Blood is gathered on my hands, so I have caked blood all over my fingers, maybe some moments where more blood comes, and it really starts to drip. So I had one of these "I'm here for hours," and then all of a sudden the veil comes up, and I see myself like this. And I see the look in my face, and I see the blood on my hands, and that's when I went to my computer, and I said, "I need fuckin' help." And I know there's gotta be something out there, and I don't know what the hell it is, but I need help. And that's when I got online and just put in words.

Paula found her first self-injury support group in 2000.

Finding and Applying the Label

One of the most critical pieces of information found by people who went online to look up self-injury was that they were not alone in doing it. For some it was a big surprise to discover that it was not their own private, personal thing. This realization was particularly powerful for people who started during the early years, before word of self-injury became widespread, or who were from sheltered environments where it might not have been discussed.

Carrie was a 29-year-old graduate student and research assistant in biology at the University of New Mexico who started injuring in 1990 at age 13. Her early forays involved pinching and sawing herself with plastic knives to see if she could take it. She described her discovery of the phenomenon:

> CARRIE: At first I thought that I was just like some weird freak person, you know, that there was no one else who did that kind of stuff, you know, and then I just started, like, just typing stuff in search engines.

Q: Like what kind of things?

CARRIE: Like I just put, like, "hurts self," or "cuts self," and self-injury came up. And I just started researching stuff and found that it was—that there was a lot of information out there. I looked at a lot of the psychological research. I just realized that a lot of people do this.

Q: How did that make you feel?

CARRIE: It made me feel a lot better. It made me feel sad that there were so many people that felt so bad, but that made me feel better that I wasn't the only one. I mean, I felt bad that I was happy to see other people's misfortunes, but I felt better still that I could talk to somebody about it, and they would know what I was feeling.

Katherine, a 23-year-old college student from Tennessee whose cutting dated back to an accidental cut first made in 1996 when she was in ninth grade, echoed Carrie's statement in noting that the most important finding to her was that she was not alone. Katherine talked about her discovery: "I also feel that this is a kind of a subculture in the sense that it is really separated from, or isolated from, the mainstream. Many people don't have any idea it exists even if it's right in front of them, even if they're doing it themselves. And there isn't language in the common culture for it yet."

A Spectrum of Internet Use

The Internet enabled different modes of communication, not all of which were used frequently by self-injurers. We discuss four of these modes and describe how people engaged the first three.

The first and most basic route involved *passive participation* with Websites. People read the information and looked at the pictures but did not respond to them. Much of this information was provided by lay experts and the psycho-medical and therapeutic communities: descriptions of the psychological and experiential factors fostering self-injury; deep secrets underlying self-injurious behavior; differentiations between suicidal behavior, religious flagellation, body modification, and self-injurious behavior; biochemical analyses of the purposes of self-injury; physical, mental, and addictive reactions; resources and literature on self-injury; and links to other related Websites.

Also common were informal sites where individuals posted their journals or accounts of their experiences. Very popular were those containing artwork or poetry created to express self-injurers' inner anguish. Liz, the 25-year-old animal trainer, was originally from a Lexington, Kentucky, horse farm and was living in California when we interviewed her in 2005. She described her reactions to some of these sites:

LIZ: I actually started looking at the Web stuff around middle school age. One of my friends had told me that she was just diagnosed bipolar, and I was looking into that. And I was like, "What? I've never even heard of this." Then I started looking at other stuff, and that's when I started looking at SI sites. And it was like, "Wow, there are lots of other people that do this."
Q: So that made you feel good?
LIZ: Validated more than good.

Others sites contained graphic pictures of open cuts, burns, words chiseled into flesh, or more extensive self-mutilation, sometimes accompanied by participants' narratives about their attitudes and rationalizations for self-injury.

Although some people were satisfied with this passive participation and never looked for more, a second way that people used the Web was to engage in the *interactive support groups* found in newsgroups or Usenet groups.[2] Nancy was a 43-year-old high school administrator who started injuring in 1991 at age 28. Originally from Ohio, she was raped so violently at a young age that the scarring prevented her from carrying a child. When Nancy and her husband discovered her infertility, he began a secret affair with the wife of a close friend whom he impregnated, subsequently divorcing Nancy. Despondent, she moved to Atlanta, but being raped again there drove her from that town to a series of cities where she had difficulty making friends. Eventually she moved to Florida to take care of her elderly parents. Feeling alone, she spent much of her evening time on the Web. Nancy expressed her frustration with the noninteractive Websites: "Journaling, like, what good does that do anybody? I mean, a lot of people have blogs, and those are kinda modern-day journals, but people aren't really interested." These people sought more active participation, as noted by Cindy, the 19-year-old retail sales clerk from Pennsylvania: "I didn't stay on those sites very long. I wanted to talk to other people."

The earliest interactive Internet forums were message boards. Rebecca, a 28-year-old bookkeeper who worked for a private nonprofit foundation in Laramie, Wyoming, explained how these worked:

Are you familiar with message boards? They used to be called bulletin boards, but now they're called message boards. They have different forums and so on. Like, I belong to one of an author I really like and some self-injury ones too. You have to go to the board itself to actually check the threads and see if anyone's posted, to read the messages that are on that. You can post a message in a certain threaded topic that has to do with a certain issue or topic.

By the early 2000s, however, groups had surpassed message boards as the most numerous interactive venues. Groups were usually public forums—anyone could go to their Websites and read the posts—but people could also apply for membership and join. Screening by list owners was lax, and members gained the convenience of having postings from the group delivered directly to their email boxes. During this time these types of Websites and groups proliferated. A simple search in 2006 of self-injury-related groups housed on Yahoo.com, one of several servers, revealed over 200 such venues. People posted news about groups-in-formation on message boards and lists to which they already belonged, trying to lure in new members, as we see in the following post:

> There is a new group just getting started...i think it could help the people in this community...it is very new...very few if any members yet...but the moderator has been through what those of you seem to be going through... from cutting ...to suicide... to having friends try to commit suicide...to finding a way out of it and other things. She can help you...so feel free to join... if you'd like to join, go to [site name]. i hope you can find some help and support here even if you just need to vent.

The ease with which people online formed virtual groups of deviants contrasts with the difficulties encountered by their counterparts in the solid world, where individuals have to identify potential members, assess the value of a particular association, work to involve others, rationalize the association, arrange communication or meetings between members, and contribute resources that facilitate group operations. Margaret McLaughlin, Kerry Osborne, and Nicole Ellison (1997) especially noted how easy it was to find like-minded others on the Internet compared to the solid world, because people were already clustered by their common interests in online bulletin boards, mailing lists, and chat rooms.

After a while, some groups banned advertising for new groups, fearing the loss of members to competing sites. Yet it was common for people to check out several different groups. Bonnie, 33, came from an abusive family and attempted suicide at age 13, for which she was hospitalized. Her first marriage started out well, but her husband became physically and sexually abusive. In therapy to deal with her issues, she worked as a bankruptcy coordinator for a student loan service. She described her movement through a variety of groups: "There's so many groups out there that it's like, how do you pick? I've gone though and joined several and unsubscribed to them because they weren't offering what I needed."

People varied in the amount of time they devoted to reading and to writing group emails, with some seeking occasional contact and others wanting more. Those with greater communication needs joined multiple groups or found busier communities, as explained by Marissa, the 43-year-old former university secretary, now a depressed shut-in, wife, and mother:

> The depression group, it's constantly active. And it's international enough that there is somebody there in the middle of the night, so if I am having a really tough night, anytime, there is somebody from Australia or New Zealand, or waking up, somebody in England, there is always somebody there to help me through the night.

The third mode of Internet use involved participation in *chat rooms*. These offered individuals the greatest and most immediate interaction, as people entered sites where others were actively online and could "talk" to each other in real time. Marissa described her most regular chat room:

> MARISSA: The depression group I am in has a chat room connected to it that is basically on whenever I am home.
>
> Q: Do you keep that open while you do other things, or are you actively participating whenever you are on?
>
> MARISSA: Usually I am actively engaged for hours on end.

In contrast, Nancy, the school administrator, an avid chat-room denizen, told us that she did other things while she was in her chat room:

> When I'm home, I turn it right on. I've moved my bed into the living room and hooked up my computer to the TV screen. I keep my chat room open, and I check the various groups that I belong to. When my friends see I'm on, they start sending me IMs. . . . I pretty much stay in the chat room, and then they instant message me separately, but I try to keep—like, I try to multitask and do the chat room while talking, and it's really very difficult. . . . I keep my chat room and IM open all night so that when I wake up I usually have five to ten instant messages that people have sent me to wake up to for the

day. . . . When you're in a chat room, to the right of the chat room is a list of everybody that's in the chat room. And if you click on their name, it'll give you some options that you can take, and one is to send an instant message.

Nancy, like many of the others with whom she interacted in chat rooms, also used a webcam, so that she could see and be seen by others while talking to them. People's access to webcam technology was visible in the list of chat-room participants through a picture of a camera next to their name.

A fourth way that people use the Internet is to participate in *virtual space* through interactive, multiuser, real-time online cyber games (MUDs, MOOs, or MMORPGs), cyber pubs, cyber cafes, or other forums that go beyond mere words to offer visual representations of characters in "textual virtual reality" or virtual reality (VR).[3] As of this writing, though, none of these forums was frequented by or specifically marked for self-injurers.

Initial Impressions

In people's initial forays into the Internet, some found things that they liked, while others were disenchanted. On the positive side, finding a community with others like themselves was very educational, as noted by Paula, the holistic massage therapist:

> What I found is that there are the cutters, the burners, the breakers, the bangers, the pickers. There's all these little groups, and there are definitely differences. There are personality-type differences, I think. And I found that there were absolutely common grounds. And I was amazed as I began to write about what my experience really was, and what I had felt the role of the behavior had been playing in my life. I was amazed to find how many other people were having that same experience. There was a huge relief in actually realizing that there were a lot of people that had the picking problem, because I didn't know. I thought I was just this freak. And just realizing that people all over the world were having the same struggle; that was amazing for me. That in itself was very healing because there was a sense of community, there was a sense of not being isolated. And through that there was the exchange, and from that came learning. I learned how to understand it more, and I learned to have compassion.

Although many people were frightened to venture into this unknown terrain, they were relieved by the acceptance and support they received there. Deborrah Frable (1993) has suggested that people with concealable stigma are especially likely to feel alienated from groups in the solid world because they hear the negative comments and opinions of others concerning their stigma. Yet in cyberspace they encounter their peers and receive advice on how to deal with their urges. Kelli, a 20-year-old college student with a history of sexual abuse, depression, and eating disorders, reflected on the value of these suggestions:

> Some of them were kind of helpful. They would give you alternatives, like if you need the release of pain, you can take a bucket of ice and stick your hand in it, and that would get it away. They gave a couple of alternatives to try. On some of my lesser urges those helped, but sometimes the urge is just too strong. I just can't get anything controlled in my head, and I didn't like sticking my hand in ice because it didn't do anything.

Others found the shared experiences immensely beneficial, not only because it made them feel less alone and abnormal but also because they were able to yell, to vent, and to scream in what they perceived to be a nonjudgmental venue.

Yet some people found the advice trite or annoying. Katherine, the college student from Tennessee, described what she found this way: "Mostly just a lot of crap that pissed me off. Just clichéd stuff like 'You're not alone; there's help.' I don't think that it's something that I want help with anymore, or need help with. I think everybody's got their thing. People drink or smoke or whatever. Everybody's got something. Like religion. I just kind of see it that way." Danielle, the 35-year-old housewife and mother who had tried several treatment facilities, complained that she went to sites looking to help people and to get help but found youngsters, aged 10 to 12 years old, who were talking very graphically about cutting. She found their experiences too different from hers because they were not interested in stopping, and they claimed that they cut just because they liked doing it. With her abuse history, she found it hard to relate to kids who were self-injuring for, as she described it, "a fashion statement." Denise, a 31-year-old Scottish woman who emailed us an online interview, noted what she most disliked about some of the self-injury cyber sites: "Worst: people who are constantly in crisis, some sites poorly run, whiny teenagers who moan that their mum won't let them go to the mall, seeing people with less insight when you are further on and not knowing how to support them." People who were disenchanted either left or moved on in search of better venues, while those who found a site they liked stuck around for more.

Finding a Community

Going to the Web did not always yield a successful community search. With self-injury growing and expanding around the world, it took years for Internet support groups to catch up to the demand for them. Kyra, the 31-year-old Bulgarian former car-rental agent, self-invented her injuring in 1988 at age 12 by scraping her arm with rough wool. By 13 she had figured out how to cut herself while in the bath and "fell in love" with the blood. She thought for many years that she was alone in her behavior. But by 2002 she had learned that there were others, and so she started searching the Web for them. She described this process:

> KYRA: I first started searching in Bulgaria around three to four years ago, but there was no such thing in Bulgaria on the Internet as self-injury, so I read most about suicide. But it did not help me because all the people just complained, complained, and there was no thinking, there was no idea how to escape it, how to deal with it.
>
> Q: And what made you look further beyond Bulgaria?
>
> KYRA: Well, I needed some relief; I needed some explanations because I haven't talked with anyone about my—what I was doing, and I needed to figure it out, to get help. So I had to go to the international groups, which are in English.

Kyra noted that strong awareness of self-injury in the cyber world had not diffused yet from America and Great Britain to some other countries.

People searched until they found a community that seemed to fit their specialized needs.[4] In this search, they considered the size, level of activity, and demographics of the group. Some groups generated no more than a few postings daily, while others hosted a hundred or more communiqués. People with the greatest communication needs gravitated toward busier communities. Smaller groups were often highly cohesive, with above-average levels of participation, while larger groups, despite their size, could feel relatively small because only a few people posted regularly.

The age demographic of the groups was also important in making people feel at home. Some groups specifically marketed themselves as teen oriented; some were for older people; most invited a mixture. Tasha was a 24-year-old first-grade teaching assistant who used to be a manager at PetsMart. Raised in a family with neglectful parents, she went from an eating disorder into self-injury, trying to grab some control over her life. It was important to her to find a group with people her own age because, as she noted, "I've heard it said many,

many times that I should have outgrown it by now." Judy, the 21-year-old music therapy major from Louisiana, also sought a community of agemates. She noted that she found it "kind of comforting to know that people [her] age still do it." Ingrid was a 21-year-old engineering student in Germany. She went online to see if there were other people such as herself who did not "fit the stereotype" of self-injurers. She described this stereotype as "being a mental disorder, a 13-year-old Goth, you name it." She settled on one that had a lot of diversity:

There's a lot of people who are older than 30, there's a lot of people in college, a lot of people who you'd never know that something was wrong with them other than the fact that they post on the message board. I mean, there's some people that their life seems completely perfect, kind of a lot like you'd think my life is completely perfect, and they don't tell anybody except for the people on the Internet.

In addition to the work they might do with their therapists or during hospitalizations, individuals relied on their cyber communities to help them with support.[5] They found it important to talk to people who knew what they were going through, since most people they knew in the solid world did not really understand self-injury. When they found a community that fit them well, it was rewarding. Paula, the holistic massage therapist, expressed the sense of community she got from her group:

It's a good feeling to find a community that can accept your darkest shadows, but it's also a really scary thing to see those shadows. So it was double-edged. But it got to where, the same way I would look forward to coming home to pick, I would look forward to getting home and getting on the computer and reading all the emails, and I would go on the chats. It's a world, it is definitely a world.

Yet many others found that no one community completely satisfied their needs. Bonnie, the bankruptcy coordinator, noted that she had "gone though and joined several and unsubscribed to them because they weren't offering what [she] needed." Linda was a 40-year-old former medical transcriptionist, who belonged to several sites and was a moderator on one. She discussed how she had to supplement one site with others to fulfill all of her expressive needs:

LINDA: I'm in another group that I'm in because sometimes I need to vent, and I need to be very explicit about what I want to do. And in the ——

group we have a "no trigger" policy, which I completely respect and understand. So if I want to write something triggering I go to another group and do that. But I really like the —— group as well, because it is based on recovering.

Q: And how did you find this other group?

LINDA: One of the other members of —— actually mentioned that he was in a venting group, and I emailed him, and I said, "What's a venting group?" And he said, "Well it's a group where people just vent about suicide and injuring, and there's not a no-trigger policy." And I said, "Really? Send me the link!"

Others used memberships in multiple communities to express different identities or aspects of their identities. Rebecca, who worked for the private, nonprofit foundation, belonged to one group that was mostly teenage girls, what she called "teenage angsters." But she was also a member of a group that had a lot of "older people," in the 20–50 age range. They ranged from individuals who had "serious mental problems like MPD [multiple personality disorder] and DID [dissociative identity disorder]" to "a lot of middle-aged people who seem to have perfect jobs and good lives, married with children and everything, and they self-harm. Because I guess the everyday stresses of life are too much for them, and that's how they take it out."

In another case, Tim, a 21-year-old college student who held various part-time jobs and who moderated his own self-injury group, felt that he had to offer a hopeful self-presentation to the people he was helping on his site, so he proclaimed himself self-injury-free for two years, when in fact he had lapsed in and out of cutting. Tim used his membership in another group to discuss his ongoing problems, presenting a different self and identity there, although he used the same screen name.

When people found a community that they liked, it opened them up to a whole new world of others. Josh, a frequent poster to one list who struggled with depression and was on a cocktail of medications, noted the joy he got from his cyber group:

For me, what I get out of the group is just a sense of community, a chance to really express my true self, my true feelings, which is something I don't get to do very often. We are all connected. We are all one to me. If one of us hurts, we all hurt. If one of us has a good day, we all have a better day. Sometimes I really need that when I'm down. I'm sure I'm not the only one that feels that way. I know I get all excited when I read about one of you that is feeling better after a bad day. It brings a smile to my face. While it might have just solved itself, it does the same thing.

Nature of the Community

Communities differed in their breadth of focus, their orientation toward self-injury, and the degree of regulation they offered. The most narrowly focused single-issue groups preferred postings by people whose primary behavior was self-injury. Participants might have eating disorders or be depressed, but these should not be their main avenues of discussion. Groups encouraged people to talk about other aspects of their lives, such as their feelings, their families, their pets, their travels, and the weather, but their main issue should be self-injury. Moreover, their orientation toward self-injury ought to be in line with other members of the group, as the following 2001 boundary-defining exchange reveals:

> POSTER1 (MALE): Hi, I just found this group so I apoligize if my posting
> method isn't correct. I just had a question. I know it sounds weird but
> I was wondering if any of you get off on harming yourself? Sexually I
> mean? I know it's a rather direct question but there's really no polite
> way to put it. The reason is that I do seem to get off on it. I noticed
> that many of you listed depression as your motive. I've never harmed
> myself because of depression. If there's anyone else and you don't want
> to respond in the group, feel free to Email me.
> POSTER2 (MALE): Although your post is about self harm, it seems that you
> self harm for sexual kicks, whereas this is a *support* group for people
> who self harm due to depression, mental health problems etc. Am I
> alone in thinking that this isn't really a suitable place to be posting this
> sort of material?
> POSTER3 (FEMALE): Getting off on pain is not a new or strange thing.
> You might want to look into BDSM and S&M groups and then look
> for topics about knife play. But for a selfharmer cutting is more akin to
> crying than to getting off.

After being rejected as outside the group's focus, Poster1 was directed to other venues.

Multifocused groups offered long laundry lists of the behaviors or conditions that could acceptably drive individuals to join their ranks. We encountered many people who belonged to multi-issue communities[6] in which people talked about topics from self-injury to suicide, depression, eating disorders, abuse, coming out as gay, social anxiety, loss of a loved one, miscarriage, unfaithfulness, and drug abuse. In fact, self-injurers often shared some of these other problems and sought out others like themselves with common backgrounds who engaged in a range of discreditable practices. People referred to their desire to talk to others who shared their multiple issues as an "addiction" and gravitated toward specific individuals within these groups with whom they had the most in common.

Beyond the focus of the groups lay the issues of orientation and regulation. Although these are two separate dimensions, they overlap to some extent. *Orientation* refers to the degree to which people were stringently anti-self-injury versus supporting of people's continuing practice. *Regulation* refers to whether boards, groups, or sites had strict rules and oversight versus being largely unmonitored. Regulated sites usually cracked down on people's explicit discussion or postings about their injury, the topics they were allowed to discuss, the level of venting that was allowed, the tenor of interaction on the site, the reliability of how people presented themselves, and the composition of members (in membership sites).

Groups that were strict in their orientation and regulation had firm rules about what could transpire and usually made sure to have many people patrolling their cyberspace for violations. The group that Linda mentioned in the preceding section had a firm no-nonsense policy. As one of the moderators posted, "The reason that this group exists is to help people in recovery. All members are asked to identify the alternatives s/he tried to use to avoid using SI as a coping mechanism. For those who are not ready to embrace recovery, this is the wrong group." The group's moderators and members accepted people's slips into self-injury as long as they only discussed their feelings about it and not their injurious acts and as long as they remained staunchly committed to quitting. Their rules not only prohibited discussions of individuals' self-injury but also any use of the actual terms. Any email that the author could construe as having the possibility of upsetting others had to have the word "trigger" in the title so that people could avoid reading it.

This type of forum appealed to people who were very fragile and easily susceptible to others' descriptions of their urges or acts or to people who could not handle conflict on the site. Certain words were banned entirely, while others were replaced with initials or euphemisms. Sets of rules were regularly posted reminding participants of the boundaries. When problems arose, members were likely to appeal to owners or moderators, either privately or through the group forum, to censure recalcitrant individuals. This kind of control gave greater feelings of safety to sensitive individuals. At the same time, it blocked the expression of various types of discussion that some people wanted or needed.

Groups or sites could also be unregulated, due either to a lack of oversight from the original creators or from a positive orientation toward self-injury. Many of the sites or lists from the early 2000s let people talk to each other without restriction and created space for graphic descriptions and pictures. One brief exchange from 2004 shows the kind of interaction that was typical at an unregulated site:

> SHARDSFORLIFE: I am not very good at this due to my razor being a piece of shit and my camera crapping out.. anywho here are some pictures of a few cuts that i did about 3 hours ago when my boyfriend, or ex, decided he was gonna be a dick and break up with me.. [*four pictures*]
>
> ARTFAG: I know what under boob cuts feel like: they don't hurt at all. or maybe i've just built a tolerance. oh well. kinda light cuts :\
>
> DENADA: hmm I'll have to agree with you on this one, they are light cuts, but if that's her thing then that's her thing! I'll post some of my pictures when they are finally developed!
>
> RIPHERTOSHREDS: I don't want to post negatively here, but those are kinda light cuts...did you use a pin/nail or something?

This accepting attitude toward injuring and toward posting vivid pictures of cuts that were still bleeding clearly encouraged people to cut and to display their own accomplishments. At the same time, the judgmentalism about what others said was accompanied by a competition that pushed individuals to engage in more severe self-injury.

An exchange from another site in 2003 shows an argument over the norms of the community and the appropriate reasons for cutting oneself:

> FASTCAR: hahahahhahahahahahhahahahahahahha
>
> why the fuck would you take pictures and POST them for everyone to see of that?
>
> thats a personal thing, you dont cut yourself for anyone else but you.
>
> so excuse me if i think you just want attention. k, sorry about that rant. i just hate when people do take pictures and show people things liek that. *sigh* ok now you hate me, but thats ok. just wanted to say sorry about that screaming up there. k bye

TORTURED: I don't hate you. it's a personal opinion. but since there is a community created for that specific purpose, i'd think i'm not the only one.

FASTCAR: haha yeah, wow your a much better person than i am. i would have hated me lol =[sorry about that, and yeah i didnt notice you were in a community until i looked at the link.

Disenfranchised by groups with strict rules and regulations, people felt free to say or do whatever they wanted in these more open spaces. Often, newcomers wandered into these sites without fully realizing their nature, finding them by Googling words such as *self-mutilation* or *self-harm*. The next short exchange, from 2004, shows this kind of misunderstanding and its correction:

LILDEVIL: I"m leaving thats it I quit there is no one there to help me any more.

FREEDOMFIRE (*LIST OWNER*): Help you? This is not a help community.

People were also free to get into "flame wars" with other posters, expressing hostility and disdain, as we see in this exchange that erupted in 2003 between two men in their 20s:

RAFE: There is no help for cutters. talk therapy does not work with this population. talking about their feelings could make matters worse and do more harm than good. treatment regimens do not work. the cutters have profound psychological disturbances. A few of the cutters I have talked to online have shown tendencies toward pathological lying and a great need to draw attention to themselves.

CHIP: I hate you Rafe. If i never have to look at your opinion again, it wont be soon enough. Fuck off, and leave everybody alone with your views. We dont need to be belittled by you, again and again and again, over and over. Your my biggest trigger by far, here in these posts, you should think about that!! I bet you've never ever cut yourself, even once.;....

RAFE: Chip thinks he OWNS this yahoogroup. You really should become moderator so you can ban people from posting. in the meantime, you should learn how to get along with others.

Some of these sites were very explicit in their avowedly pro-self-injury orientation. These approached self-injury in much the same way as the pro-ana and pro-suicide movements,[7] treating it as a voluntary lifestyle choice and a long-term coping mechanism. Considering individuals' decision to injure themselves rather than injuring others constructive, they encouraged people to help themselves embrace their self-injury and, like others in a tertiary deviant stage,[8] to shed the stigma. Along with this support, they offered practical suggestions for engaging in self-injury, managing relationships with friends and family members, and dealing with the physical problems this behavior generally causes. Zoe, a member of an unregulated Website, posted the following view of self-injury:

> I honestly dont see what is so wrong with cutting. I think Im kinda looking to see if anyone agrees. I mean, instead of punching a pillow, you just take it out on yourself. As long as you dont do it too deep, whats the big deal??? Its better than abusing the people around you. The real problem with it is the emotions and the depression BEHIND the cutting, right? If it isnt "adversely affecting one's life," as is required for anything to be a legal disorder, then why does everyone else think it is wrong...
>
> Am I making any sense to anyone???

She received the following response from Angie: "Hi there!! Nice to hear from you, welcome! As I was reading your posts, I couldn't help but feel as tho I was reading something that I had written!!! I don't see too much wrong with it either, it doesn't hurt anyone but myself."

Tina Deshotels and Craig Forsyth (2007, p. 212) and James Quinn and Forsyth (2005, p. 199) have called these deviant cyber subcultures Goffmanian "back places" (1963), where people of similar preferences feel no need to conceal their pathology and openly seek out one another for support and advice. They note that "socially proscribed and severely sanctioned behavior that was once relegated largely to secrecy among isolated individuals is now at the center of a cyber-community in which all manner of support is readily available" (Quinn and Forsyth, 2005, 193). Philip Jenkins (2001) has discussed the feeling of freedom and safety among child pornographers who were loner deviants in the solid world but members of an online subculture.

Many self-injurers found these unregulated groups too triggering. Hannah, a 19-year-old college student who had struggled with a severe case of self-injury and eventually sought help in a specialized self-injury inpatient clinic, explained what she disliked about unregulated sites and the people who frequented them:

They love that they have Internet friends who do the same thing as they do and they can confide in them all of the horrible, horrible things that they do to themselves. There's more than one of these groups where they would just egg each other on, and that can be good to have people who understand, but that's also detrimental in the long run.

As a result, beginning in the mid-2000s unregulated sites started to decline in popularity. Participants visited them less often, and servers that hosted them began taking steps to shut them down. Many were driven underground, only to resurface under different names on different servers, forcing users to engage in a frequent search for new cyber locations.

Other sites were more moderate in their orientation and control. By the mid-2000s, most sites had moved into this category, offering a broader orientation toward self-injury and supervision; this served to mediate interaction but did not stifle communication. These sites ranged from ones that were generally recovery oriented to others that were somewhat but not too venting. People flocked to these sites who found the unregulated groups too triggering. They had everything, from people who loved cutting to those who were ambivalent about their self-injury, to those who had quit. If people wanted to stop, there were those who would support them. If people wanted to continue, others would accept them. Penelope was a 20-year-old college student who also worked as a graphic designer. She indicated that the mild orientation of the group toward recovery was particularly important to her, noting, "I was looking for people who hurt themselves who weren't so focused on stopping it because I didn't know that I could stop it at that point."

Many of these sites fostered conversations among participants about their daily problems in dealing with friends and family members who did not understand them, about individuals' various psycho-medical conditions and medications, and about self-injurious problems and practices. At age 53, Susan had been injuring herself for 15 years. She had experienced depressive incidents dating back to her teenage years that progressed into what she called body dysmorphic disorder, an excessive preoccupation with her physical defects that impaired her functioning. By the time her daughter reached the teenage years, she, too, was suffering from clinical depression. Both of them had been in and out of psychiatric hospitals. Despite these difficulties, Susan completed a master's degree in early childhood education and swung back and forth between working and receiving disability. She described the moderate regulation and approach to self-injury in her site as embodying a philosophical orientation that was dedicated to the view of self-injury as adverse behavior that ought to stop but that fell short of demonizing the behavior or the individuals who engaged in it. A moderator on another group in this middle range welcomed a new member by informing her that the site was open to a range of recovery perspectives: "Welcome to the group. I hope you find some comfort here in being with people who really do understand where you are coming from. We are all in different places, but have many things in common. We are not judgmental and try to be supportive." Tasha, the 21-year-old teaching assistant, said that she felt comfortable in her community because the moderators read and approved most of the postings before they went online. She chose this group after trying out a few others because this preapproving cut down on people telling "crazy stories that were usually not true" and people yelling at or cursing each other. Yet, as one new member made sure to initially ascertain, people could still discuss their troubles:

> Hello my name is Sheila and I am not new but I've been in a hospital for the past 2 weeks. I was trying to work up the courage to talk to people about it but I've already been deleted from one group and would not like to be deleted from anymore. i need people to talk to, do I still have your support?

Identification with the Community

Although people belonged to various sites and sometimes went for long periods between postings, when they found a community that fit them well, they identified with it. They experienced this identification whether or not they were actively self-injuring. Steve Jones (1997) has noted that our sense of identity is derived not only from identification with the group but from our understanding of the group identity. Erica was an 18-year-old college freshman who was sexually abused by her brother at age 7. By age 12 she was trying a range of different injurious behaviors, progressing from scratching herself to using paper clips, to using toothpicks, keys, safety pins, scissors, X-Acto knives, blades, and knife sharpeners to cut herself. She discussed with us the importance to her of finding a community where there were other people who had been through things similar to herself:

> You've been there; you know what it's like. I have traits in common with other members of the community: being sexually abused, being a perfectionist, having an ED [eating disorder]. Always like, trying to help other people, doing community service, volunteer work—I'm really into that.

Like everything they say on those Websites is completely me. I don't think it's all cutters; I think it's the majority of cutters. I just happen to fit. So it makes me feel more connected to the community as a member.

Identifying with members of the community was vitally important to most people we encountered, whether they had fully functioning work and social lives and hid their self-injury or whether they were trapped in their houses or bedrooms, unable to make contacts with people in the solid world. Katelyn McKenna and John Bargh (1998) have suggested that people with concealable stigmas identify more strongly with these Internet support groups and consider them more important to their identities. As a result, they are also more likely to achieve greater self-acceptance, decreased estrangement from society, and decreased social isolation. Deshotels and Forsyth (2007) have proposed that identities forged with the aid of Internet groups may help people disengage themselves from normative social control. Yet while people found these sites helpful, their identification with the community might also reinforce their self-injurious behavior,[9] as noted by Gwen, a 20-year-old college junior:

If you go to, like, the same chat room and stay there, you kind of get this group of friends, maybe. I guess you could get a sense of belonging or something. It's like you need to cut to stay in that group, you know? Because that's what the chat rooms are for. It's a cutting chat room I guess, even though it says it's a no-cutting chat room. And so I think it just escalates people because we're kind of codependent in a way, because, like, say someone tells their friends the experience of it in that group: everyone will try it, and they'll just keep on doing it, and it'll just keep on escalating because, like, that's what's expected in that group. And it just gets worse because there's no outside force preventing you from doing that, I guess.

Just as with any other group, some people fit in and others did not. Those who fit in but saw their group going in directions they did not like dropped out, deciding not to belong anymore. However, between all of these self-injury communities, members found some strong connection. Identifying with each other was easier because they all knew what it felt like to be in each other's shoes.

The cyber world of self-injury constituted an international arena populated by individuals of widely varied ages, backgrounds, problems, desires, and interests. What differentiated those who went online and found or joined cyber communities from others who did not was not always clear. It may be that those who reached beyond the bounds of their solid-world lives to seek out information and contacts on the Web were likely to be people actively or intensely involved in the behavior who viewed it as a more significant part of their lives and selves. These individuals sought something that they deemed missing in their everyday lives.

This self-injury cyber world prompts us to modify our typological conceptualization of the social organization of deviance. While self-injurers without Internet associations remained loner deviants in their everyday lives, those who joined cyber communities lived the classic stigma-management strategy of the "double life":[10] they were closeted to people around them yet open about their behavior in cyberspace. As such, they reaped the benefits of membership in a global cyber subculture without the associated risk of exposure, stigma, or rejection, gaining practical advice, legitimation for their behavior, social support, and a set of nonjudgmental cyber friends and acquaintances.

Although these categories of deviant association were originally intended to be mutually exclusive, this no longer appears to be the case, since people may simultaneously enact multiple forms, living as loners in the solid world and colleagues in cyberspace. This also fundamentally challenges our views about the necessity of loner deviants' isolation, since the Internet is such a fertile ground for spawning and supporting communities formed around extreme behaviors, which characterize much loner deviance.[11] The concept of loner deviance in the era of the cyber world may thus be moving toward obsolescence.

8

Self-Injury Communities

Once self-injurers ventured into the postmodern world of cyber-space, they found an arena that mirrored their solid world in many ways but had more ephemeral features. In this chapter we examine the characteristics of self-injury cyber communities and the people who inhabited them. Participation in social communities such as these can be very beneficial, offering individuals who join them multiple resources. They give members increased value, or social capital, by enhancing their social networks, offering social norms that govern how members interact, and providing sanctions that ensure members adhere to these norms. It took a while for the self-injurers in our study to learn the characteristics, norms, and values of the different communities they found. As they did so, they created a cyber persona, or possibly multiple personae, for themselves. They then had to navigate their existence in the numerous realities of these new cyber realms.

Cyber Group Roles

The population that frequented different cyber self-injury sites varied, but there were certain common types of participants and posting styles that emerged across these sites. Four of them appeared most repeatedly.

Drama Kings and Queens

Many people took the role of drama kings and queens. They vented or cried for help in an emotional manner, sometimes spewing out stream-of-consciousness ramblings. They worried and reacted harshly to small things. They repeatedly presented their life occurrences and agonized over them. Wendy, a 24-year-old graduate student who cut and burned herself when she did not achieve the perfection she sought, described the irritation she felt toward people who seemed desperate for attention, noting that they just "said the same things over and over and over but never really did anything proactive to help themselves. They just kind of sit there and wallow in self-pity but never really do anything," a complaint commonly voiced. An example of a dramatic post gives some sense of them:

> Sorry I haven't wrote in the longest time. I've been busy. Well I need to rant on so here I go... Well today I was totally like depressed and I was telling my friend who's an SI that I don't know what to do and that I don't want to go to this stupid pyschatrist who makes "educated" guesses on what the fucks my problem. But then she started yelling at me that I'm never going to get better and that I shouldn't judge a shrink without ever seeing one and that I shouldn't be bitching when I'm not even getting help. And ya it does make kind of sense but the way she went on friken made me want to cry. I mean people treat me different but she was always there for me 100% and now it feels like she just doesn't care anymore. And practically everyone in my class now is lecturing me on how I could be helped but I don't want there help they don't realize that treating me like a psyco freak doesn't make me feel any better. And they were all saying that I can make a cure for myself and that they can help me. This girl actually sat me down and wanted to know everything aobut me and shes the new girl in the class. I probly sound like I'm the wrong one which I probly am because I am all the time but I just so confused. I stopped cutting but now I'm scaratching. I don't know what to do. I'm so confused I need someone to help me out.

These posts usually reached out for help at the end, asking for advice, compassion, or at least interest. Some members noted that they had a hard time opening "whiney" posts when they were depressed.

Teenyboppers

A second type of poster who frequented self-injury cyber sites was the teenybopper. Labeled as such by the older posters we interviewed, these middle or high school students were typically also very dramatic. But in contrast to adults, who seemed to either gear themselves toward relationships or recovery, many teenage posters sought ways of injuring and not getting caught. They also recounted their social troubles at school:

> I know just how you feel! I'm 13..and I told 2 or 3 ppl in May...and now my whole grade knows! (its ——). She told everyone! It sucks! And now I'm going to a couselers!! And my family knows..and I might get on anti-depres-

sants and I might goto a freaking pycho helper! I'm not freaking pycho! I hate it! I wish I wouldn't of told anyone..because I still do it and everyone asks me 20 freaking times a week if I still cut...I say no now so they'll stop all the rumors...i'm only 13...i don't need this crap yet. Its like...leave me alone! I'm just like you! I feel like I can't do anything anymore..i feel so lost.

This post is typical of the age that young people usually first started posting to the Internet. In contrast to the adults we interviewed, teenagers were more likely to be driven to self-injury by social factors related to their friendship circles, caught in the drama of adolescence.

Children

Others who posted to these sites assumed childlike roles. No matter their age, they looked for motherly support and advice. Some came from backgrounds where parents were absent, unkind, or conflictual. Their lack of attachment to family members led them to reach out to surrogates. Others had once had strong parents but lost them either temporarily or permanently. The despair they felt from this loss drove them to self-injure. One college-aged girl wrote that since her mother left the country to visit her sister in Brazil she had become severely depressed. She lay in bed all day trying to overcome her depression and thinking about suicide. She ended by saying, "I'm trying to overcome this, but it's hard. Please someone help me!!!!!" Another wrote that even though she had a family and children, she was so depressed over the loss of her mother that she had covered her arms with cuts, and they were bleeding; all she wanted was to join her mother in heaven. She ended with a cry, saying, "Yes, I'm 27 and still love stuffed animals." People offering childlike posts were looking for a maternal support system and a group that embraced them.

Sage Adults

Finally, an abundance of individuals filled the role of the sage adult. When people in trouble posted cries for help, the sage adults offered comfort. Many community members had been in similar situations and knew what desperate posters felt like; they could draw on a strong base of experience to frame their help. Regular posters often assumed these sage roles, as did moderators and list owners. In a sense, these people took the posture of uncertified, lay "cutting professionals," dispensing informal counseling. One moderator replied to the student whose mother had left town, saying that people were listening to her, that her words were not going to be "lost in space." She comforted her, maternally, by saying, "I hope you're not ignoring all our efforts to make to feel better... you're not a little girl......just be yourself... it will be enough!"

A regular poster replied to another person in need by drawing on her own experience to generate advice:

> You're numb hun. Been there lots of times and all I can say is hang in there because it will pass but if you're really worried you might hurt yourself call your doctor. He may need to adjust your meds. Just know if you suddenly get violently angry to call him immediately. I had that happen when I first started wellbrutin and tried killing myself because nobody seemed to be taking me seriously. It was like I'm screaming I need help but wasn't saying it.

Some sage adult postings were extremely mature, filled with grounded wisdom. These posters cared for lost and desperate souls. They reached out and drew people into conversations by asking specific questions about their drug use, their therapeutic support, and their familial relations. Then they offered assessments and advice, as we see in this post by a moderator:

> Sixteen is a very critical and difficult age even in the best of circumstances. The problems you face and the decisions you make about them can have far reaching consequences and it makes me glad that you are moving towards health at such a young age. You have your whole life ahead of you and it can be all that you want it to be. I heard you speak a litlle of what you do not want in your life and this is very good .At the same time try thinking of what you do want ...what are your goals...your dreams...what does a good life for you look like? It helps me to look at both sides of the coin. As hard as things may be for you at this time try to remember that your future is wide open and this can be so exciting. Nice to meet you and please post again.

Some moderators even went beyond just answering posts that came in over the transom to reach out to the "silent members of the group," encouraging them to speak up and to write. One noted that their group had over 300 members but only 30 of them posted regularly. "Where are you all?" she asked. She pushed them to ask for help if they needed it, to give advice if they could, or just even to let others know that they were there.

However, the moderator role was wearing and difficult to sustain over long periods, especially for people still struggling with their own self-injury. Paula, the holistic massage therapist, found herself drawn into the advice-giving role because she had a high degree of self-awareness and could articulate well. Moved into the supportive role of one of the "wiser folks," which she enjoyed, she ultimately encountered the typical dilemma of being triggered by other people's problems and not being able to ask for and to receive the support she needed. As a result she had to take a step back from the group for a while to just take care of herself.

Functions of the Community

Self-injury cyber communities served several functions for all these various types of members.

Helping Themselves by Helping Others

Probably the most important function that people sought was to help themselves by helping others. David Brown (1991) notes in his study of alcohol and drug counselors that many people who had been through drug and alcohol problems turned during their early stages of sobriety to counseling other drug addicts and alcoholics. They went through the training to get professionally certified and worked in the field helping others. In this way they capitalized on their former deviance to build a new occupational avenue, becoming what Brown calls a "professional ex-." A side benefit of the time they spent in this pastime was that being in the setting reinforced their abstinence. Thus, by helping others, they also helped themselves.

Many self-injurers posted to sites about their desire to help others and expressed this sentiment strongly to us as well. Assisting others gave them a sense of value and purpose when their lives were feeling tenuous. They wanted to be there for others as people had been for them. They deeply believed that they were best equipped to understand and to give advice to self-injurers, that their words would have greater resonance to other practitioners because of their own struggles. At the same time, they hoped that by motivating others, they would strengthen their own resolve. We see this well articulated by Sally's post and her response to a query:

SALLY: Hi there, my name is Sally and I am a former cutter. I have not cut in over
4 years now after cutting for 7 years and I would to like to help others out
there who need someone to talk to who understands what they are going
through. I know how hard it is to find people who actually understand
what is going on in our head when we do this stuff. Please e-mail [address]

BECCA: Have you helped anyone else Sally? Are you sure it wouldn't trigger you to do it again?

SALLY: In the last two years, I have helped 6 young women and one young man to understand what they are doing with themselves and to be there and mentor them. If anything, the experience has helped me to not want to cut even more. As I look into the eyes of these people with such bright important roles to play in the future, I realize that I to was one of them. That is why I am here, to help others on here who might need help getting through what I got through. There is hope and people who understand. If I made it through, and can help others, than I am sure that others can too.

Defining the Act

A second, critically important, function of cyber communities lay in defining the act for members. How did various people seek to legitimize their feelings and acts? The way they defined their behavior, often with the help of others, affected their feelings about themselves as well as the way others thought of them. As loners in the solid world, self-injurers often lacked the support of others like them to interpret and account for their behaviors. These social definitions fell into what we characterize as the three S's of deviance: sin, sickness, and selected.[1]

Some people regarded their self-injury as sinful and chastised themselves for it. Their interpretation of their act as involving a religious or moral failing could take one of three forms. Some looked on themselves as morally unworthy because they lacked the will power to stop the behavior. Others thought they were committing a sin against their bodies, God, or the church. A third group believed they were driven to self-injury by evil religious forces.

People who considered themselves morally inferior because they wanted to quit injuring themselves but could not muster the resolve to do so or fell quickly into relapses imagined that they had a stain on their character. Some prayed for help, while others continued to think that putting their faith in God would get them through this difficult period. They posted messages to listservs that referred to God's role in their lives. Yet they felt like they were not living up to what God wanted. One poster tried to console others by suggesting that their self-injury played out as a struggle between God and the devil:

God doesn't want you too suffer. The devil is the one causes the torment and pain that we suffer. I tend to wonder why we tend to blame God for all our troubles and tribulations when it was Satan that causes all our problems. God tries to fix them maybe not the way we want him too or even fix them in the 5mins that you want him too. He works on his time and in his own way. I know it may not feel that way. I think we all question our purpose and what exactly God's will is for us.

Others preached or were preached to by fellow self-injurers, people they knew in the solid world, or people who went onto self-injury sites for the express purpose of railing against the "wicked" about their sinfulness. This bothered many people, triggering them, although others were able to slough it off. Some sites closed their membership to shut out inveterate preachers or evicted them from their sites after members complained.

Many self-injurers who defined the act as sinful suspected themselves or were accused by others of being influenced by ungodly elements. One woman posted to a self-injury Website about the conflict she felt about the origin of voices she heard in her head. Her pastor, she noted, "believes that the voices I hear are demons, and when I have hallucinations he says that I am somehow associating myself too closely with the devil or something? Oh and my parents also kinda agree and think that dark spirits are speaking to me." Yet she noted that she often could not help herself from sometimes speaking back to the voices or from believing what they said. She was confused and tormented by their origin. Molly, who came from the highly religious family in Texas, suffered severe consequences due to her family's assessment of her acts:

My parents shut me away, took me out of school, and took me out of church. I was like Jane Eyre, very secretive. They were like, "If somebody finds out, then we're no longer going to be accepted in our church. Everybody's going to think we're raising the daughter of Satan." It was just pretty much, "You're not allowed to go on trips with your church, you're not allowed to do this, you're not allowed to do that." At that point church was my life because I didn't have any social life anywhere else. And being told, "You can't go to church because you did this, and we don't agree with it," so that made me do it [self-injury] more.

Not only did her parents force her to undergo an exorcism performed by the local minister, but they often left her at home alone, even when they left town on vacation, as we saw in chapter 1. Lacking the skills and knowledge to get a job or go to college, she had a bleak future.

People who viewed their self-injury as addictive, or beyond their control, often spoke about it medically, as a sickness. We encountered a plethora of psycho-medical discussion in interviews and online about people's psychiatric diagnoses, therapy, hospitalizations, and struggles with medications. Someone posted to a Website saying, "A psychiatrist once told me that because of the extreme chemical imbalance in my brain that I would probably always fight with suicidal impulses and SI, even with medication. He said there was no way to fight those for me." Rafe, from the "flame war" in the preceding chapter, believed, "There is most likely injury to the brain that prevents the cutter from being able to regulate their emotional states. I have heard that prolong mental illnesses can permanently alter the brain chemistry of neurotransmitters." Some people accepted these definitions, while others were energized to fight their urges to prove the medical establishment wrong. Those who acquiesced to the medical perspective tended to have a fairly passive view of their own agency in struggling with their self-injury, as one posting to a group illustrates:

> Do you or do you know shome one that has an addiction? It is the same as smoking/drinking/stealing/lying/SI.... no matter what it is, if you feel that you cannot live without doing it/ have to do it. Then it is an addiction, not so much a choice. I have been SI for 6 years, going on 7. I have been this way since I was 13 years old. This is the only way I know how to cope. Sometimes I have to do it even though I do not want to...I really cannot explain the feelings... but something inside tells me that I have to, I have no choice in the matter so then it begins again, the cycle of SI. And breaks my record. I do not SI because I choose to, I do it because I have to.

The addiction model was widely cited, although people held different views on what this exactly entailed. One young woman suggested that her addiction could be viewed as a "habit," similar to drugs and alcohol. She noted that she started self-injuring to deal with stress, but as she progressed through the stages, it became addicting. Yet her descriptions of her urges lacked the intensity often associated with clinical definitions of addiction, often falling into the realm of what she described as "unseemly fascination." Similarly, Gwen, a college student who tried to use the Web to stop her cutting yet was often triggered by chat-room conversations she encountered there, explained the way she viewed it as addictive:

> GWEN: I remember getting this high from it—not necessarily this happy-high, but it was a high. It's like that adrenaline rush I was talking about. Like, you cut yourself, and your blood pressure would go up, and your

heart rate would go faster, and you get flushed, and it would—there was no pain, and then it would start bleeding, and it'd sting, and then you'd come down from it. It was kind of like this emotional high too, but I don't know—it's more physical. You're feeling so much.

Q: So is it a physical or a psychological sensation?

GWEN: A psychological one. I think when it becomes a habit, it's like, I don't know, whatever tool you use to cut yourself or to injure yourself, that's like the best friend you go crying to. And so you go, and I think the addictive part is the release of the emotions, and you keep on wanting to go back, because sometimes I just did it just to feel. And I think that's why it was addictive for me. It was the only way I could really feel. And I hated feeling numb all the time.

These definitions of addiction reflect the casual way people in the culture used the concept, rather than any scientific formulation.

Self-injurers who experienced psycho-medical treatment were often profoundly shaped by their diagnoses and then turned around and readily dispensed their opinions and advice to others as lay experts. One person posted, "I know you don't really see your drinking as a problem, but that might be part of the problem. a lot of people see si as a type of addiction as well, so you might be just trading one addiction for another, which really isn't helpful in the long run." Predictably, she urged the person she was counseling to see a therapist.

Finally, the third perspective on self-injury visible in cyber space defined it as selected, or a voluntary choice. In contrast to the sin ideology that viewed people as succumbing to temptations or being controlled by forces of good or evil, or the sickness ideology that viewed people as driven by biological, chemical, or psychological disorders beyond their influence, the selected model put forth the notion that self-injurers controlled their own agency and made the conscious decision to practice this behavior. Someone posting to a self-injury group asserted her rejection of the addiction model as well, noting, "In time and with proper therapy you will see that you do have a choice, you are just not ready to give it up yet." She cited a friend of hers who was an alcoholic and struggled with self-injury who had given up these behaviors, noting that people did not have to give in to their urges. Several people also discussed how cyber support groups operated under the belief, just as treatment centers did, that individuals could be helped, could learn to give up their injury and replace it with alternatives, despite claims to having susceptible "brain chemistry" or "being wired to be that way." They were working, collectively, to help people get the support and understanding to develop the tools to quit if they so desired. These examples were used to argue for an agentic model of behavior.

The selected model especially differed from the other perspectives in arguing against the notion that self-injury was a bad thing; instead, proponents saw it as something helpful, at least for the present. A poster from Australia suggested that people self-injured because they did not have the skills or motivations to use other means to cope. She saw it as a default because it worked and was quick, and she considered it unnecessary for people to struggle with uncomfortable feelings. Jimmy, the Alaskan college student, went beyond that, arguing that cutting was not a problem and suggesting that it was the way he dealt with his problems. In order for him to stop, he would have to stop the things that caused it. Although he would rather not injure himself, he pronounced himself "content with it." A Canadian poster even noted that his therapist approved of this method:

> But si is also not some terrible evil in my opinion. It's just a bad coping strategy. It's funny but I've had this conversation with my T. I'm a recovering alcoholic and when I drink I drink dangerously, so we've made a deal that if I ever get so overwhelmed emotionally that I can't handle it and all my other coping mechanisms have failed, I'll si before I drink, because that for me is harm reduction.

He viewed self-injury as a more acceptable way of dealing with his problems than others available to him.

Finally, some people indicated that they liked their self-injury. One poster said she had been going over the ins and outs of her cutting with her therapist and had come to the conclusion that she simply liked to hurt herself. It was not just that she enjoyed the release of tension or putting the hurt on the outside where she could see and control it, but her therapist pointed out to her how relaxed, enthusiastic, and happy she looked when she was talking about cutting herself. She closed her remarks by wondering if she should really be using the site on which she was posting, a recovery-oriented venue, at all.

Forging Identities as Self-Injurers

A third function of these cyber support groups lay in leading people to develop identities as self-injurers. Membership in cyber self-injury communities often made this behavior more central to individuals' self-conceptions. In our interviews, we noted clear differences in the way people who belonged to cyber communities self-identified as injurers compared to those who eschewed these groups. This difference could be partly due to a self-selection factor, since people who injured more and felt it was a central part of themselves were increasingly likely to go online for a support group. Yet we suspect that their cyber interactions advanced this aspect of their selves further. People we interviewed in person without cyber support were apt to accept the behavior but to reject the identity. Gwen noted that it was "part" of her "but not the whole" of her, "not even the main part." Kelli, with a history of sexual abuse and eating disorders, regarded it this way: "a temptation I still have to resist, but I don't think it is my master status or anything. Like, I am not a cutter, but I am a person who has cut."

Edwin Lemert (1967) discussed how primary deviants, who keep their deviance hidden from others, have the luxury of denying self-identification with their behavior. Howard Becker (1963) expressed this theme as well, arguing that "secret deviants" are unlikely to conceive of themselves through the deviant lens. Nicola, a college freshman, knew a cutter who flaunted his injuries. She distinguished herself from him by explaining, "No one ever really found out; thus, I was never labeled. I never saw it as part of my identity."

In contrast, people who joined online communities revealed their behavior. Bonnie, the 33-year-old bankruptcy coordinator, said that this revelation felt like a significant coming out in her life, even though she knew she would never see these people face to face. Erica, who was sexually abused by her brother and had cut and broken bones by slamming her hand in the door, discussed how going to the Internet changed the way she thought of herself:

Q: At this point did you identify yourself, any part of your identity, as connected to that behavior?
ERICA: No. Actually I always just thought I wasn't actually a cutter. I was just utilizing it.
Q: That's interesting. Tell me how you see the difference.
ERICA: I guess I thought cutters couldn't control themselves. And I thought I had major control, which I didn't. I just thought cutters are addicted; I'm not. Cutters always need to cut; I don't. I just do it for fun, which really wasn't true actually, at all.
Q: When was it that you started to identify more with being a cutter?
ERICA: I'd say my sophomore/junior year [of high school].
Q: And what made the difference that you embraced that more as an identity?
ERICA: I think just the fact that during my sophomore year I was, like, looking on the Internet, looking at stuff, reading about it. Everything was just like, "You're not alone."

Q: Tell me what about this site helped you change your identity, to incorporate that more into it?

ERICA: Just the fact that there were other people doing it. Maybe, like, there's a group of people. I *am* part of this group, obviously. That helped me connect my identity to a self-abuser. Whereas before I was just, like, one of two people doing it, so it wasn't really an identity; it was more of a habit. Whereas on the Internet it's a lifestyle, almost.

Tasha, the teaching assistant, agreed with this sentiment, noting that she had gone for many years viewing her injury as a private thing that was not a problem. She knew that it was not a good thing, but since it worked "really well" for her, she kept quiet and compartmentalized it to herself as just something she did. Even as she took psychology classes in college and read literature that touched on self-injury, she never told any friends about it, fundamentally refusing to deal with it. For her, joining her community signified an admission that her self-injury was real, was a problem, and had to be addressed.

Jimmy, the Alaskan college student, noted that registering to join a group meant acknowledging that his self-injury was not a quick passing thing but something with which he was dealing. Diana, the 44-year-old Swedish woman on disability, said that it caused her to feel a change because she was part of a group of people who would understand what she was talking about. Darcy, whose parents had an ugly divorce, added that spending hours daily interacting with other self-injurers online increased the likelihood of people identifying with the behavior.

Oscillating In and Out of Communities

As many scholars have noted, a common feature of cyber communities, much more than in the solid world, is members' transience.[2] This transience might relate to people's active involvement in or desistance from self-injury, but it was not necessarily dependent on that condition. People moved fluidly through groups, looking for one that felt right.[3] As their lives evolved and changed, what had once been a good fit might no longer suit them. Paula, the holistic massage therapist, noted that oscillating in and out of cyber communities was common:

The basic group is an open door. It's a place where anybody needing support can come, and they can disappear days later, if that's what they do. There's people like me who come for six months or whatever and then move on. And who knows, in 10 years, I may come and go and come and go many times, or I may at some point want to make a commitment and stick around. These communities are built around these very complex personal issues that people are having, so they're complex. What plays out in them is very multilayered. And why someone would stay and why someone would go and what that means and how that affects people—and I think it's hard for people to see someone come in and then just disappear and think about them for the rest of their life: "What happened to that person?" Or someone who does something like writes a suicide note and never writes again. And some people make a commitment to sticking around, and others take a step back because they're not handling it so well.

Taking a Time-Out

It was common for people to take time-outs from their cyber communities. They might do so because of other engagements or a deliberate need to detach from the group. Some people did so quietly, with no fanfare, for their own personal reasons. Sarah, a 34-year-old bookkeeper, noted, "Life got a bit hectic, and I needed to take a step away. I didn't post about it because I wasn't really been involved with anyone there." Several people mentioned that once they started feeling emotionally connected to a group, they had an urge to leave, because they felt like they became too attached and were uncomfortable with it. Many self-injurers had issues and found it hard to fully trust people they never met personally, especially if they divulged more than they had planned. Sometimes the camaraderie that cyber communities offered felt like too much for them.

Other people announced that they were going to either leave or take a break from the group. One online poster said,

> Just wanted everyone to know that I am going into hiding for an indefinite about of time. I want to thank all of those who have responded to my posts and I would like to thank everyone for all of the support that they have given me. Things are just too overwhelming and confusing that I just don't want to be around anyone or anything, so I think the best thing that I can do right now is to just disappear. Those of you who know me, know how to get ahold of me if you need me for some reason. I hope that I have not triggered anyone with the things that I have been posting and if I have, I would like to send my upmost appology. That was never my intension. All of you are great people and all deserve to happy and healthy. I hope that everyone is going to be able to continue to be safe. Take care.

Paula withdrew from her group, after having been deeply involved in it, because it was triggering her; it got too intense. She had ceased her picking and was helping others, but she felt like the group was pulling her back in. Eventually, she posted a letter that said "just disappeared."

Oscillations in and out of participation were an expected characteristic of these communities. Denise, from Scotland, commented, "Most lists are relatively fluid, but I would guess a good list has long-term members. On the UK list a lot of people leave for a short time and come back because they miss it. Most people who leave come back at some point."

Returning

People returned to posting for various reasons. Some vacillated back and forth between being active posters, being intermittent posters, lurking, or avoiding reading posts altogether. It was common to see people introducing their posts with a disclaimer about their recent absence:

I haven't posted here in months now I think.. well may maybe!!
Dunno if anyone remembers who I am, but oh well people usually never do so that's no biggie!!

After posting about problems with her family, this poster closed with the following:

Dunno what made me sign in and write her again.. just felt like doing it! I've often been here to read, but well it's only know I've felt like posting..!! sorry for all this boring babbling.. hehe!! But no one forced u to read it all!!
*hugs *

Others offered more serious explanations related to recent hospital stays, emotional breakdowns, or other traumas. People who had been away for quite a while often reintroduced themselves for new members and for old members who might not remember them.

Ingrid, the 21-year-old German engineering student, noted that although people dropped in and out of cyber friendships more easily than solid-world relationships, maintaining relationships on the Internet was easier because it was a portable community. She planned to leave school in another year but knew that wherever she went, her community would follow her, would always be accessible.

Leaving for Good

Eventually, some people quit their communities permanently. Several left because they became dissatisfied with the interaction in their venue. Bonnie, the bankruptcy coordinator, commented that she was ready to leave for specific reasons, wanting a different kind of group:

> And I think —— is a good group, and I've met a lot of really nice people there. But there's also a lot of that constant crisis, like "help me right now, right now, right now" kind of thing. And I'm trying to avoid being in that situation again, because I was in that situation. So I have a little harder time with that group now.

She noted that people moved through different groups as their career of self-injury evolved. Others quit with more rancor:

> I wonder what all of the newbies think of all the bickering and back stabbing?? :(
> I'm a newbie. I joined this list because I thought it may be a place where I could feel safe talking about SI, the stigma and impulses that still arise. In the past 4 days that I have been observing this list I've come to realize that this list will be MORE harmful to me than helpful. There is supposed to be a no SI triggering policy yet I saw several posts that said *warning may trigger*, I see bickering among members and lots of wasted time talking about the weather. This is not for me, I know what my boundaries are and what is helpful and what is hurtful to me. The bickering, the frivolous posts, and the overall negative feeling on this list is the reason I am leaving this list. I wish you all good luck in finding your way thru this world and coping with SI.

Still others held on long after they had (allegedly) desisted from self-injuring for months or years, enjoying the outreach they provided to those still in the throes of the behavior or reducing their posting but remaining for a while as lurkers. But as people increasingly found stability and joy in their solid-world lives, they left their cyber communities behind. Cindy, the retail sales clerk, found a better job, got into therapy, and met a boyfriend, and her life improved significantly. She no longer felt the need to self-injure, and although her group had been a huge part of her life for three years, she gradually faded out of the picture. At first she did not write as often but did read some of the posts, but eventually she found people's stories depressing and self-absorbed. She stayed with the group for as long as she felt strong urges to self-injure, but as these weakened, she was able to leave. Reflecting on her life after self-injury, she noted that if she had a problem or got upset, she was likely to turn to her boyfriend or to find some other way of dealing with it.

Cyber self-injury communities were complex entities, with rules, roles, and responsibilities. They attracted vastly different people who often arrived with no previous cyber group membership or experience. These groups tended to evolve from their early beginnings, becoming more regulated, more structured, and more complex. Smaller and simpler venues tended to fade away. With a highly transient population, sites that did not keep up with the changing needs of cyberspace denizens lost the interest of current members and did not have the features to attract and to hold the continuous array of potential new members.

At the same time, cyber communities had multiple and conflicting effects on their members, providing them with permanence and change, safety and danger, solace and aggravation. Most important, they provided the opportunity to interact with others about their common behavior in ways the solid world did not, to ground their behavior within a fluid and developing frame of interpretation, and to satisfy their ongoing needs through a readily available and exchangeable array of groups or sites that fit their current situations and stages of self-injury.

9

Self-Injury Relationships

One of the key byproducts of entering the cyber world and participating in groups or chat rooms is forming relationships with other cyber denizens. These relationships constitute the types of associations that differentiate deviant loners from deviant colleagues, even if they only (or primarily) exist in cyberspace. In this chapter we examine the nature of the relationships self-injurers formed online, how these compared to their solid-world relationships, the effects these had on their solid-world relationships and lives, and how these affected their self-injury.

Making Relationships

Relationships that were formed in online venues differed significantly from those made in the solid world. They developed in different ways, took dissimilar forms, and were based on unlike sets of assumptions, knowledge, and needs.

Rapid Growth of Intimacy

Relationships in cyberspace seemed to form nearly instantly.[1] Once people posted to groups or boards about their issues, the responses began to flood in immediately. From that point, the correspondence between individuals became continually more personal. People seeking cyber support often drew close to those who responded instantly to their posts, sometimes favoring them, as one poster noted, over longer-term solid-world relationships. Bonnie, the bankruptcy coordinator, commented on how relationships arose:

> BONNIE: It's a lot easier to talk to these people online because they don't see you, because you don't have to beat around the bush. The terms you use or the way you explain what happened—you don't have to tiptoe

around these people because they've all been there, they know exactly what you're saying.

Q: Do you think that it's a type of relationship and type of interaction that people have to learn?

BONNIE: I had to learn. It was hard for me. It's weird to talk about your problems to people you don't know at first. And then on the other side, it's easy to talk to people who don't know you, because they can judge you, but it's almost like it doesn't matter if they're judging you. But it matters if your friends and family are judging you.

Most group chat focused primarily on self-injurious behavior: its causes, its triggers, issues associated with concealing it, problems that arose with others because of it, therapy, drugs, and hospitalization. From people's interactions on these sites, these cyber relationships only attained a certain level of intimacy, because they were based solely on group conversation and lacked many of the intricacies and nuances of solid-world relationships. Expectations between members were low, with no real obligation on others' part to reply to postings. Therefore, although people said private and painful things about themselves, the relationships mediated through the group lists encompassed a strange mixture of intimacy and superficiality.

When people found others they liked or with whom they found commonalities, they usually initiated additional, more private, exchanges. Individuals could have immediate and unrestricted conversation in the chat rooms associated with many message boards and groups. Where chat rooms were not structurally established, people often assembled IM addresses and posted them to the whole group. Individuals added their new cyber friends to their buddy lists and could then track each other's presence at their computers, since their arrivals and departures were marked by pop-up screens. People who found their IM or chat-room interactions satisfying often exchanged phone numbers and called each other. Rebecca, at the private, nonprofit foundation, noted that cyber relationships could intensify faster than solid-world relationships.

Depth of Revelations

Several factors drove the immediacy of cyber friendship formation. First, people could talk truthfully to their cyber friends about their self-injury, an important component of their lives that they could not discuss in the solid world.[2] This brought down the wall of secrecy separating people from face-to-face others and forged bonds of trust and understanding. Second, the anonymity and distance of the cyber world brought with it a certain kind of intimacy.[3] Steve Jones (1997) has remarked that community and relationships rest on a foundation of sustained, reflexive, personal intimacy, and this is what self-injurers found online. Denise, from Scotland, felt that she could be more honest on the Web, so that people online knew more about her than most of her solid-world friends. Paula noted the irony of feeling freer to come out to a group of people she did not even know and yet feeling more like she belonged there than anywhere: "It's a scary thing to come out to the world, a bunch of people you don't even know, and it's ironic that on the one hand there was this anonymity and on the other hand I felt more like I belonged there than I had anywhere. It was just such a sense of recognition."[4] Nancy, the school administrator, noted,

> I would confide my deepest, darkest secrets to a stranger on the Web. I think there's, you know, there's a sense of liberty about being able to. I mean, I could tell a complete stranger of my wildest fantasy and not worry about judgment, and he would never know who I was, and I would never have to look him in the face.

Kyra, the 31-year-old Bulgarian former car-rental agent, echoed this sentiment, noting that she had fewer troubles talking by phone or even writing than talking to others face to face. She suggested that people would share less if they had to see each other face to face: "I think people are more, not open, more true in the cyber world, because they can share and they can choose the moment when they share. In the true world you actually act; most of the time you have to pretend in front of people. You have to hide who you really are." Katelyn McKenna, Amie Green, and Marci Gleason (2002) have suggested that the self-relevant information people usually disclose on the Internet is different than it is in the solid world; in face-to-face interaction, people usually disclose the widely known features of their public self, but in cyber relationships they are more likely to reveal aspects of the "real me": those identity-important but usually unexpressed aspects of the self.[5]

Many serious cyber frequenters commented that the cyber world became more real to them than the solid world.[6] People found kindred spirits and were accepted with all their warts. When their warts were too overwhelming, they disguised or omitted them, because they were free to present themselves however they chose. Individuals who had experienced hurt, pain, and rejection in the solid world were the most likely to leave it behind and enter wholeheartedly into cyberspace. Nancy, who held a full-time job, noted, "I don't leave my house much, to be honest. I really don't. Pretty much I'm stuck to the computer." Marissa, the depressed shut-in, noted that she did not have any friends except online: "When I posted that I had no real-life friends, people said that I had *them*, which was nice." Randy, a victim of bad experiences in therapeutic communities, would not even do a phone interview with us, despite our having been cyber acquaintances for years. He said, "I don't talk to people in RL [real life] except for dire emergencies. Just these online connections, and what a learning experience it's been." For him, the cyber world was the *only* reality, yet analysis of his posting suggests that he has experienced problems there as well.

Trust and Misrepresentation in Cyber Relationships

Most cyber relationships were supportive and nonjudgmental. People gave emotional energy to their cyber friends and acquaintances and got it back in return. They could feel secure in knowing that when they needed a friendly remark or piece of advice, one would be forthcoming shortly. Although this support could not compensate for the face-to-face value of a hug or concrete and immediate help in the solid world, people felt that their cyber friends related to and accepted them at a deep level. Bonnie noted that the most important thing to her was for someone to just say, "I understand, and I'm sorry that you're going through this."

Most people accepted others' postings as genuine. Ingrid, the German engineering student, asserted,

> I think that self injury is such a personal thing that when people get on there and start talking about it, it's pretty evident when somebody's just there for the attention, and it's pretty evident when somebody's actually there because they have a reason to be. And so, yeah, I think for the most part people are genuine.

Jimmy, the Alaskan college student, felt that the authenticity of postings on message boards was not an issue. In talking about how he might speak to someone who was making things up just to get attention, he noted, "I'll respond to them the same way I would respond to somebody being absolutely honest, because somebody who comes on and is willing to make something like that up, they still have a problem."

It was precisely this atmosphere, however, that created the trust that opened people up to potential exploitation by others.[7] Randy wrote that trust, extended through shared intimacies, could then be withdrawn during "flame wars": "Sometimes, group members threaten to expose each others' true identities during heated disagreements. Power-plays by the moderators, influence-peddling, mind games, control/censoring, rulemaking, derision, banning. All part of the cyber communities." Marissa noted that when people got into disputes on her site, they sometimes threw offenders out of the group. But individuals could easily rejoin under a different name and persona. She claimed that regular participants knew each other so well, however, that after a while they could recognize old offenders in their new, fraudulent identities. They then busted them publicly and removed them again.

Much has been written about people's ability to misrepresent themselves in the cyber world. This is most prevalent in the virtual spaces,[8] where people are apt to create and enact multiple characters, and in the social networking sites such as MySpace and Facebook that appeal to the young because they represent an escape from a world that does not, and does not want to, understand or provide for them.[9] Although we noted that we encountered no self-injury virtual cafes, pubs, or MUDs, the greatest level of misrepresentation we found was in the chat rooms and their associated IMs.[10] Penelope, a 20-year-old graphic designer, mentioned that the chat rooms made her more nervous because in contrast to a message board, where people had little reason to lie, people could have "alternative motives" in chat rooms, leading them to be fake or phony.

This happened to Molly, the homeschooled shut-in from the religious family. Although she was left to founder in her literacy, math, and knowledge base, she was allowed to use the family computer. At 15 she met Ben on a multi-issue site and became his girlfriend. Although they never actually met in person, they "talked" regularly, and after three and a half years he proposed to her. She accepted, and they planned the wedding. A year later she flew out to join him to pick out the dress and the rings and to meet him and his family. When she got to his door, a guy met her there:

> MOLLY: [He said,] "There's something I have to tell you now. I'm Ben. The guy you fell in love with, and the guy who proposed to you's name is Jason." I was like, "So what is this?" He says, "Well, see, I'm not cute enough to get a girl, so Jason builds all these relationships with girls for me."
>
> Q: And was he doing this with more than one person at a time?
>
> MOLLY: Yeah, five years on the phone and email. What a scam artist!

These kinds of betrayals are so common that they are referred to as "masquerades."[11]

Nancy, the school administrator, spent five years in a chat room where she and another member became "like the mother and father of the chat room." He became her online boyfriend, and they spoke often. When he finally arrived for a planned visit, he showed up with a female "friend." Unnerved, Nancy agreed to the woman's presence. But when she left for work the next day, they cleaned out her apartment, stole her identity, and ended up making charges of $30,000 against her credit cards and bank account. These stories reveal the incomplete aspects of cyber relationships and support Sherry Turkle's (1995) assertion that offline rules about identity do not necessarily apply online.

Yet at the same time, the cyber worlds of self-injury were not rife with exploitation. Rather, they provided an environment where people could "bend" their identities. In an email correspondence, Barbara, a 41-year-old dimensional inspector at a factory, whose primary experiences lay in the bulletin boards and groups, offered her assessment of the degree to which people presented genuine versus altered selves in the self-injury cyber world:

> To be honest I think a lot of people bend their self-presentations as to who they really are. Some people go a little too overboard, and you have those out there who are nothing but storytellers. They think they can say whatever they want, as no one will ever find out the truth about them, as they will never meet this person face to face. Don't get me wrong, there are a lot of people out there who are genuine and very sincere about who they are and who feel alone and are just seeking for help or for someone to understand or to talk to. But I really believe that there is also a lot of bending on the cyber world.

In the following email, Nancy, with a wider range of cyber experience, contrasted the impressions she had about people's authenticity in the chat rooms with that in the group listservs and bulletin boards:

> In the SI rooms, because you are not there looking for acceptance, expecting to gain acceptance—because you can feel a connection because people in there are SI's, it's a bit different. But travel through MySpace and you will see tons of frauds and posers. Y? Because attention is a very hard thing to get in this world people may have experienced little contact in the real world and cyberspaces liberates their alteregos. Maybe their alters can get attention they cannot get as themselves in real life. Invisibility kills.
>
> I would say in a forum or chat group u will most likely find fragmented flexible personalities that bend and tailor themselves to the audience. But most people that post to a BB or group list are truly trying to be themselves.

Self-injury chat rooms (and to a lesser extent message boards and groups), then, primarily drew people whose self-presentations were freer to differ from their solid-world selves but were not as likely to be as wholly invented as those found in cyber pubs and cafes.[12]

Leaving Cyber Relationships

People entered cyber relationships expecting to trust and be trusted, until they got burned. They then, like Randy, Molly, and Nancy, became more cautious and caustic with even their cyber friends. Some distanced themselves from cyber relationships for other reasons. Diana, at 44, the longtime self-injurer from Sweden who was on disability, pulled back from a close friendship she had formed in her group because her friend had an accident and could not stop dwelling on it. No matter how hard Diana tried to distract her, to cheer her up, or to tell her she was not to blame, the woman refused to be helped. After eight or nine months of offering support Diana got so frustrated that she relapsed into cutting. She described her reaction:

> I felt like she's pulling me down because I can't help her. Finally I decided to stop writing at all in the group, and I was finally able to stop cutting. And after a while I felt okay, but even now I am very careful with [my friend]. I know that she can cause a scene, so I'm trying to be very careful, what I say, what I write.

Cyber relationships, while easily acquired, might be just as easily lost, turned off with the flick of a switch or the click of a mouse. Bonnie described her cyber relationships as "disposable,"[13] noting that if she left any of the lists, there would be a few people with whom she would stay in contact but that she would abandon the rest of them. She would be glad to lose the "trouble makers or people always stirring up something." Rebecca, from the private, nonprofit foundation, described cyber relationships as "easily acquired, easily lost." She noted that when she dropped off a message board for a few months, she stopped corresponding with her best friend there, with whom she had been having "really kind of intense" frequent conversations. They happened to reconnect by chance when they encountered each other in a different cyber venue and had to catch up on what they had missed in each other's lives. Rebecca noted that she could not imagine that kind of a break ever happening with one of her solid-world friends. Yet during the time when she was out of communication with her most intimate cyber friend, she felt no need to seek her out, nor did Rebecca's friend contact her.

People felt remarkably unperturbed about abandoning cyber relationships into which they had heavily invested emotionality and intimacy. Although these relationships were deep, they were situational. Paula felt no pangs about periods of time when she withdrew from her cyber community of many years, because she felt she "needed isolation in order to be safe and okay." Bonnie anticipated that she would eventually walk away from her cyber relationships and cast them off, because, she said, "that's what I did in the past." Although she wanted to make a commitment and to stick to her community of friends, she found these groups "multilayered." People dropped in, but then they left. They made appeals for help and got it, but they also left suicide notes and disappeared. As Lori Kendall (2002) has noted about the fragility of these kinds of relationships in general, for self-injurers having friendships in cyberspace meant learning to have different types and levels of expectations than in the solid world. Rebecca compared her cyber friendships to those she had in the solid world and decided that the two were more alike than different but that she had "less to lose" with her cyber friendships. She explained this attitude with regard to her most intimate cyber relationship: "Because if she were to really react negatively or if something were to happen and she decided that she didn't want to be friends with me or something like that, I wouldn't have to necessarily see her anymore. It just wouldn't be as, I guess, lasting as real-life relationships are." Mitch, a 42-year-old groundskeeper who left one group and moved to another, described the relationships he lost as expendable. Discussing his new group, he explained it this way:

MITCH: It's a whole new site, new people. I made a bunch of new friends, left the old friends behind.
Q: How do you feel about these friendships?
MITCH: They've fleeting at best, but they're good enough.

These remarks illustrate the dual nature of cyber relationships: they were intimate and deep but situational and transient. Ironically, some of their strongest features made them easier to abandon.

Cyber and Solid-World Relationships

People grew dependent, to varying degrees, on their cyber relationships. They talked about the differences between these relationships and those with people in the solid world. Not surprisingly, their thoughts on these differences varied.

Solid-World Relationships

Many self-injurers thought that a close, meaningful friend in the solid world offered them the greatest friendship advantages. People in the solid world could be there physically, could do things with them, and could have fun with whole groups of people at a time. Friends in the solid world had many more kinds of things they could discuss together, could be there for the good times, and could last for years. When things got rough for self-injurers, they often wished they had solid-world friends who would show up to help them. A friend who offered support in the solid world seemed more valuable to some people than one whose support only took the form of the written word. Darcy, who started cutting at 15 when her parents were going through a bad breakup, noted, "I really like hearing a voice as compared to type, type, type. It's more effective at preventing me from cutting myself."

Albeit rare, the most helpful kind of solid-world friends were those with personal experience of self-injury. Unlike other solid-world friends, these people could understand what the pain, the drives, and the cravings were like. Bonnie, the 33-year-old bankruptcy coordinator, noted that she had one friend who had been a cutter, so she could be more honest with her. She said, "She is my first choice supportwise, obviously. But for people who have never done it, or don't understand it, it's very hard to call and ask for help, because they don't know what to do." Although people in the solid world offered many different facets to their relationships (they went to the same school, they had similar interests and activities, they spent time together), what was usually missing was the ability to talk about self-injury. That subject ended up being, for many self-injurers, the one thing that they would never consider discussing with solid-world friends.

Cyber Relationships

Cyber friends, in contrast, offered an avenue to discuss this highly sensitive and important topic. Many self-injurers found it easier to reveal delicate aspects of themselves to cyber friends precisely because of their lack of corporeality. People who were scared to come out of the closet about their self-injury knew they could find people in online support groups who would not judge them but would accept them. Robin, who at 33 years old belonged to an online group specifically for people over 30, worked doing data entry. She had self-invented harming herself in the 1980s as a child but became aware of it as a phenomenon and sought others on the Internet much later. Robin made a friendship with someone in her group that was deeper than any she had been able to establish in the solid world:

> I guess it was a lot easier for me because it wasn't a face-to-face thing. So, I mean, as soon as I met her I was much more comfortable with her than I will ever be with anyone in my life. She knows a lot more about me than anyone needs to know in my life. And we are close in age, and we talk about other things, and we like to have fun. But it's—it's a lot more intense, because we don't have to deal with each other in real life. So we can tell a lot more crazy shit than we can ever, ever share with anyone.[14]

Robin routinely spent an hour or two "talking" with her online friend every day.

MaryBeth, who had run out of sympathy margin from her high school friends because of her repeated drama and neediness, similarly welcomed the opportunity to forge the kind of relationships on the Web that she lacked in the solid world. She had three cyber girlfriends who regularly kept in touch with each other via email. Part of their interaction every few days involved just catching up with what was going on in each other's lives, the small details. She said,

> We'll have personal conversations and things like that. There's nobody that I've met face to face and probably never will like that. And that's part of the comfort of the group is knowing that, you know, we're all here and we talk about this kind of thing, but we don't really have to deal with it in real life, so to speak.

MaryBeth kept thinking about revealing her self-injury to people she knew in the solid world, but she never could, because her self-injury had been such a comfortable and private thing for so long that the idea of changing that scared her. For her, the online relationships were safer because they were compartmentalized.

Marissa, the depressed shut-in, spent about 80 percent of her time in her room, in her bed, with her computer for company. For her, another benefit of having cyber relationships was the fact that at any time she could just walk away from a conversation. "If I don't feel like talking, I don't need to. I can come back tomorrow, and that's fine. If I want to work on how I am going to word something very precisely, that's a lot easier than in a face-to-face conversation." Judy, the music therapy major in Louisiana, noted that her online social interactions were easier for her, because she could pick them up when she chose; they were not as demanding. Chloe, an engineering student from Nova Scotia who worked in tech support, also mentioned the safety of online relationships. She discussed her difficulty in raising the issue of self-injury with her friends: "It still feels like a hot topic area; bringing it up still makes me feel rather exposed. I can't handle that face-to-face reaction." She preferred the safety of the cyber world, where she could easily disengage from a conversation that made her feel uncomfortable. She said, "Any type of reaction you get online is filtered to a certain extent, without all the content and facial expressions and tone of voice, so it's somewhat muted." This limiting factor offered her protection.

Others were troubled by the temporal delays associated with the Internet. Cyber friends were not always reachable; people took their time before checking their email, their groups, and their boards, and they then took additional time to think about the responses they wanted to compose. Although people in the solid world had jobs and commitments, they might be more readily available in times of crisis.

People sought out cyber-world friendships, then, not only for the benefits they offered but partly to avoid rejection in the solid world. Rejection was easier to take when there was no physically present person doing the rejecting. Rejection over the Internet could be blamed on people not checking their email or changing their email address. People found it easier to be in denial about the rejection when it did not happen face to face.

The Spectrum of Isolation/Integration

Individuals who participated in Internet support groups ranged in their solid-world relationships over a spectrum, from those who lived in relative isolation and lacked friends to those who had many friends and active social lives. Their placement along this spectrum was partly, but not completely, related to the extent of the disclosure versus closeting of their self-injurious behavior.[15]

Complete Isolates

The most extremely isolated individuals were those who could not function in the solid world, could not hold a job, and rarely left the house. Complete isolates spent nearly all their time on Internet sites; their real life existed in the cyber world. Randy fell into this category, as he refused to communicate with anyone via any venue other than email. Marissa fell here as well, for despite her husband and children, she had retreated to her bedroom and used her computer as a window onto the world. Marcy rarely left her apartment except to get food. Out of work, she maintained a friendship circle through support groups. But when she developed emotional crises, she dropped out of communication with even these people. Sandy spent hours daily talking on the Internet to a friend in Denmark. When her friend planned a visit to the United States, they talked about meeting. Yet she described this encounter as a "scary proposition" for her: "I mean, because I—the only person that I even speak to face to face would be the therapist, and I've rarely see him for like two months." Kyra, the Bulgarian former car-rental agent, described her highly visible scars as partial impediments to interacting with people. She quit her job and just stayed at home. Kyra talked about her fears of interacting with people:

KYRA: I still cut my face or my arms, visible places.
Q: And what do people say to you when they see these cuts on your face now?
KYRA: Well, I'm kind of very cold person. So I usually I don't like to talk about it or something like that. I refuse to talk about it.
Q: Has that ever been a problem for you? Does it stop you from having a relationship, from having friends or a job?
KYRA: Definitely, I mean I feel like an alien. I don't, like—I'm not interested in making new relationships. I'm not interested in even talking with people. I feel like I'm—sometimes I wonder what I should do with the rest of my life, because I have fears to talk with people, I have fears to do anything. I feel like a, I don't know, stone. So I'm really confused about my future. No matter that I try so hard to get well and to stop it.

When people withdrew because they became depressed or fearful of interacting with others, they tended to lose the friends they had. They turned to the Web for relationships, ones that they could safely control. Marnie, at 51, suffered from such severe dissociative identity disorder (DID) that she lived on disability. Her two grown sons lived nearby but never saw her. Dropped by several therapists, she was missing huge chunks of her life and could not remember anything before the age of 18. She spent several hours a day online in a DID online group and one for self-injury. Over this time she formed two close Internet friendships, but one of these friends died, leaving her with only one friend. Another woman described her depression and isolation on the Internet:

I know God doesn't give us more then we can handle but dammit I just don't want to go on another fucking second. I can't do nothing right in my life, i'm a complete and utter failure at everything I do and a lost cause. I can't work,

I can't get myself to shower regularly, I can't sleep and I ran my husband off into the arms of another woman. How much more do I have to endure before he finally just takes me away from this hellhole called life? I want to cut so bad. I was up all damn night typing when I couldn't sleep. It's been all day and less then two hours of sleep. Up all night again. . . . I'm 34 dammit, my marriage is over, i'm a failure, want to die, to end it all and i'm lonely. I love Mo with all my heart but i'm tired of waiting on him to realize he loves me enough to come home. My life is slipping away. . . . I can't sleep but what does it matter. I'm nobody. Nothing. I think I need the hospital again. I ws fine 'til this weekend and now that's it coming to an end i just wnt to disappear into nothingness. I'm ashamed that i feel this way, that i want to die, to cry, to be alone and push everyone away. I guessni'll go. Ain't like I matter.

Jobbers

A second category of individuals' interaction with the solid world was the jobbers, people who functioned and went to work but had few solid-world friends. All their social life existed on the Net. Several of the older people we observed or interacted with online fell into this category. Most of them had few close friends in the solid world and were often alienated from their families. Self-injury lists were full of people like this who had cats and treated them as children. Nancy was a good example of this type, because she held a job as a school administrator but wandered through the support groups and chat rooms every moment she was not at work. Paula worked as a holistic massage therapist but lived her real life through the Internet. She said,

> I would say that the feeling that I would have when I was on that list, it was like with every other part of my life: most of me would be there, and then I would go to that list and be like, "Okay, this is the real deal. This is me." And you know, I would write, like in my emails, I would write; I would really bring all of who I am. This was a place where I just truly fit it. But the same way I would look forward to coming home to pick, I would look forward to getting home and getting on the computer and reading all the emails, and I would go on the chats. It was a world; it was definitely a world.

The other group that fit this description was the younger people, in junior high or high school. They had a certain amount of contacts from their forced interactions in school. But they had few relationships in the solid world and came home to pour their hearts out on the Web.

Dual-Lifers

A wall of separation divided the two different spheres of dual-lifers, each sphere lacking something. These people had both solid-world and online friends, but they guarded information about their self-injury secretly, to be revealed only to their cyber friends. In their dual lives, they talked to their solid-world friends about one set of interests and to their online friends about a completely different set. They had solid-world lives, but their injuries were not publicly a part of them; they were hidden. They talked online about their solid-world lives and the issues they faced, but as one person remarked, "This could all be a lie, and no one would know." Riikka, the Dutch premedical student, spoke about her different kinds of friendships:

> I don't think I've made, well, any friends, not real-life friends. I mean, I have lots of friends, but I cannot talk with them about the things that I have—self-harm, because it's too personal. And there are very many people which I can go out with and which I can go to the movies, but I cannot talk to them about what's wrong with me or what I feel. And that's what I use the Internet for, because it gives me more anonymity, so they do not know who I am. But there are some people with whom I have a better bond with than others over the Internet.

Having one type of outer life and a different secret life sometimes created a wall of separation between people and their solid-world friends, as noted by Carrie, the 29-year-old graduate student in biology and research assistant in Albuquerque:

> Well, 'cause it's like they don't know there is a secret between us, so that's kind of like what I think about. Like, it's always like I'm trying to hide something, like I'll think about the angle of my arm in the sunlight, or maybe I shouldn't wear a bathing suit because of my leg. Do you know what I'm talking about?

To her, both kinds of friends had an aura of superficiality, because none of them encompassed fully rounded relationships. The wall of secrecy separated her from her solid-world friends, and the fact that she did not know her online friends in person made her think of them as not "like real-life people."

For these people, life might appear to outsiders to be going well, but on the inside they were suffering. Things in the solid world, from either their past or their present, caused them stress that was too great for them to manage. Externally they might appear quiet and reserved, with blinders on to avoid bringing out their emotionality, but internally they could be extremely emotional, fragile, and vulnerable. Internet groups and relationships filled this void and became a critical component of completing their lives.

Flaunters

A final group we identified consisted of those who brought the signs of their inner pain outward, revealing their self-injury and their scars. They were forthright about revealing their self-injury. These people were rare, because most self-injurers lived with a high degree of daily secrecy to conceal this inner turmoil, especially if it was currently ongoing. Brianna, who cut in high school after her father committed suicide but quit when she discovered that the behavior had become trendy, had a friend who was very overt about her injuries: "She cut more because she wanted people to know about it. You could tell, she was just screaming for help—you know, wear short-sleeve shirts or colorful Band-Aids on her arms which screamed 'I am a cutter.' She ended up going away to rehab school." People who could not express their pain in other ways sometimes resorted to flaunting to get the help and attention they needed.

For others, attention was not something they specifically sought. Chloe, the engineering student, remarked that she had met a few people who flaunted their scars but that it was definitely not very common. For her, "Those people tend to stand out, just because even when describing how they go about it, they tend to be quite assertive, sort of 'I'm not ashamed of going around with short sleeves.'"

Flaunting was sometimes a gendered act. Several people recalled boys from high school who cut or burned themselves publicly, as an act of defiance or manliness. Mandy, who rejected a friend's cry for help but eventually joined an alternative Goth subculture and became a cutter, talked about a boy from her grade: "He would do it, like, in the lunch room. It was more for show and 'Look how badass I am' sort of thing. He would take a lighter or something and put it on his hand or his arm or something like that." This boy was two years older than she was, and she interpreted his behavior as anger that he did not know how to handle, so he took it out on himself. The next year, when she became a member of a Goth subculture, she saw a lot of kids in her social group who publicly performed self-injurious acts for the shock of it.

Boys' self-injuries were regarded differently from girls'. Nicola knew a boy in high school who had "really big scars on his upper arms." Once she got to know him a bit better, she asked about them, and he told her point blank that he used to cut himself all the time. He mentioned his "really bad experiences with his parents: his dad beat him when he was young and then he left." All his friends were aware of this history, and so he wore his scars, rows of highly raised welts, openly on his arms. Nicola, who struggled inwardly with eating disorders and secret cutting, was surprised at how little stigma he experienced, while she was afraid things would be very different if her acts were discovered.

People who were in recovery, whose self-injuring was a thing of the past, sometimes lived more openly, wearing short-sleeved shirts and bathing suits in public. Scars that were older lost their raised texture and reddish color, fading to white lines, and even burns eventually melded into the skin. If people looked closely, they could recognize what these were, but some people who had quit decided to leave their concealment behind and move on with their lives. Marsha often wore short sleeves to remind herself of all she had been through. The many scars covering both sides of both arms testified to the emotional pain she had endured and had survived. "It's a big part of my history," she said. "I'm not ashamed of it. It makes me see where I've been and where I am now. When I feel like doing it, I look down and say, 'Do I really want another scar?'"

This final group comprised people who openly acknowledged their self-injury.[16] They moved beyond stigma and shame to accepting or embracing it. Linda, a 40-year-old moderator of a popular site, described these people:

Well, they want to flaunt it. They flaunt their scars; they don't try to hide them. They kind of dare people to ask them. Actually, I feel bad for the people in recovery who really, you know, would like to wear short sleeves and are afraid to because of their scars. And my philosophy is, just do what you want, and if people have the nerve to come up to you and ask, just come up with an answer but don't let them tell you that you have to wear long sleeves. I mean, it was a part of your life, and you're at a different place now.

Effect of Cyber World on Relationships

Still a relatively young terrain, the cyber world's influence on solid-world relationships, and vice versa, is still evolving. Scholars debate whether these fragmented, ephemeral, and physically distant but intimate relationships pull people away from the solid world or whether they act as a staging ground for individuals' future solid-world selves.

Supporting Solid-World Life

When individuals were injuring and experiencing inner turmoil that they could not manage, they started spending more time online. Their cyber friendships could serve as temporary bridges, supporting them through difficult periods of crisis and readjustment. Molly, who spent quite a lot of time online, made the following observation:

> MOLLY: These people drop into these worlds when they're, you know, like, having trouble, and then when they kinda like pull their shit together, they leave again.
> Q: They go back to real life?
> MOLLY: Yeah.
> Q: And is that okay?
> MOLLY: Oh, yeah! Sure. I mean, I think it's kind of expected.

Beyond temporary havens, cyber communities offered places for people to experiment with their selves, to try out different identities,[17] and to portray themselves as they ideally saw themselves or wished to be. Nancy thought that this kind of experimentation was especially prevalent among younger cyberists. She suggested that adolescents do this "to find out how to fit in and become accepted. It is a place that can be so accepting and when u screw up, you can, in an instant, reinvent yourself and find acceptance." These cyber interactions, then, prepared them for both solid-world work and relationships.

People differed, though, on whether they thought lessons learned transferred from the online to the offline world. McKenna, Green, and Gleason (2002) have suggested that the more people express their true self over the Internet, the more they are likely to form close online relationships and to be able to move these friendships to a face-to-face basis. Nancy regarded online relationships as "a big educator of how and what is expected in order to gain acceptance, and these lessons transfer into RL." Tim, the college student, agreed, poignantly reflecting to us in an email on the way his cyber experiences helped him improve his solid-world life:

> First I was a loner in real life so I was glued to the cyber world and even I made up a fake me. Tall muscles so on. But now I honestly have a group of friends that we do stuff well when we have money and thats like never. Lol But being in the cyber world helped me be me and yes I have a cyber girlfriend and its funny because my friend emma in cyber space once told me

she was in a relationship with a guy in Canada. I was like what that wont never work hes a guy so he has a girl in real life you know. Well now I have a girl in cyber and were in love not like oh your so sweet. We known each other for 2 years and weve talked tons and tons.

What do you think about me being with kyra who we never met in person but share feelings. Do you think its real love??? For me and her it is I say.

Tim, whose solid-world experiences with family members and friends had been troubled, was able to create a more accurate self-persona in cyberspace than he had been able to in the solid world, and this cyber interaction enabled his solid-world friendships. His level of cyber interaction eventually diminished considerably, although at the time he wrote the email he held on to key friends and his online girlfriend. Yet we see from his message that he prioritized solid-world relationships over cyber relationships, casting the latter as a transitory "staging ground" for the formation of the former.[18] David Shaw (1997) found something similar in the gay chat room he studied, where people used their virtual selves as an integral part of their coming-out process and gay identity formulation. A month after Tim wrote us his email, he went on his first date in the solid world. By several years later he had repaired his relationship with his mother and had a serious girlfriend.

The cyber world, then, can act as a bridge between having no friendships and forming them. People who were not yet ready to make friends in the solid world might use their groups as a stepping stone for forming relationships. Diana even made one close friend online who she saw in the solid world. Although her friend had quit the board where they met, they continued to talk on the phone and sometimes visited when either of them made out-of-town trips. Scared to meet this friend for the first time, Diana arranged to get together in a public place. Diana formed several solid-world friendships with women she met on the Web. One poster from another group even met someone with whom she formed a romantic relationship, saying, "I would never have met Dan (my soon to be husband) if it hadn't been for my having depression. We met on an online support group similar to this [self-injury group]."

Detracting from Solid-World Life

Others had been less fortunate in transferring their cyber selves and cyber relationships into the solid world. Despite the success of the poster quoted at the end of the preceding section, the most difficult relationships and skills to transfer into the solid world were romantic ones.[19] Molly and Nancy were but two of several people who reported tales of disaster when they attempted to meet people in the solid world to whom they were attracted in the cyber world. These kinds of experiences rooted people even more firmly in their cyber communities and relationships, where they were safer and more satisfied. Turkle (1995) and Kendall (2002) have questioned the effect of cyber interactions and online bonds on people's level of commitment to their offline relationships, and Barbara similarly noted that she thought people's cyber lives took away from their solid-world lives: "I really have to say that I believe that people who are in a cyber community or cyber relationship make them less committed and less real. It would have a great impact on their real-world commitments and relationships." She thought that people found spicy possibilities in the cyber world that could weaken a lot of marriages:

> Because you get a bunch of bored housewives bashing their husbands, and the next thing you know . . . I mean, it's because you get those instant messages so quickly and suddenly. Juan—the very sexy Juan, 33, Peru—thinks that you're the goddess of the kitchen and the bedroom, and suddenly your husband's looking frumpy and old, and we haven't had sex in three months. All the sudden Juan from Peru keeps saying how beautiful and sexy you are, and you start—you think, you know, "I could be happier. I deserve . . ." And then you start talking to women who go, "You do deserve it, girl. You deserve to be happier. You should just seize the moment." It's a circus.

Some people, she thought, fell into the trap of wanting to believe that the cyber world was more real than the solid world, because people could be in the cyber world what they were not in the solid world. If they found acceptance in the cyber world that they might not in the solid world, they could have a hard time separating from it. One person emailed us that she had gotten sucked into this feeling and had to kick herself: "I had to go 'EWWW snap out of it!' I mean luckily, you know, I'm talented enough to do that and I've got some grip on reality. It's a small one, but for kids I can so see how they get sucked in."

One online poster described how her time spent on the board pulled her away from dealing with her solid-world problems. She realized that she spent "entirely too much time on this board alone." Not only did she communicate through self-injury groups and boards, but she also looked at sites related to eating disorders. Although she claimed, in fact, to love the support she got from the pro-ana sites, she realized that she relied entirely too much on these kinds of places and acknowledged,

I guess the internet does fuel my isolation. Especially considering the fact that the more time I spend on the net, the less time I'm spending on taking care of my priorities, the more I feel like I'm failing my husband, daughter and students, the more depressed I get, the more time I spend on the net 'cause I don't want to deal with everything else that has now become such a burden for me...it's all a vicious cycle. As a matter of fact, I should be cleaning or working on a major project for the teacher professional development program I am required to do. Argh.

Nancy agreed, writing,

our ideas and opinions find their way into cyberspace shaping it into what it has become. it is so full of fantasy which becomes reality and transforms people. we are exposed to so much that we are so desensitized. it has robbed us of some joy, innocence, and confused us, challenged us, and created addictions on a much grander scale it often replaces RL contact which is a shame. we use the very tool we think connects us to others to isolate us from spending time in RL with real people.

Nancy here notes the fundamental irony that although people sought out online interaction to bond into relationships and communities, they did so in a physical space of separateness. Embarking on the journey into cyberspace was a simultaneously communal and lonely experience. The technology of the Internet thus offers us separation and connection,[20] a time to be alone yet to be with others,[21] leading people to spend their days alone at their computers trying to retribalize.[22]

These conflicting viewpoints existed, and for some the cyber world became their whole world, at least for a time. But few really gave up on the solid world, which shaped them and surrounded them, and they ultimately had to deal with its physical reality, for both their bodies and their relationships. The solid world thus bounded and framed their technical skills at cyber navigating and their social skills at interacting with others.[23] Scholarly research suggests, and our findings support, that the majority of people who venture into cyber worlds remain ultimately grounded in the reality outside.[24]

Effect of Cyber World on Self-Injury

The final question that must be raised about cyber-world relationships involves their effect on participants' self-injury: does the cyber world help them desist or draw them into continuing or increasing this behavior?

Reinforcing

On the negative side, many of the sites, especially the early ones, were highly triggering for self-injurers. When people posted their injury pictures, egged each other on, and even wrote about their blood dripping on the keyboard, participants considered this activity supportive of self-injuring. Even as late as this writing, sites still exist for posting photos that can be accessed by non-members. When people post these with captions such as "my recent cutting," it reinforces people's urges to cut. Jimmy, from Alaska, said, "On [pro-SI site] I almost found it becoming competitive. I mean, when you are doing pictures, you're looking, and you say, 'Oh, my God, he's got the—the control to do that to himself. I wonder if I can?'" Darcy, another college student, compared self-injury Websites to commercials:

> The more you're exposed to anything, the more you do it. Like watching commercials: their goal is to make you do things, and you're trying to quit smoking, and you're watching commercials, and you're like, "Hmm, cigarettes." I think the exposure has that effect inherently. Don't think about a pink elephant, whatever you do. . . . Okay.

The sites that most supported self-injury were the pro-SI sites. Erica, who slammed her hand in the doors, noted that she liked going to these sites when she was happy about her injuring. She read people's postings about their injuries, how to keep them clean, how to manage their cuts so they did not go too deep, how to deal with drugs and therapists. Her view of these kinds of sites was, "I see nothing wrong with it; it's what I would say too."

Finally, having self-injuring friends reinforced self-injury. Cody observed, "When you have a group of people who cut and no one else, it's not very good." Gwen, in college, suggested, "You keep on doing it because that's what's expected in that group, and it just gets worse because there's no outside force preventing you from doing that, I guess." Hannah, who had been to a self-injury clinic, talked about how she saw people encouraging each other on some of the sites:

> They probably just egg each other on, be like, "Oh, I did this last night, and I lost this much blood." And then someone would be like, "Oh, what are you talking about? I passed out last night from losing so much blood. You're a pussy!" And I feel like they just egg each other on, I don't know.

Then there's the other one, where they understand the problem, and they love that they have Internet friends who do the same thing as they do, and they can confide in them all of the horrible, horrible things that they do to themselves. That's more of one of the groups, where they would just egg each other on. And that can be good to have people who understand, but that's also detrimental in the long run.

Self-injury cyber subcultures may also reinforce members' acts by sharing techniques and motives and by normalizing and encouraging these.[25]

Quitting

On the positive side, many of the people with whom self-injurers formed relationships offered helpful suggestions and support for recovery. When people felt the urge to injure, sometimes they went to the groups, boards, or chat rooms to distract themselves. Any time that they spent there talking was time that they were not cutting or burning. People offered them helpful suggestions, from the shallowest ones to deep assistance for their cyber-revealed selves. People supported each other, like in solid-world support groups, encouraging and congratulating individuals who passed significant markers in their desistance, such as yearly anniversaries. One person posted online,

> I am happy to report that in 3 weeks it will be officially 1 year since I last self injured! Gah! This is HUGE 4 me! Just wanted to tell you all this, I wouldnt be here if not 4 you guys. *tear*
> Thanks!
> Live life like a rock, strong and grounded!

And when people slipped up and reverted, their online friends told them to start fresh, to take it one day at a time. One day was good; one week was good; one month was better. They all knew that healing was about ups and downs. They offered relief from the isolation and loneliness that people faced in their moments of inner turmoil and feelings of addiction. Jessie, living in Germany and working with a special-needs child wrote, "When you find a safe board where there's not that many triggers it can actually be a really positive thing. It can be a supportive environment that actually helps you to stop or supports you when you're trying to stop."

Mixed Effects

In the end, these cyber contacts had mixed effects, triggering some and helping others. Erica noted that people made their own choices about how self-injury sites affected them: "You can go to that site, and it will help you to cut because you see it and want to do it. Or you can go to that site and help you not do it. I think it's, like, whatever you're feeling, whatever you're going to that site for." The effect of the cyber contact really depended on the stage where people were in their self-injury careers, whether they wanted the support to continue or the support to stop. Bonnie, the bankruptcy coordinator, reflected on this dynamic: "I think there's good and bad, and at one time I needed a pro-cutting, and now I don't, and I don't look for it. So I think that depending on the stage that people are in they need certain things."

The relationships that self-injurers formed in these groups and sites were thus layered and complex, ephemeral and transitory while at the same time deep and meaningful. People treated their cyber friends differently, depending on their current needs and strengths. For some, cyber contact pulled them away from relationships in the solid world, but for many more, it supplemented these relationships and either helped them bridge from a difficult period to one when they felt better or helped them move themselves through these stages. People got out of their cyber relationships and support groups what they invested there, and they usually found people whose interests and goals mirrored their own. As such, these relationships could have rather different effects on their solid-world lives and behavior.

10

The Social Transformation
of Self-Injury

In this book we have highlighted the evolution of self-injury. We argued in chapter 2 that whereas the behavior was for a long time defined and treated by the psycho-medical community according to their clinical view of its cause and population, things changed significantly over the course of our research. In this chapter we extend our discussion of these ongoing developments in self-injury's practice that took it further beyond the psycho-medical bounds and established it more firmly as a sociological phenomenon. Self-injury has become demedicalized in its practice, changing from being primarily a mental disorder, or a disease, into a social trend.

The Social Transmission of Self-Injury

One of the ways self-injury evolved as it morphed into a more widespread practice involves its social contagion. In chapter 4 we discussed how people heard about self-injury from the sources available during the late 1990s and turn of the twenty-first century. But as the first decade of this century unfolded, the types of social learning about it expanded and changed.

Interpretations

People not only discovered and were encouraged to self-injure from others, but they also learned the way to interpret the changing social meanings of this behavior. Joanna, who started to self-injure after her brother's hospitalization, had a friend who casually mentioned that she wanted to cut herself right then. When Joanna asked her friend why she did it, the girl talked about the way it made her feel and said it was "just such a relief." Joanna was excited by this revelation because it was the first time she had talked to someone about why she did it and its effects. She realized that her cutting produced an adrenaline rush that took away her frustration and replaced it with a better sensation, just what she was seeking. She recognized, "The rush was probably the best part of the whole thing. And I didn't realize that until I talked to her."

Gwen learned about self-injury in 2000 from a Website that contained personal testimonials and medical facts about it. She said, "I didn't understand it, so I just Googled it and just read all I could on it to try and understand it." Even though she found the descriptions graphic and disgusting, she was intrigued, so she cut herself on her ankle. From there, she began to self-injure regularly.

These people heard from friends that self-injury was, as Kim said, "not about hating who you are; it's not trying to get out of your life. It's about pain and having no other outlet for emotional pain." Kim said that her friend taught her "not to do it where people will see you and not to cut too deep."

Sponsorship

People who came to self-injury either because they were curious, because they wanted to be cool, or because they wanted to belong were much less likely to exhibit the impulse-disorder symptoms and pathological family backgrounds described in the psycho-medical literature. More often, they were *sponsored* into self-injury, learning how, why, and when to do it. Although it was less common for people actually to cut together, the social contagion effect became more pronounced over time as groups of high school students self-injured and formed identities, social groups, and clusters[1] around it. Gwen talked about how it became a practice of her high school social group:

> But I think my friend Julie got into a whole cutting thing because of Caitlin and I. She was the last of our little group that got into it. She said that she just wanted to define herself in some way, because everyone else was doing it. I think it gives you a sense of belonging to do something other people are doing. So you're in a group or something like that.

Self-injury became, in the early 2000s, a behavior that people got into through copycatting.[2] Valerie, a college student, knew two girls she called the "depression twins," who both self-injured. They would hang out and take naps together because they did not know what else to do. Between them, she identified one as the leader and the other as the follower. Though she did not imagine that they cut together, she occasionally caught enough snatches of their conversation to convince her that the two girls were discussing their self-injury. According to her analysis, this union fostered their cutting: "The second one, she was a follower. She didn't really have—she was a follower. She didn't do things on her own: she always needed someone else's support, she always needed someone's approval. And she got that from the first girl, and they got it from each other." Vanessa also described a girl who followed her crowd around, unsuccessfully trying to become accepted by imitating them: "Once she found out about it [the self-injury], she tried it just to try and fit in better with my friends. And I really despised her for that, because she didn't have any reason to."

In certain groups, friends were especially open about discussing their self-injuring. In Connie's alternative clique, a lower-income crowd in her suburban high school, a lot of her friends openly displayed the cuts on their arms. By her senior year in 2003, she and some other girls wore tank tops to school and flaunted their injuries. No one ever openly challenged them about these scars because what they were doing was a known phenomenon. She discussed the size of her group of injurers: "I probably knew about 10. And that's just people that I knew. I didn't know if maybe more other people in the school were doing it."

From Hardcore Punk to Goth to Emo

Over the course of self-injury's more public career there have been three social movements associated with it: the hardcore punks, the Goths, and the emo punks. These groups represent one strain of the self-injuring population: those who did it more openly, who were more driven by their connection to a music, style, or ideological movement, and who were more neutralized in their attitudes about it.

The punk-rock subculture emerged in the 1970s in major American and British cities but evolved by the 1980s into a hardcore punk scene that engaged nihilistic and antiestablishment philosophies. Hardcore punks expressed their identity, as Lack (1995) has noted, through the use of "harder, more self-destructive, consciousness-obliterating substances like heroin or . . . methamphetamine and by the 'mutilation of the body' with razor blades." Hardcore punk bands, unconcerned for their future and disaffected from middle-class values, gave the most outward public displays of self-injury. Their followers, mostly male, rejected the showy fashion style of the British punks, with their dyed, Mohawk hairstyles and safety pins through their ears and noses.

Instead, they moved back to more mainstream jeans and punk-band T-shirts to avoid verbal and physical harassment.[3] The earliest people we interviewed, such as Gary and Robert, spoke about going to punk concerts and raves in the early 1990s, events that were characterized by showy cutting.

In the early 1980s the Gothic rock movement branched off from the punk/hardcore scene.[4] Goths worshiped Halloween and dressed in vampire style, with black clothing, corpse paint, and blood dripping down their arms, faces, and bodies. By the 1990s the Goth scene embraced the more morbid aspects of mid-nineteenth-century Victorian fashion and culture.

From this base, the Goth movement expanded beyond the punk-music subculture into a high school custom, fashion, and style subculture with loose boundaries.[5] Many participants self-identified as "thespians" or other offbeat artsy types. They used a "romance of darkness" to displays toughness, creativity, and emotional authenticity.[6] Gary described the showiness of adolescents in his old Goth crowd from high school:

> A lot of people would cut, like, slogans, really cheesy, like "love" or "hate," that sort of thing; it took quite a lot of time. Most people were hackers, causing lacerations rather than really slashing and opening up a wound, because a lot of these kids were pretty young and hadn't really dealt with really major pain a whole lot. . . . You'd see that a lot in public, people slashing their chest. They were really showy.

Mandy was into the Goth scene during her senior year of high school (in 1999). She followed Ozzy Osborne, Kiss, Marilyn Manson, and Nine Inch Nails. They projected an aura of "death, violence, gruesome things" that attracted her, spilling their own blood onstage. She described a self-injury culture surrounding this music scene as drawing

> kids who are disaffected, and they feel like they don't belong, kind of a thing, moving toward that music, because it's the anthem for the weirdos of the world. They feel so left out, and here's something that they finally can belong to. I'd say kids anywhere from thirteen, fourteen, to my age would be doing it more often.

She described the people drawn to this crowd as also potentially into sadomasochism, religious violence, or racial violence. They kept their skin white and wore black. When they saw each other's cuts, "they understood them." Anya, who also hung out with the Goth scene at that time, began injuring a few years before she discovered a group of about eight people in her high school who were into cutting. She spoke about them as posers: "A lot of them were Goths, so they had to act that way to be, like, a Goth. I think the majority of the people who dress and act like a Goth are kind of pretending on almost every level. They are very pretentious people."

But by the middle of the first decade of 2000, most of these people had moved out of the Goth scene.[7] In its place the emo ("emotional," "emotional hardcore," or "emocore") subculture emerged, moving away from its musical punk origin to a rock sound featuring melodic musicianship and expressive, often confessional lyrics. People belonging to the emo subculture displayed a strong style of fashion, culture, and behavior that was visually prominent online and in high schools. Mostly a teenage phenomenon, the "emo kids" often wore skinny jeans, tight short-sleeved T-shirts bearing the names of emo bands (e.g., Death Cab for Cutie), studded belts, black wristbands, black Converse sneakers or Vans, and (especially among guys) thick, black, horn-rimmed glasses.[8] Being emo connoted that a person was particularly emotional, sensitive, shy, introverted, or angst ridden. Emo kids, especially guys, thus violated the hypermasculine dictate of suppressing emotionality. The emo subculture has also been associated with outward displays of depression, self-injury, and suicide.[9]

Adam, whose father locked him in his room, described himself as belonging to an "emo crew," a group of outcast guys who were disassociated from the high school cliques and recognized each other's self-injuries. They displayed their affiliation in their accessories: "We always wore, like, the thick sweatband stuff and bandanas. It's a flair on my wrist and whatnot. It almost became kind of the style, and you accepted the style, and everyone knew who we were and kind of knew [that we self-injured] but turned a blind eye to what we did."

We described in chapter 7 how one cyber community rejected a poster's inquiry about a sexual dimension to his self-injuring, drawing a boundary line around "legitimate" members as driven by depression. Many people we interviewed, both in person and on the telephone, drew a similar boundary between themselves and people who self-injured because of their membership in the punk, Goth, or emo movements. Many private self-injurers disdained the emo kids for the stigma they brought. Like other disadvantaged groups, they distanced themselves from the most visibly or doubly deviant among themselves by denigrating those as "others" in an attempt to enhance their own legitimacy.[10] People who viewed themselves as "serious cutters," who felt they only engaged in the behavior because they *had* to, denounced the people they saw as injuring because it was "trendy."

The Practice of Self-Injury

Individuals who tried and liked self-injury practiced it in varying ways. According to the psycho-medical community, these acts were most likely to occur because people could not control their impulses, they were histrionic, they sought attention, they needed to alleviate frustration, and they acted in the here-and-now. Yet those we observed were not restricted to this clinically defined style of behavior. Some found the need to harm themselves overwhelming, while others approached it much more sociologically.

Impulse versus Planned

We found many people who self-injured impulsively, ducking into school restrooms to cut in toilet stalls, getting drunk and depressed and then cutting, or doing it whenever the mood struck them. One person posted in desperation from her computer at work:

> I don't have anything, I'm at work, and I cannot find anything sharp. I took my razor out of my purse last week and now I could almost kill myself for it. I feel so dispirited that I am fixing to excuse myself to go outside in the pouring ran to break this glass bottle of white tea so I can cut myself.

Whether the practice of self-injury occurs because of an impulsive urge or as the result of a conscious decision is a source of serious disagreement on self-injury Websites. There are many people who condemn others who do *not* do it out of impulse, arguing that the behavior is so bad that anyone who can resist the overwhelming urge to do it should do so. In an online debate about the nature of self-injury, one person followed the psycho-medical definition and posted, "If SI is really an impulse than where is the impulse?"

More often, however, we found people who injured themselves in an intentional, planned, and deferred manner. They rejected the irresistible-impulse model and defended their behavior as rational, debating, evaluating, and assessing the decision to self-injure, both in the initial phases of their involvement and in later returns to the behavior. Responding to the previous post, another person wrote, "I read your post, it all made sense in a way but in a way it did not. I try to put it off as long as possible as I really do not want to SI but then I have to give in once there is no more excuses to not do it."

Many people who followed this instrumental mode delayed their self-injury until they were ready to do it. They picked a time that was convenient because they could hide it better or they would enjoy it more.[11] Some waited until they could get away from parents, until summer was over and they could wear long-sleeved shirts, or until they felt they deserved it. Matt, a 20-year-old college student, postponed his self-injury while he let the desire build up. After waiting, he got to the point where he did not even need something to trigger him. It was not quite so much of a release anymore; he just did it because it felt good. He described his thinking:

MATT: So this was a rational decision to me. I'd think about it, and I'd always remember how good it felt to do it, so I'd keep doing it. I guess it's kind of the same way that I would do just about anything else. Delayed gratification, I guess.

Q: So you never sat down and weighed the pros and cons?

MATT: Well, a little bit. I'd know that I had to do certain things, like I'd have to make sure I was always wearing long sleeves or that I'd put something over it when I was asleep to make sure it didn't open up again and have, like, blood all over my sheets and stuff, because that would be bad.

Q: So that would be on the cons side?

MATT: Yeah, but generally I weighed the cons. The cons were pretty easy to get over, but then I guess the cons began to outweigh the pros when I started losing some of my best friends. . . . So I was like, "I have to stop. As much as I want to do it, I shouldn't." And so I made a conscious decision to stop for a while. The pros weren't good enough to outweigh those cons.

Like Matt, many people weighed the benefits they got from their self-injury against the personal, physical, and social costs. When they felt bad, they knew it would make them feel better. But many thought that self-injury was an unhealthy way to deal with their emotions, so they brushed away their desires and resisted the urge. As they became unhappy, they reevaluated their decision, adding more items to the pros and cons list. When they finally decided that the pros outweighed the cons, they began again. After Matt gave up self-injury during his senior year of high school, he made a conscious decision to reengage it. For him, the return to self-injury was not prompted by any specific event but was because he missed it. "I think I wanted to have that feeling again, that release that I could only get from doing that, that calming sensation. And I'm not sure if there was anything really all that upsetting going on at that time." At the time of our interview, Matt was still self-injuring.

Like Matt, Liz, the 25-year-old animal trainer who was still engaged in her self-injury, thought ahead about doing it. She discussed her philosophy of planning:

> LIZ: I don't like being impulsive. I like making decisions, choosing how I'm going to live, how I'm going to do everything. It gives me a sense of control.
>
> Q: How would you plan it? How far in advance would you start thinking about it?
>
> LIZ: Anything from a few hours to a few days, depending on how long I can hold it off for.
>
> Q: So then do you think like, "Thursday would be a good night for it," or how does that work?
>
> LIZ: Kind of, yeah. It sounds really weird just talking about it. Like, I'll know what days I have to work with certain people, and I'll know that ahead of time and be like, "Well, okay, I know I'm going to be really stressed here. I might as well start thinking about it because I'm going to want to do it anyway."

Unlike Matt, who deferred his gratification indefinitely, Liz oriented herself to specific days that would be good.

Another way of practicing self-injury nonimpulsively was to do it routinely. Hannah, the college sophomore, established a routine for herself shortly after she began to self-injure. Nightly, she read for a while, injured, and then went to sleep. The evenings were her time to reflect on upsetting things from the day, but this pattern eventually became so routinized that she self-injured every night, regardless of her feelings. Many people described the release they got from self-injury, much like people who have a nightcap as a sleep aid.

Finally, some people made bargains with themselves about how and when they would self-injure. Lindsay, a 32-year-old nurse's aide, described her thinking process:

> LINDSAY: Like, I'll sometimes think, "Okay, well I can't cut now, so I'll promise to cut on a certain date." Even if I don't feel like it anymore, I've made myself that promise, and to be able to trust myself, then I have to keep it. . . .
>
> Q: Is it more or less satisfying when you do it that way?
>
> LINDSAY: Then it's more like it's something that has to be done, and you do it because it has to be done. It's not something that you really look forward to. It's more like a chore, but you have to do it. And I've often

done it sort of in rituals too, where I've done it for so many different reasons and everything that, I don't know, it's just different all the time.

Self-Injuring with Others

Occasionally, although rarely, people began to self-injure in the company of others. Nina, who first saw self-injury during her hospital visits to her brother, advanced in practicing this behavior due to influence from friends. Drawn to an alternative crowd because she had "low self-esteem," she found a boyfriend in the group, a "cool, troubled guy." Together they progressed in their self-injury:

> It was very ritualistic, because he had rosemary, and he'd been doing this a long time. So I was the rookie, and he was just drawing me in, like some kind of Hitler or Manson. And I enjoyed it because it was very intimate. And also the rosemary that we applied to the cuts, actually to the burns, afterwards—we did both cutting and burning. He would suck—he would drink my blood, and he expressed a lot of desire for that.

An ongoing fascination with vampires led some people to engage in imitative blood sucking or sexual blood play.[12] Penelope began her cutting in junior high with two friends who went through "this whole vampire phase" and cut herself with them a couple of times. But then she realized that the intensity of cutting herself helped her to break through her everyday numbness, so she spun off on her own. Recognizing this behavior as a whole different thing, she knew she could not mention it to her friends. Hannah found a guy who also cut, and they did it together a few times. More commonly, they would cut separately and show each other the results:

> We would get to school in the morning—we were freshman in high school—and we'd go down an empty hallway, and I'd be like, "Hey Mike, come look at what I did last night." And he'd be like, "Phh. Look at what I did last night." It was kind of like a game. And I had a lot of friends at that time who injured and who were very vocal about it within our group.

But then Hannah began to do it with more frequency and severity. When people discovered this, she said, "it quickly went from like half the kids in our group doing it and just kind of like joking around about it and not that big of a deal to everyone being like, 'Okay, Hannah has a problem.' And they kind of stopped doing it as much." She then had to hide her actions.

Lindsay, the private nurse's aide with the traumatic background and severe psychological problems, found someone hanging out on the streets with whom she would occasionally cut. Sometimes they went to her house and hid in her room from her "messed up family" so they could cut together:

> It was just like sort of, well, we'd ask each other, "Do you feel like cutting?" and the other would say yes or no or whatever. It was like, "Well, okay, I have to be at work in 20 minutes, so I can't do it really bad. But we can squeeze it in." It was just really crazy. We'd sit there as if we were just having coffee or whatever, and we'd sit there and be talking regularly. At that time we weren't cutting bad. I don't think we hardly ever needed stitches or anything. We'd sit there with a tea towel on our laps, and we'd just be talking back and forth and cutting ourselves. And I think once we burned ourselves together too.

Embracing Self-Injury

Many Internet support groups had rules prohibiting positive expressions about self-injury, and sites that fostered or triggered the behavior with photographs, suggestions for how to do it, or reinforcement were often closed. Yet a percentage of the self-injuring population remained positively committed to it. They went beyond accepting this behavior to embracing it.

Passively Positive

A first group took a passively positive position on their self-injury. Sue, a 28-year-old elementary school teacher, managed a neutral stance to self-injury by never thinking about it. When we asked Marnie, a 51-year-old bank teller, about her future relationship with it, she stated that she focused her thoughts, instead, on the present. It just was not a part of her thinking process. Those who did think about it sometimes had thoughts of remorse or regret, but when they needed self-injury, they were grateful it was there. They let nothing stand between them and the relief they wanted; as long as they felt they needed it, they were committed to doing it, no matter the consequences.

Actively Positive

A larger (although still small) group expressed steady and outwardly active positive attitudes about self-injury. They took the pros that they weighed in their decision-making and forged them into a more unified philosophy. These people represented an informal pro-SI movement, similar to the pro-ana (anorexia) and pro-mia (bulimia) movements.[13] Pro-ED movements viewed eating disorders as a lifestyle choice and not a medical or deviant issue. Many Web postings and sites offered tips on how to avoid eating and hide eating disorders from friends and family and how to calculate body mass index (BMI) and basal metabolic rate (BMR), "thinspiration" pictures, reverse triggers, recipes, fasting suggestions, poetry, photographs of extremely thin models and actresses, and support for resisting recovery.[14]

Philosophy

The existence of a pro-SI movement is still somewhat controversial. Eva, a 30-year-old cashier, disputed its existence. Although she acknowledged that people openly expressed support to others who self-injured, she distinguished between people who were "not willing to recover just yet" and more outright encouragement of the behavior. Some suggested that people hid their pro-SI orientation because they found expressions of these views unacceptable. Bonnie, the bankruptcy loan coordinator, compared the pro-SI movement to others:

Q: So do you think there's a pro-cutting movement just like there's a pro-ana movement?

BONNIE: I think so. I don't think it's as large, because I think self-injury is so hush-hush. And I think people are becoming more knowledgeable about it, but at the same time I think it's just as big a problem, but there's just not as much treatment. People just don't know how to handle it.

Q: How would you rate the pro-suicide compared to the pro-cutting and the pro-eating-disorder movements?

BONNIE: Oh, pro-suicide is huge, really bigger than pro-SI. Pro-ana is bigger too. But it's [pro-SI is] there.

The formation of a pro-SI movement was impeded by the censorship of Internet sites that avoided condemning the behavior. Many people spoke about the high turnover of such groups, message boards, and chat rooms where they congregated. Liz, the animal trainer, offered her guess as to why these sites tended to disappear so quickly:[15]

LIZ: I think it has to do with the negativity surrounding it. Like with pro-ana stuff, they just take it off. Their Web servers do, and I think they're probably doing the same thing with that. . . .

Q: How do *you* find new sites?

LIZ: Usually one of the people from the sites before tells me, "Oh, hey, look there's one over here." And you're like, "Okay, I'm coming." Or the email group I'm on will mention one.

People were aided in their pro-SI attitude by the community of people they encountered on the Internet. Cindy, the 19-year-old retail salesperson, noted that by going online, she found others out there doing the same things. That convinced her that she was not so abnormal and made her feel better. At pro-SI sites on the Internet, people also found tips for improving their behavior. Cindy mentioned, for example, that she learned how to make a cleaner cut so she healed with less scarring. Bonnie learned to view her SI as better than hurting others and hence as a strength rather than a weakness.

Lifestyle Choice

People espousing a loosely pro-SI orientation began by accepting it as a lifestyle choice. Vanessa, the 20-year-old college student, expressed this philosophy:

It was on the *Today Show* or something, and they were doing this "seven-part series," which is so beating a dead horse, on self-injury, and they bring all these teenagers that are like, "I had a problem." And they're bringing all these psychiatrists, and they're like, "These kids, they need help. It's a mental disorder." I was like, "That is *so* not it." It's just—it's a personal way of express-ing emotion. It is a lifestyle choice. It's just the way you choose to express your emotions. I mean, everybody has to have an outlet. You can go and do martial arts as your expression, or you can do art, or you can cut yourself. If some people view it as a problem, if a cutter views it as a problem, then yes, they should get help, because if they view it as a problem, then it is a prob-lem. I never saw it as a problem. I just saw it as the way that I chose to do it.

Erin discussed her view about how self-injury was accepted on the Internet and featured as a lifestyle choice: "I guess the reason I would say that it was a life-style is because they had tips on, like how to stop bleeding, what to buy, what to use—just a lifestyle: the way you are instead of just a habit. It could be more of a central focus of people's lives. It was the central focus of mine for quite a while."

Coping Mechanism

Sienna, a 28-year-old shoe salesperson, compared self-injuring to other cop-ing mechanisms: "Some people drink, some people do drugs, some people kill people." She regarded life as difficult, although manageable. Her way of dealing with issues was to self-injure, and she decided that she might as well take a positive attitude about it. Her perspective was, "It's not a 'Oh, my God, I just cut myself, I feel like shit' kind of thing. It's a 'Oh, hey, this kind of stuff is going on in my life. How else can I deal with it?'" For Sienna, self-injuring represented an effective coping tool: "Yeah, I think it's effective. I mean, I'm not dead yet." Sienna offered an "only harming myself" account, rationalizing that people who injured themselves were better than those who injured others.[16]

For Molly, the homeschooled shut-in, self-injury was her only way to escape. Oppressed by her parents' rejection and isolation, she felt numb. Self-injury gave her a way to let out her suppressed feelings. She often found herself tuning out when people were talking to her; she had disembodied experiences, which alienated her from those she reached out to on the phone. When she realized she was feeling this way, she would hang up, cut, and call them back. One time a friend said to her, "You're a different person. What'd you do?" And Molly said she told her, "I just had to go think about something." For Molly, self-injury was one of her only and most reliable friends: "Cutting is the only thing that likes me right now. And it's not killin' me yet and definitely not killing me as bad as being anorexic is. And it's my way out. Nobody has to know. It's just between me and the box cutter or the X-Acto knife or the scissors."

Rejecting the Stigma

Part of the pro-SI attitude involved rejecting the stigma. Lance, a 28-year-old furniture salesman, explained how people could flip the stigma away from themselves and onto others. "Everybody knows that there's a lot of really bad stigma, but a lot of our views are that once you get past that, they're just getting after you or being upset because they don't understand what's going on. It could be a lot worse. So it's *their* problem, not *your* problem." By putting the problem onto others, he distanced himself from the stigma.

Long-Term View

People espousing a loosely pro-SI orientation also took a long-term view of the practice. Heather, a 42-year-old receptionist, asserted her intention to continue self-injuring forever: "Probably the only thing that will get me to change is if I die. That would be it." Others noted that they could sustain it over a lifetime because they were not doing it to kill themselves; they were doing it to survive. Robin, 33, said that although she would not recommend self-injury to anyone else, it was part of who she was, and she was not convinced she wanted to stop.

For Susan, a 53-year-old Internet group moderator, self-injury was a tool that kept her alive. She did not care about the stigma; if she could cope with her job, her friends, and her husband, her choice would be to continue it forever. She saw herself as always having "one foot over the line" but as managing to hang on to the right side of the line (life) with the help of this primitive tool. Since it allowed her not to commit suicide, she respected it. For her, if it worked, then it was all right.

Scar Acceptance

As we saw in chapters 8 and 9, acceptance of scars was part of flaunting the behavior. Lindsay saw encouragement to display her scars on a chat room that was pro-cutting. Someone urged her to show her scars, to "go right out there," and, as Lance said, to leave it up to others to accept it. When people got over the stigma and shame of their behavior, they became less fearful of showing their scars. Lindsay, the nurse's aide, expressed this view: "Well, don't be ashamed to show your scars, and people all just have to accept it, and you go out there, you know." People who flaunted disreputable identities[17] might engage in these displays as expressions of freedom or defiance.

Bonnie struggled with self-esteem. Her many scars often got in the way of a more "normal life." A few weeks before our talk she had moved to not wearing long sleeves all the time. Living at home, she asked her parents if it would bother them if she stopped hiding the scars on her arms, because she always wore long sleeves or a jacket around them. She found them very open to the idea, encouraging her to wear whatever she wanted. She knew her self-injury bothered them, but they did not make her hide it.

Pro-SI attitudes only coalesced into a loosely forming movement with the greater communication among self-injurers facilitated by the Internet. These value orientations and behaviors stood in stark contrast to the impulsive and pathological psycho-medical model of self-injury. These developments changed the social meaning of self-injury. It became transformed from a bizarre, highly stigmatized behavior associated expressly with the mentally ill into a more normalized activity practiced by a wider swath of people, in socially acknowledged circles, and with multiple interpretations. As this happened, it moved away from its exclusively medicalized context into a more broadly social one.

11

Careers in Self-Injury

One of the most fascinating ways to analyze people's involvement with self-injury is to look at it as a *career*. Individual testimonials, postings, or blogs can offer only a frozen snapshot in time that fails to capture the typical patterns that commonly evolve over the stages of people's involvement. Yet through our in-depth life-history interviews and the longitudinal nature of our research design we were able to trace individuals' transformations over their years of self-injuring. Whereas the psycho-medical community tends to focus on the traumas or disorders that lead individuals to self-injure and the treatments available for desistence, sociologists have a long history of observing the way people change over the span of their careers in deviance.[1] In this chapter we examine the way people's attitudes toward and practice of self-injury evolved over the course of their engagement.

Entry

We have already discussed the entry phase in several chapters, noting the differences between people who self-invented the behavior during the hidden years, those who were drawn into it through punk, Goth, or emo subcultures, and those who tried it knowing in advance how it was viewed and having an eye toward using it for stress management.

Rapid Escalation

Some people took longer than others to increase their involvement with this deviance. The stigma of self-injury often led individuals in their teens and older to move cautiously in increasing the frequency of their acts. However, young people commonly feel a sense of invulnerability, live in the moment, and face emotional stresses that make them seek immediate gratification, unconcerned and/or unaware of the ramifications of slashing or burning themselves for their later lives. Many people described a rather rapid escalation of their behavior, from occasional use to fairly repeated involvement. Bonnie estimated that within a month she was cutting daily. Penelope said that her cutting "became pretty frequent pretty fast." By "pretty frequent" she meant every day or a couple of times a day. Cindy started cutting herself over the summer, and when she returned to school, she went to her computer to learn more about it. "Yeah, I just went to Google and Yahoo and started typing stuff in. I used to have pictures downloaded on my computer and everything. It was almost like an addiction. I just couldn't stop." One Internet poster sought out others with whom to share her experience:

> Hi my name is denise...i am new to this. I am 20 years old and I am a cutter...i haven't been cutting that long (roughly 6 months). But it has totally consumed my life...i went from cutting just when I am really really upset, to cutting even if i am tense or stressed out. well you wanna talk, I would love to!

Another blogged for help:

> I haven't been SIing for that long, but for me it's is a coping mechanism to regain control. If emotions get too intense, it brings me back to a balance. If the numbness gets too intense, it helps me feel. If I have a panic attack, it diverts my focus and helps me snap out of it. But it's losing its "magic" and things are getting worse quickly. I have to do it more often and more times. How do I stop this? I feel like I'm on a roller coaster and it's going out of control?

Spinning Out Quickly

Several people we talked to spun out of injuring moderately quickly. Just as fast as they ramped up into it, they went through the stages and got out.[2] It seemed easier for some to stop if they had not been involved with it for a long time and did not identify as self-injurers. Spinning out rapidly was often a pattern associated with teenagers. Crystal was in and out over three months at age 16 in 1998. When she met her boyfriend, after this period, she replaced cutting with doing drugs, since this was his preferred mode. Robert tried self-injury at 14 in a 1995 punk subculture, but after two weeks he decided that his arm was starting to look pretty "messed up." Getting tired of trying to hide it, he determined to move away from the "abnormal friends" he had because he thought these people were headed toward doing serious damage to their lives. He did not want to take on the "negative side effects" he saw in these others.

Leith was in a high school group in which cutting was tolerated but not encouraged. He did it first socially and then moved on to an individual practice. After a year and a half he felt he had gotten to the point where he saw little purpose to it. It was something he needed to prove, to fit in, but he realized that it did not help with any of his convictions. Cindy's self-harming career lasted a year and a half as well, but she progressed through the typical stages quickly. She rapidly became a heavy user, was hospitalized, got out and sought support from several online groups, became an avid member of these groups, and found a way out.

Some people involved in the scene postulated that younger, trendier people tended to get in and to spin out easier. From participating in online groups over several years, Penelope observed that some young people self-injured to be cool, because their friends were doing it, or because "it was the whole 'emo' thing." These people lacked a meaningful involvement in the behavior, she thought, and because it was more of a phase they were going through, they found it less problematic to drop. Paula also thought that young people did it as a fad:

> I would be interested to see, to actually track the people that get into it in the more shallow, fad kind of way as teens, and then stop. Because when I was a teenager, there was this kind of coolness, somehow, "We have the dibs on that. We're here in the realness of life, and grownups don't know anything." I think every generation has a version of that kind of thing. So maybe some of these kids are like that.

Reversing this pattern, some people who developed self-injury on their own quit when it became a popular phenomenon. Anya thought the change that led her to spin out did not occur in her but in society. She had always regarded self-injuring as her own personal secret. But once other people started to do it, it lost its specialness. She wanted her own thing that no one knew about. Brianna quit when people started doing it for the trend:

> I think another reason I got over my cutting was it became trendy. It lost its value for me because so many girls were doing it for attention. They would cut their arms and wear an ace bandage around it—and obviously say, "What is wrong with your arm?" And they would just be like, "Oh, I had some problems." They took away the meaning of me doing it by just kind of doing it because it was popular.

Many self-injurers reading the postings and accounts on the Internet suggested that some young people *grew out* of it in their twenties.[3] They went to college or got a job, moved away from home, and left their high school scene behind. They escaped from being trapped in their rooms, isolated. Their raging hormones died down. They found other ways to manage their anger and depression. Melanie thought that once she matured, she realized that self-injuring was a childish way to escape her problems. Looking back, she reflected, "Like, who cuts themselves to feel better? That makes you feel worse."

Several people mused that people's social anxieties in high school became alleviated as they matured, got a better sense of themselves, and forged more meaningful friendships. They were not chasing a popular crowd of people whose behavior they had to emulate for acceptance. Nicola described her difficulty relating to people, which led her to cut: "In high school I just kind of had shitty friends and obviously was never going to go to my parents and be like, "Hey, guess what? I'm doing this, and I feel like this." And I don't know, I bottled up, like, the anger, and I was holding everything in. But now I have people that I talk to."

Mandy, like Nicola, used cutting to deal with her unhappy life: "I'm lonely. I have no friends. What am I going to do with my life? I don't want to be me anymore. Let's cut." But eventually she got involved in activities, she met people, she made deeper connections, and she learned how to deal with herself.

Developing more positive interests was also a way that young people drew away from their cycle of self-injuring. Maggie, a 25-year-old nurse, grew up in a Mormon household and felt suffocated. She recognized that her behavior and the scars it left might make her feel less confident when she tried to go out on her own. She described her spin out:

> I think I was 16 when I kind of grew out of it. I got into cycling, and I was racing semi-pro. Junior year of high school, '94, I started traveling with my cycling team. I was able to see other people out there; nobody else in the cycling world was Mormon. I was so much more comfortable here. I feel good here. I didn't need to do those kinds of things. I felt healthier, positive outlets for that.

Getting out of a bad situation helped some adolescents to grow out of self-injuring. Sally's self-injury started in eighth grade and continued over the summer and into ninth grade. That year she moved to a new school, a private school, and she got away from a friend who was also injuring. Noting the effect of her transition, she said, "I don't think it was reinforcing me that much, but it did kind of. I had no one around to talk to about it or who would think it was halfway normal." In her new school she dropped out of her highly competitive ballet program and moved to a more recreational level. This enabled her to play soccer, which she loved. She reflected, "I finally was feeling that I was living my own life."

Brianna's bad situation was her family life. She called her parents "dysfunctional." They went through a bad divorce, and her brother had severe drinking problems. All the weight of the family fell on her to be the "good girl." She explained, "There was just this period in my life in high school where so many bad things were happening all at once that . . . that at that time I needed the cutting. My parents divorced, my father committed suicide my junior year, I didn't have friends I could trust; things were rough." But after that passed, she went through "all of that adolescent trying to find out" who she was. She figured it out, developed confidence, and stopped cutting.

Joanna, trapped in her house with her stepfather who called her fat and ugly, blackened her eyes and did other things to get her mother's help. She finally got a new perspective on herself when she spent some inpatient time in a hospital. Away from her family, her biggest stress, she did not feel the need to self-injure, and she was able to take that feeling of removal back when she returned home. In the hospital she saw people in much worse situations than she, such as with mental disorders or living in foster homes, people who she felt would not be able to make the kind of recovery she had. Listening to their trapped situations, she feared they were "pretty much a lost cause."

Many people, like Crystal, *replaced their self-injuring with alcohol and drugs,* especially as they got older. Mandy noted that alcohol and drugs numbed the pain and gave her something else to focus on. Drinking and smoking pot, for her, was the next step when she moved from high school into college. Liz, the animal trainer, alternated cutting with doing drugs, but she did not do the two at the same time. Drugs offered her similar relief, although she said, "I didn't dissociate as much when I was on drugs all the time." She would use one method of relief for a while, and then she would feel like, as she explained it, "'Ohh, I shouldn't be doing so many drugs.' Then I'd quit and start cutting again. Then I'd be like, 'Ohh, I'm cutting. I should be doing drugs instead.'" This became a habitual pattern for her.[4]

A few young people needed to *hit rock bottom* before they could quit self-injuring. Melanie, like Cindy and Joanna, wound up in the hospital. Eight months after she began self-injuring, a giant cutting episode landed her in the emergency room. She cursed at her parents, calling them "motherfuckers," and screamed to be released. "All night I was in intensive care, I was straight-jacketed to the bed. That was when I think it hit me, that I kind of hit rock bottom." Hitting bottom made her look inward and decide that she was "here for a reason," that she did not want to die. In just that one day she switched her mind-set and decided she "needed to live happy."

Thus, in addition to hitting rock bottom, Melanie *thought about the future* and decided she wanted to have a normal, fun teenage life: "Not people seeing your arms or how you're going to get drugs the next day or anything like that." Dana turned her perspective toward the future when her counselor pointed out the practical problems she would encounter. She explained how she thought about it: "'Am I going to go to a job interview with a big scar or a cut on my arm?' And that really freaked me out. 'I don't want anyone to know. No one can know. No! This is my thing.' And that just sort of scared me. 'Wait a minute, no, I don't want it to be a long-term thing; I don't want scars and stuff.'"

Longer-Term Involvement

A big difference existed between those who spun out quickly and those who continued for longer. Several people, in explaining what they saw on the Internet, described a *bimodal population*. They differentiated longer-term involvement from the early spin-outs. Hannah gave her view: "There are people who are trendy and do it, like I said, to be like, 'Oh, I'm so fucked up, look at me. Haha! I'm crazy I hang out with the punks.' And then there are people who—and I identify with the second group—people who really do have a problem with it and have struggled with it for years." All these people used self-injury as a coping mechanism, she believed, but the earlier spin-outs did not have "as much to cope with." The younger folk made her angry. "I don't like the trendy kids, and I want to punch them in the face a lot of times." But the people who progressed to the second group had real problems they could not resolve. She explained how she viewed her self-injury: "something that I'm addicted to and I will struggle with for years and years and years."

Whether people fell into the first or the second group might be affected by the *age of onset* of their self-injury. Many self-injurers believed that those who began early had a more benign course to tread and an easier time quitting.[5] Loner teens often had stress in their lives that they could not discuss with their parents, but when they developed the emotional tools to deal with this stress, they left self-injury behind. Gary believed that these people used self-injury for escapism, but their social scene was "less pathological." People who started later or lasted longer might have more deeply ingrained issues.

Self-injurers analyzed the difference between shorter- and longer-term careers as an issue of *serious trauma or depression versus angst*. Those who posted to the Internet that they were long-term injurers sometimes claimed to have chemical predispositions or more problematic emotional issues. Linda, the 40-year-old group moderator, suggested that people with severe anxiety or depression, or who were still struggling to cope with psychological problems rooted in youthful abuse from family members, might evolve into using self-injury as a coping mechanism over the long term. The same might apply to individuals who only commenced self-injuring (usually because they discovered it late) as adults. Once they made it to adulthood, they might be stuck in structural life situations, like the people Joanna saw during her hospital stay. They might lack better alternatives into which to grow. In a rut, with no visible means of escape, they might feel like this online poster:

I have been on medications since the age of 14, I am now 43 i have also been in therapy consistently for 10+ years I have talked and have tried and I am just tired I have kept living because of my kids who are 22 and 20 I have to try to live for myself and i can't. eveyday is a struggle i just hate myelf so much. I never see what others say they see in me I have fought with life and death for 30 years and I am tired of fighting I really believe there is only one way to go.......................

For others, the cyber support groups offered a means of self-sustenance. One 31-year-old, fairly regular group member lived with her mother in a one-bedroom apartment. On medication and in group therapy for bipolar disorder, she dated the start of her self-injury to age 12. In and out of hospitals for much of her life, sometimes for months, she had quit and come back many times. Yet despite the fact that she still struggled and was miserable, she continued to try again. She posted the gratitude she felt for the group support, writing, "THANK YOU ALL FROM the BOTTOM of MY HEART!!!" Just as for some people drugs could substitute for the succor they got from self-injuring, these cyber support groups played the same role.

Many people, especially those in their late 20s, 30s, 40s, and beyond, expressed the view that they would *always be doing it*, especially since it brought them relief and helped them function in society. At 39, Ed saw no relief in sight. "Old habits die hard," he said: "When I'm really upset, that will always be the first thing that my mind always goes to." Nancy recognized that her cutting was both therapeutic and harmful. When she was feeling logical, she could talk herself out of it, but when depression absolutely took over her, she went back to it. At 43, she expected that cutting would be a part of her life forever because it was "just like an old friend." Frustrated, she asked, "What the hell am I thinking?" One online poster embraced her self-injury openly. She declared,

> I have no desire to stop SI anytime soon, which I know is not the best way to face things, but the worst part is not the wounds/scars, it's the immense emotional torture I feel when I can't do it because of a person or situation in my life. I've even been through periods where I've severed all contact with everyone—just so I knew I had the freedom to do it whenever I liked.

Marnie, the 51-year-old with severe dissociative disorder, talked about her ongoing self-injury with more emotional detachment. For her it was not a coping strategy or a means of managing her disorder; it was just a part of herself. Asked what would have to change for her give it up, she replied, "Never thought about it. Probably the only thing that will get me to change is if I die; that would be it."

Managing

People who kept at their self-injuring for a longer period, beyond the adolescent spin-out phase, usually encountered more issues with maintaining the behavior. Scholars have noted the difficulty and sometimes instability in maintaining a deviant career over the life course.[6] Several types of constraints served to hold people to a long-term career of self-injury, such as structural, personal, and moral commitments. Many of these people ceased to think of self-injury as a problem, considering it just their way of being able to function in life.

As these people's career evolved, there was often a tendency for them to "notch up" their behavior beyond the kind of simple progression described in chapter 4. Danielle, the 35-year-old housewife, remarked, "Timewise, as I got older, the deeper the cuts got. The more blood I would lose, right afterwards I would fall asleep just from sheer exhaustion." Darcy said that she needed to see more blood. Starting with shallow cuts, she progressed to cutting deeper over the years. A small trace of blood no longer satisfied her, and she needed a substantial amount. Barb continually challenged herself to handle more pain, to prove that she was not a "wuss," and so she looked for implements that were sharper, that would do more damage.

Escalating the severity of their acts, longtime self-injurers usually encountered more serious consequences. Heather, the 42-year-old receptionist, noted that she visited hospital emergency rooms often. Lindsay, the 32-year-old severe self-injurer, went to the emergency room regularly. "I think I was going for stitches three to five times a week. . . . I circulated between the emergency room and some walk-in clinics, and I would do different parts of my body so that it wouldn't look like I had so many stitches at one time." At 53, Susan got to the point where she did not want to deal with the whole emergency-room routine. Having been sutured there many times, she even sutured herself once.

Managing self-injury over the length of its career, then, usually required *developing medical skills*. The ability of self-injurers to stitch themselves up was one of the most needed proficiencies. Like many patients in the United States, Liz, the animal trainer, found the medical treatment she received for self-inflicted wounds degrading: "If you came in because you were disso-ciative, and you cut your wrist to the ligament, and you needed surgery or stitches, they completely blacklist you. They won't talk to you; they'll never come check on you. That makes it hard." She, like others who had been "at it" a long time, innovated her own adaptive ways. While working with horses during her younger years, she learned how to take care of herself:

Q: And have you ever cut so much or so deep that it wouldn't stop bleeding?
LIZ: Yes. I've gone to the ER a couple of times for that, and luckily my boy-friend knew how to stitch, so I went to him a lot too.
Q: What'd he stitch you with?
LIZ: Just the same stuff that they do in the ER. You can get it pretty easily in Kentucky because of all the horses. We'd stitch up our own horses when something would happen. So we learned to stitch each other up.

Homeschooled Molly learned how to repair herself from an old boyfriend, whom she called one day after she cut. "He was like, 'Okay, I'm a graduated Boy Scout; this is what you're going to do.' He kinda just made me laugh about it. So he told me how to get it to stop bleeding and how to clean it and every-thing." If Liz was by herself and could reach the spot, she could practice self-stitchery. Being left-handed, she could only suture wounds on her right arm. She kept moving the cuts around to make repair easier: "Okay, an episode on the leg. The next episode better go to the stomach." One person posted to the Internet, "Getting stitches vs not getting them: I use super glue. It works."

Marnie got by with regular thread (Coats and Clark) and a needle. Over years of watching doctors stitch her up in the emergency room, she figured out how to do it herself. That offered the advantage that she would "not have to deal with people who looked at you weird and stuff like that." She had a medical kit in which she kept alcohol, peroxide, and other implements. Molly's kit included Lidocaine patches filled with antibiotics. Working like Steri-Strips, they stuck to her once she pulled off the tabs on the sides and were available over the counter. These were "repair kits" that had evolved beyond the simple cutting kits that individuals constructed during their younger years.

Over the years, long-term self-injurers learned to *tolerate worse damage*. Amy offered a theory of progression that people became acclimated or habituated to pain and thus needed greater stimulation to achieve the same emotional satisfaction. Lindsay, the nurse's aide, explained that she also learned to tolerate more serious injury without medical intervention. For her, just needing one layer of stitches became a relatively minor injury:

> LINDSAY: I won't go to the hospital if I just need a few stitches. If I'm cutting a whole bunch of times, I won't go to the hospital until I need between 45 and 50 unless it's life threatening or unless it's really going to complicate my life later on. Like when I surgery [cut] myself now, I know that I need to go.
>
> Q: What do you surgery yourself with now?
>
> LINDSAY: Razor blades.
>
> Q: So how deep are these cuts?
>
> LINDSAY: I have—honestly, 100 percent, literally—had my whole hand inside my leg, up to my wrist.
>
> Q: When you have a cutting episode, how do you know that enough is enough, that you should stop?
>
> LINDSAY: I'm usually out of control. I'll phone somebody in a more controlled moment, and I'll keep going until they come to pick me up to take me to the hospital.
>
> Q: And were people trying to stop you from self-injuring at this time?
>
> LINDSAY: I don't think really. Like, the medical field for a long time really gave up on me. I've been in the mental a few times, so usually what they'll do is just sew me up and send me home.

Quitting

Past the point of spinning out after adolescence, people broke free of their dependence on self-injury for reasons and at points in their careers that displayed certain patterns.[7] The population winnowed down, with a gradually shrinking number of self-harmers from their teens to their 20s, 30s, 40s, 50s, and beyond. Alice noted that the longer she self-injured, the more of an issue it became. When people's attitudes toward self-injury reached this point, many of them tried to taper down their involvement.

One of the strongest reasons people cited that drove them to cessation was *quitting for others,* an external "pull factor." People experienced a lot of pressure from friends and loved ones to turn away from this behavior. At 44 Susan married a therapist who, she said, thought he could "fix her." He gave her a point-blank ultimatum that their relationship could only last as long as her abstinence. Asked how she was able to quit, she sighed and said, "I think it's mostly been as a direct response to wanting to maintain this marriage and knowing how much pain this has caused my husband. He said, 'You know that would end things; I will not live with a cutter.'" She had gone nine years without it. But should their marriage ever end, she noted, she would go right back to it. Bea's boyfriend never put it to her quite so definitively, but he felt so bad about her hurting herself that she stopped. She explained, "I didn't necessarily want to stop, but the stress of hiding it, coupled with the fact that it was hurting him, didn't seem like it was worth it anymore."

Elaine quit at 19 after a 10-year career, following a particularly violent episode in which she cut herself so aggressively that the bleeding would not stop. After two hours she finally left her room and went downstairs, where her parents were shocked to find her covered in blood. Their reaction pushed her over the edge to stop. She noted, "It definitely wasn't *me* driven; it was *other people* driven." Mandy quit for her best friend. Once, fighting cravings, she reached out for support to her friend, who helped talk her down from them. The conversation ended with her friend telling her that if she ever did it again, she would never speak to her. Mandy felt so grateful for the emotional burden her friend took on that she quit: "It is not that I'm afraid that she won't speak to me—I'm afraid that if I do it again, it's going to hurt her more. And it's such a private thing to begin with, to have them saying that they'll take care of you, you feel like you owe them so much, it makes them so afraid for you."

Other times people *quit for themselves,* being "pushed" out of deviance by their own involvement with it. Cari, 39, mused, "Anyways, a piece of advice: if you stop for others, you're not really stopping, more just postponing. To really stop you have to stop for yourself." Jenny had always blamed others for her problems, but she finally took a really hard look at herself and decided her self-injury was not helping her. Once she realized this, she was able to gather the strength to move on with her life. Kim finally stopped seeing a point to her injuring. She turned herself around on her own: "I started seeing a benefit with being healthy and being a good person and being good to other people. People will stop on their own, I think."

Tracy, the 31-year-old librarian, *tapered off*. When given ultimatums by men she dated, she broke up with them rather than being pressured to quit by others. Again, the man she was currently living with freaked out about it the last time she injured. She then decided, "Well, I can't stop because of him, but I can stop because I realize that this is not a coping mechanism that, I guess—I realize that this isn't something that's going to help me have solid relationships with anybody, including myself." People knew that leaving a reliable crutch would be hard, yet sometimes something made them reevaluate their point of view, and they decided that, for themselves, they should get on with their lives.

Many times people quit for themselves because of emotions they felt. One emotional impetus was *fear*. People quit because they were afraid they were going to get sent to the hospital, they were going to get discovered, their friends would drop them, or their scars would show on a job interview. Another emotional impetus to stop was *guilt*. Mandy felt guilty after her best friend put herself on the line for her, and she would have felt guiltier had she self-injured again. Jane felt guilty each time she cut, looking at her arm and not wanting to see bigger and bigger scars. The mixture of feeling guilty toward herself and feeling guilty for hurting friends and family pushed her to give it up.

Shame was another emotional impetus toward desistance. After years of self-injuring, Hannah looked at all her scars and began to feel ashamed. She decided that she should have been dealing with her issues better. She reflected, "Although shame isn't a good emotion, it's been good in the sense that I know that it's not what I need to do anymore." One of Kim's co-workers saw her scars after an incident when she ran out of concealed places to cut. The way the co-worker looked at Kim made her feel ashamed, the first time she had ever felt that way about it. This helped her to see herself through another person's eyes and to decide that she should turn toward a healthier path, that she should find more "normal" ways of dealing with her problems. Mindy got shamed by a stranger in public who turned her away from the behavior. After a long cutting career she, like Kim, ran out of places where she could hide her fresh injuries. She was ordering a car wash from an attendant, when he busted her:

> He looked down and saw that my arm was, like, all mutilated up. And he sat there, and he was just, like, "Why did you do this to yourself? You are such a pretty girl, blah, blah, blah"—like some random guy in the carwash. Then I am, like, giving this guy every denial point, everything that I can possibly give that, like—I am just trying to get him out of my car, you know? He's just driving me crazy. This guy is like, "You have such a big life

ahead of you," and he is trying to get stuff out of me. And you know, like, I didn't want to share with just some random guy in the car wash. And then he kneeled by my car and started praying. He was like, "I am going to pray for you. Don't worry. I know that you are going to get better. God is going to take care of you. I am going to pray for you every day, and I am going to make sure that this doesn't happen to you again." And to be going through the car wash—like, that was a big deal for me. This outside random person is, like, kneeling by my car trying to, like, save me. It was so embarrassing; I felt horrible. I was lying through my teeth to this guy, and he was praying for me. And just, like, he wouldn't stop, he would not stop. That was like a big milestone for me, you know. I think that was a big shift in my act.

Rather than having an impetus to quit suddenly, a lot of people quit their self-injury gradually because they *got tired of it*. Over the years, they got tired of having to hide it, of having to talk to people who became close to them and who saw the scars. They got tired of fighting the urges, of dealing with the stigma, of leading a double life, of being lonely and alone. Although Alice had earlier relished her scars, she eventually started to dislike them. An Internet poster wrote, "I never thought that in a million years that I would say these words, but I am so tired of fighting my uges to harm. It is so difficult everyday to get up and consciously remind myself not to harm, to be careful not to be triggered by someone, not to give into any urges or feelings today. I've got to find a better way." Tasha, who inflicted chemical burns on herself, got tired of hiding:

The younger population, with them I think a lot of the times they quit because they've been caught and realize they need to stop this, you know, because they're going to get in trouble for it or something. But as far as my age group goes, I know a lot of us have said that we're tired of hiding it: I'm tired of always having to hide my stomach because I'm not overweight, and people are always saying you should wear this or that. There's been too many cases where I have to hide this aspect of myself—not just physically, but I have to hide this part of myself emotionally too. I can't let anybody else know what's going on, and I think that starts to take its toll after a while. We also realize that this is a horrible behavior and probably a damaging mental process for the long run.

Life transitions often weeded out the population of self-injurers. Many people quit as they aged and went through the stages of life. Some quit when they moved from high school to college or when they graduated from college and got a job. Others fell away because they were in a serious relationship or they had children. Several mentioned that they were more worried that their children would find out about what they did than that their spouse would, that their children would be upset with them, or that maybe they might be bad role models and pass the behavior on to their children. As people aged, thus, the group of those still injuring got smaller and smaller.

People used a variety of techniques for quitting. *Therapists* helped some people break away by equipping them with other coping skills, giving them specific treatments or cognitive practices. Therapists delved into the root of self-injurers' past issues and helped them work their way through traumatic or emotionally difficult feelings. For people who turned their anger or shame inward, therapists taught them how to redirect these feelings outward.

Many individuals were helped by a variety of *psychiatric medications*. People we interviewed recounted the prescriptions they were taking, often in combination with each other. Antidepressants were especially prevalent among the self-injuring population because they helped people tamp down their mood fluctuations and extreme emotions. Vickie said that her medications helped calm her life down so she could deal with things better.

Finally, people quit *without therapy*. Although the psycho-medical community promotes therapy, hospitalization, and drugs, these were not the only ways that people found the strength to quit.[8] Chelsea, in a "cold turkey" quit herself, thought that a lot of people quit on their own, without treatment. She got the support that helped her recovery from her mother and from an online group called Sanctuary of Love. Bonnie said that the most helpful thing she learned was how to "surf the urge to cut":

> It kind of comes in waves for me. I get these big tidal waves of emotion that rush through me, and my first reaction for a long time was to cut, to make it stop. But now, if it's sadness, cry; if I'm angry, scream; if I'm ashamed, accept it. It's more about being mindful about whatever's happening to my body or my mind or my emotions at the time. But if I surf that urge, let it happen, it always passes. And that's actually been the most helpful for me.

Oscillations

People's deviant careers did not always end definitively. Individuals oscillated in and out of their deviance, just as they had with their support groups, quitting and coming back. It was hard to pinpoint what kind of stimulus might cause a permanent endpoint versus a temporary cessation.

Many tried, often repeatedly, to quit. Unsuccessful efforts, which ended in renewed self-injuring, could be called *relapses*. People rarely stopped self-injuring cold turkey, as Chelsea did, but were triggered again and again. In fact, self-injury may resemble cigarette smoking in having such a large percentage of the participants in some active stage of trying to quit. "Slips" were one of the most common topics of Internet discussion and were met with patience and understanding. A typical message looked like this one: "Unfortunately, I hit some major stress about 8 months ago, and it all started up again. Someone in a previous post said that she/he did not see relapse as a failure. I am trying to live that piece of advice." People responded with suggestions on how to go get over the disappointment and shared their stories in return:

> i want to respond to your angry feelings of relapsing. i too am feeling very angry. i went 14 mos with no si. that is the longest time i have ever gone since i started si 16 years ago. when i succumbed to the overwhelming pressure the other night i was very upset and angry with myself. i talked to my therapist about it and she said that beating myself up over a mistake will only cause more mistakes. i think she may be right. if i accept the fact that i si'd and begin working at not si'ing i will be able to build up another 14 months of freedom. i am pretty sure that you can do the same thing if you put your mind to it. good luck and please be patient with yourself.

People quit for days, months, or years and then slipped back into it, usually multiple times. They counted the length of time they had been "self-injury free" by the days, weeks, and months, just as they kept track of their desistance date. Vanessa noted that drama, hatred, and fights with her classmates in her senior year of high school were responsible for her relapsing.

Like many of the solid-world support groups, particularly the Alcoholics Anonymous model, cyber communities encouraged people to take their desistance *one day at a time.* This helped them avoid compounding their frustration in life with self-anger over losing their sobriety. In fact, since most people expected each other to quit and relapse repeatedly, they developed a host of strategies and legitimations for not getting crushed by this occurrence. Those who subscribed to the medical model could always externalize the blame for their relapses on uncontrollable urges or mental disorders.

The self-injuring career, then, was typically marked by people's *phasing in and out,* and they absolved each other of shame. Many believed they were more prone to relapse because they had found relief from this behavior in the past. Diana, at 44, remarked, "I mean it's—once you have [*sighs*] . . . once it's in your head, it's not something you can forget about. You can't totally erase the whole experience." Instead of talking about total elimination, people often talked about pathways to desistance that incorporated diminished cutting and burning. One poster wrote, "Well, I've been si-free with just a two or three 'slips' for seven months." This person proudly listed her goal as a month free of self-injury. For some, the return to self-injuring came quickly, whereas others had years of inactivity marked by a return later in life. An Internet poster wrote,

> I was a cutter for 15 years, then somehow I don't remember what I did, I stopped. So here I am 9 years out and the need is back. I have a 4 1/2 yr old and don't want him to know. I have bipolar but nothing new happening just the old stressors I always have. Why am I still so drawn to it? I just want to do it again. It's an addiction I know but I thought by now it would be gone. My 19 year old birthson also cuts so I wonder about the genetics of it. My question is does the want, the desire ever really leave??

For some people, the *last quit* was no different from any of the others; it just was not followed by a relapse. Those who built up to their exit gradually learned, along the way, how to manage their triggers better. For one online poster the trick to stopping was learning his "point of no return," coming to recognize the feelings that pushed him over the edge to injury. It took a series of major traumas to teach him these signs, but he then used them as a guide and tried to protect himself from such things. This awareness made it easier for him to get through the tough times. When he made it through one of these periods, he rewarded himself. The longer he was able to divert himself, the easier it got each time. Jane worked her way up to the last quit by making a conscious effort to put up with the hurt, and she eventually built toward being able to withstand more stress.

The Post- Phase

Just as it is difficult to assess the final cessation of self-injurers' careers, it is hard to describe the postinjurious phase of their deviance.[9] Many people on the Internet referred to their deviant careers as a "journey" or a "journey of quitting." For some there was not really a post- phase; there were just periods during which they did not do it.

Many people who had quit still found themselves *thinking about it*. Some boards, groups, or listservs were dedicated to people "in recovery." They still self-identified in their online signatures with their cessation date or the length of time they had gone without self-injuring. Reading other people's success stories was inspirational for them, but when they saw that someone who had been free for several years relapsed, they were discouraged. Yet they drew on their groups like any type of group support, talking their way through problems that continued even if their acute need to self-injure had subsided.

One poster who had been abstinent for six or seven years wrote about the anxiety she had in dealing with people, even superficially. Frustrated with her lack of progress in overcoming this anxiety, she was considering going back to injuring. She wrote, "I really feel, whats the difference if I start to cut again? It will help me when I'm out with people. It's like a defense against them, what they think about me won't bother me. Why did I work so hard to quit anyway? It's like I can't remember what was so bad about SI." She knew how many cuts it would take her to deal with any given situation, and these thoughts became increasingly intrusive. She posted to the group asking for someone to help her deal with the temptation to start again, to give her some reasons "why not."

Scar management was an important component of the post- phase. When people were in their actively injuring phase, they were often so wrapped up in their emotional needs and releases that they overlooked the damage they might be causing that might last into the future. Once they quit, they became more conscious about this damage. They then had to manage the shame and embarrassment they had ignored previously. People relied on the subcultural transmission of information in this area about how to use vitamins, ointments, chemicals, or peels to diminish the intensity and visibility of their scars. They talked in depth about the tattoos they used to hide scars and the skin grafts used for repair. One poster referred to getting a skin graft as being "granted a new lease on life." Several people we interviewed emailed us photos of their serious, lasting scars.

People were conflicted about their attitudes toward their scars. One person felt grateful but horrible at the same time. Others suffered from the shame and struggled to conceal the scars. Another wrote, "This is who I am, this is a part of my story and I have no shame of my scars and my history with SI because it makes me who I am today." Susan told us that she could handle her scars as long as they did not determine who she was. An Internet poster quoted a line from Hannibal Lector in *Silence of the Lambs,* writing, "Our scars have the power to remind us that the past was real." Here we are, people announced, scarred but stronger. Moving past scar shame was an important component of the post- phase.

Ironically, despite the prevalence of relapsing, some people who were abstinent for a while tried to self-injure again and did *not get the same effect*. Bonnie noted that, like sucking her thumb as a child, it no longer gave her the same rush or relief as previously. Alice, who had been self-injury free for almost a year, made an unsuccessful attempt at a "comeback." She described the experience:

> I was feeling really down and crying and kind of hysterical, and I—it's hard to say this, because it almost sounds kind of silly [*choking up*], but I think I tried doing it to see if it made me feel better the way it used to. And it really didn't. It felt awful. And once I came out of the depression and I had done that, it made me feel worse then too. And I left another scar.

This experience made her realize that she never wanted to do it again. Without the same effect, she no longer had the strong inner urge to self-injure. At the end, she walked away from the scene and said, "That's it. The end. Good-bye."

Self-injurious careers followed some common and some unique patterns. They resembled pathways through other forms of deviance in their types of entry, their various modes of escalation, and their oscillations in and out. But they were unusual in having such a bimodal career pattern, with one population running through and moving away from the behavior in such a more compressed and rapid manner than the other group. This difference may be attributed to the variations in types of people drawn to self-injury and the social contexts and meanings surrounding their engagement with its practice.

12

Understanding Self-Injury

In this book, we have charted the rise and evolution of self-injury since the early 1990s to the end of the twenty-first century's first decade. Our research makes a rare contribution to the literature on this topic because it is the first in-depth, sociological, longitudinal study of self-injurers living in their natural worlds, neither in psychiatric treatment nor in institutional settings. We add here to empirical knowledge about noninpatient groups alternative youth movements, adolescents, adults, and cyber populations, a previously untapped mass of individuals who manage their self-injury on their own, largely without recourse to clinical observation.

We gathered life histories from over 135 people who reflected on their childhood backgrounds, their often troubled adolescence, and their adult lives. In addition, we followed many of these people personally, both in the solid world and through continuing cyber communication, so we have been able to see how the people we knew evolved as they aged and as their lives and social relationships developed. These communications were supplemented by a near decade of thousands of Internet postings.

These longitudinal data give us a picture of how people manage their self-injury and what part it plays or has played in their everyday lives. Many of the people we initially interviewed, both in the solid world and in cyberspace, have quit self-injuring and moved on to more sanguine places in their lives. Others have continued to self-injure. The world around them has undergone rapid social change, yet self-injurers' behavior remains hidden, and the population is still elusive to pinpoint.

We have documented here, through the empirical accounts of past and present self-injurers and through our own observations, three historical periods in the evolution of self-injury, as its awareness and meaning have transformed from the ancient and ritualistic or hidden period to its phase of burgeoning awareness and finally to its development as a trendy fad, a recognized mode of expressing inner angst for people going through the challenges of adolescence and a way for troubled individuals of all ages to alleviate otherwise seemingly unmanageable stress in their lives. We have discussed the cyber world of self-injury that has drawn unconnected individuals together and helped them to create meaning and community in their lives.

Yet this research offers only a glimpse into other hidden populations of self-injurers that fell outside our reach, people of more limited socioeconomic means who lacked access to computers and the Internet and who were unable to go to college. Although our population falls squarely within the psycho-medical literature's primary demographic and may thus represent a large percentage of the actual people who self-injure, a group of unknown size remains understudied, potentially including structurally disadvantaged people such as homeless youth, fostered youth, families thrown out of work and into crisis by recession, the incarcerated, the military, ordinary lower-class people, deinstitutionalized populations, those lacking control over their lives, and more.

Psycho-Medical and Feminist Theory

Reconsidering the models of self-injury offered by the psycho-medical and feminist literatures, we see that the former is still useful in defining the scope of this behavior and differentiating among the levels of its severity, especially Favazza's (1987) early categorizations of moderate or superficial self-mutilation with its three distinct subtypes (compulsive, episodic, and repetitive), which gave a primary emphasis to skin cutting and burning. Psychiatrists have categorized self-injury as an outcome of mental disorders that are environmentally rather than organically caused, rooted in psychological or situational problems incurred during people's maladaptive childhoods. We saw many people who suffered traumatic childhoods, and some percentage of these formed the longer-lasting group of people who were unable to grow out of this practice and replace it with more socially accepted and useful means of coping or who stayed with it for much longer periods of time.

However, we add to this literature by expanding the understanding of how this behavior is practiced by people who do not have diagnosed mental disorders. This research has illuminated the ways that self-injurers were influenced by other environmental factors within the social realm. This shift and expansion has transformed self-injury from a strictly psychological phenomenon into a more broadly sociological one. Groups of people who are poor, weak, and powerless may have high prevalence rates because they are structurally disadvantaged. Teenagers and young adults frequently learn about this behavior through interaction with their peers, from adults close to them, and through the media. They learn to recognize and to interpret it, via their subcultures, as an acceptable, albeit deviant, way of dealing with the anger, confusion, and frustration so common at their age. They also learn how to do it and how to understand its social meaning. Older, long-term self-injurers have learned how to manage it. While the psycho-medical model individual- izes the problem and deflects responsibility away from social structure,[1] our analysis, grounded in the perceptions and interpretations of real-life partici- pants, highlights the role of interactional, cultural, and structural forces and their contributions to the spread of self-injury. Self-injury can now be seen as a practice of individuals who lack severe trauma in their lives but who turn to this behavior as a means of self-expression, comfort, affiliation, identifica- tion, sexuality, and rebellion, for myriad reasons.

Addressing the feminist model, we add to the arguments against Sheila Jeffreys's (2000, 2005) radicalized feminist view of self-injury, joining schol- ars such as Alison Guy and Maura Banim (2000) in their writing on fashion, Deborah Pollack (2003) on eating disorders, and Sarah Riley (2002) on body art. Like them, we employ the plurality of both a top-down and bottom-up approach to self-injury. We recognize this behavior as an outcome of cul- tural and structural oppression but do not box it within a strictly patriarchal mode or a discourse of oppression disguised as liberation. Disadvantages other than gender left some people so structurally oppressed and unable to cope with their life situations that they self-injured; these other disadvan- tages included their race/ethnicity, social class, family situations, and age. Self-injurious acts, moreover, were not limited to women, men with sub- ordinated masculinities, the disabled, or other disadvantaged and despised groups. Rather, they extended over a broader and growing population. The framework of the meanings of self-injurious acts was forged in the context of their production by the contingencies of people's structural life situations, the cultural constructions of their male and female gender roles, and by their interactional, agentic choices.

We contribute to and expand a feminist understanding of self-injury by describing its gendered population, practice, and reception. Women commit more of these acts, as most studies show and as our research confirms. They do them in more secretive ways and places. Women's gender socialization leads them to turn their stress inward and to harm themselves, while men are taught to express their stress through anger, outwardly. Yet this research shows that self-injury is not the "female disease" that it was originally con- sidered. Intentionally self-injurious acts committed by men are not always perceived and interpreted into the same categories that they are for women.

At the same time, though, that gender norms lead more women to self-injure, they also foster its greater acceptance when it is done by men. Women are more socially stigmatized for self-injuring than men are. When men are confronted with the same structural, cultural, and interactional stresses and their socialization leads them to self-burning, branding, or cutting (sometimes in groups) or even more commonly to punching walls or trees, this is interpreted as masculine venting, bonding, or typical masculine behavior ("boys will be boys"). But because women's bodies serve as the text of their femininity,[2] any damage or misuse of these bodies violates strong gender roles and generally leads women to more severely negative self-images than it does for men who self-injure.[3] The panopticon of institutional control demands that women enact more "docile"[4] bodies than men. Women thus disempower and discipline their bodies-as-objects by conforming to social strictures governing their size and shape, their gestures, posture, movement, and general bodily comportment, and their ornamental surfaces including their clothes, hair, dress, and (most especially, for our purposes) skin.[5]

Both men and women extend the harsh patriarchal social gaze against female acts of self-injury, condemning them as harmful, damaging, mentally disordered, and wrong. In doing so, both genders identify too closely with what Abigail Bray (1996) has called the "social text," subscribing to the deviance label and enforcing the oppression associated with it. Their judgments are too often poisoned not only by the oppression of the Foucauldian institutions that discipline and punish, including schools, hospitals, and workplaces, but by the "unbounded" institutional control rooted in the discourse of the dominating psycho-medical establishment. This paradigm pervades not only their treatment by the counseling and therapy professionals to whom they are subjected but the larger society's psycho-biologically determined model of the actor, weakening their capacity for critical structural, cultural, or situational interpretation.

There are also gendered ways of committing self-injurious acts. When men conform to these gender roles, by cutting or burning themselves visibly and harshly, flaunting their behavior, and thrusting it into the public gaze, they are defined as manly and tough. Men who hide these acts like women violate their gender role and sacrifice their masculine image. Women who hide their acts and seek out others to comfort them in subculturally appropriate places and ways are more welcomed and supported. But when women make larger, more serious cuts or display them too openly, they violate their gender role and are regarded by their peers as needy, showy, whiney, unstable, disturbing, and potentially socially contagious.

Yet at the same time, self-injurers, both alone in private and through semipublic cyber subcultures, have challenged these meanings. They have created and shared multiple explanations and social connotations for their acts, defining them as self-empowering. Although Jeffreys (2000, 2005) has challenged these interpretations as the false consciousness of neoliberal rationalization, suggesting that self-injurers are buying their logic of choice when their actions are more culturally and structurally constrained than they recognize, these interpretations are real to them and guide them in their lives. These interpretations represent social constructions created from the bottom up of society, forged by people in the context of exercising their free will.

Through their own acts, self-injurers achieve the ethic and aesthetic of self-mastery and self-transcendence through which they experience and present themselves as exhibiting superior self-control.[6] In this way, self-injurers also accord with the newer discourses of public health, in which people are structurally accorded the responsibility for regulating their own bodies.[7] Yet these social meanings may evolve and change over the course of individuals' self-injurious careers, as they transition out of dependence on cutting and burning toward other forms of self-soothing and self-expression. They thus move away from the "justifications" of their active self-injuring periods, during which they assert their claim to being responsible for their actions while denying the wrongfulness of their acts, to the "excuses" of their postinjurious careers, when they reflexively look back on their earlier actions as less legitimate and suggest that they were not fully in control of themselves.[8]

Self-Injury and the Body

Having raised the duality of the body as subject and object in chapter 1, we now reflect on the role that self-injurers' bodies have for them. Do they make their bodies, or do their bodies construct them? Do they nourish their bodies, or do their bodies nourish them? Do they sacrifice themselves for their bodies or their bodies for their selves? Do they become themselves in their bodies or through their bodies? Do self-injurers detach from their bodies to salve their inner selves or use their bodies to find their inner selves? Do their bodies empower them, or do they disempower themselves through their bodies? How, then, do they make or spend the asset that is their body?

Self-injurers' bodies represent the site of contested social control, the site of struggle between the realm of the symbolic (the self) and the realm of the physiological (the corporeal). People who practice this behavior semiotically and subjectively inscribe their inner selves onto their corporeal bodies, freeing themselves, yet in doing so they brand and objectify themselves with a mark that stigmatizes them in the gaze of others as belonging to a damaged, devalued caste. The skin can be viewed, thus, as the nexus where the self intersects with society, where ownership and judgment coincide and sometimes clash between competing domains.

As a contested site, the body social also represents an instrument of communication about how people view the locus of their selves and where they place themselves in society. Some bodily practices value-enhance those who engage in them. Individuals may bring their bodies into conformity with social norms through the moderate use of eating disorders and plastic surgery, using deviant means to achieve socially approved ends. People who get hip and trendy tattoos and piercings convey their identities and affiliate with communities of like others, finding acceptance, camaraderie, and social status.[9] These *enhancers* objectify their bodies to serve their selves, demonstrating the value of their bodies through the work they invest in shaping, decorating, and flaunting them. Yet at the same time, their adherence to social body norms marks their internalization of the social gaze, with its panopticon of control, and their acknowledgment of social dominion over their bodies. These people inscribe society onto themselves.

This is very different from self-injurers, who would rather conceal the marks they leave on their bodies. Self-injurers may be considered *depleters*, as they expend their body capital to enhance their selves. They set aside their concern about social location and stigma for their personal or social rebellion, in their desperate search for self-control, or to self-nurture, and thereby assert the primacy of their claim to bodily ownership over that of society. For people who feel bad or who lack social power, the body is one of the few things they can own and control. They thus locate their selves in their inner, subjective experience. Yet although they externally sacrifice their bodies to salve their selves, they ironically do so to seek inner normalcy. They crave the solace, the relief from anguish, the feeling of release that they ascribe to typical, ordinary people. They thus cast themselves as bodies-as-subject while at another level being simultaneously and reflexively constrained by the objectification of normative internal, emotional scripts.

But this unshackling from social claims for bodily dominion may have a temporal dimension. As individuals progress through their self-injurious careers, their priorities evolve. The resources they have for asserting their identity or assuaging their feelings of uncertainty, insecurity, anguish, and trauma are limited, and they employ what is available. As they age, they often find other sources of identity or support and are able to use these to supplement or eventually to replace the role of self-injury. For all but the most extreme practitioners, the body regenerates itself, healing over burns, cuts, and other scars and reducing them to faded or fine lines. It then renews them externally as it had previously done internally, physically rehabilitating them so that it can once again serve as the interface between society and themselves.

The Cyber World

The cyber world presents an ephemeral space of creation and destruction. It offers people who are dispossessed by mainstream society a reservoir of hiding places where they can form their own cultures and communities, even though these are framed by normative standards and assumptions. In the postmodern world, space refers not only to physical but also to social proximity, to how far from or close to others we feel, the connections between people.[10] It imbues everything with the character of "beside-each-otherness."[11]

This postmodern medium has increasingly had transformative effects on the cyber communities, cyber relationships, and cyber selves that flourish within it. In an era when we have become concerned about the loss of community,[12] civic participation and neighborhood communities have been replaced with membership in these socially constructed virtual communities. As such, they represent enclaves of *Gemeinschaft* (community) within a *Gesellschaft* (society) world.[13] Some sociologists have argued that hyperindividualism, rather than urbanization or a lack of morality, has obscured the idea of community in contemporary society, with the rhetoric of individualism becoming our primary language.[14] The resultant "communities of interest" are simply aggregations of self-interested, self-seeking individuals who join together to augment each individual's good. Yet we find that these cyber self-injury communities offer a context within which self-awareness develops and personal identities are formed. Although they are ephemeral and transient, with many members lurking silently or flitting in and out, they display norms with sanctions, and they offer a forum that joins people together to form a social order, enabling cooperation and association. They also provide resistance to the dominant psycho-medical discourses about self-injury, giving space to people to define the meaning of this behavior on their own terms.[15]

These cyber communities vary by the type of media supporting them, with very different kinds taking shape in the passive Websites, the more active bulletin board and group discussions, and the interactive chat rooms. As people engage in more dynamic and virtual interaction, they find more compelling and engaging venues that progressively offer greater potential for a real community feel, for identity construction and self-lodging, and for cyber absorption to the exclusion of the solid world. These virtual self-injury communities lack authentic embodiment, spatial grounding, the commitment associated with the permanence and obligation of social roles and relationships, and some even temporal "telecopresence" (being able to see each other in real time).[16] Yet at the same time, they offer the freedom from risk provided by anonymity,[17] the temporal lag for people to compose themselves, the intimacy of privacy, the forgiveness of self-re-creation, the ease of point-and-click interaction, and the multiplicity of overlapping simultaneous participation in different venues. For many people, especially those reared with the convenience of this type of interaction, the web of community offered in the virtual world is preferable to the solid world.

Virtual relationships are also similar to and different from those found in the solid world. People are heavily impacted in the physical world by appearance, so that initial impressions, physical chemistry, and overall attractiveness[18] play a large part in influencing interrelations. This outward superficiality is discarded in the virtual world, as people's images are rarely seen.[19] Instead, their speech and actions are more prominent, so that they and their relationships become the narratives that they construct. Sociologists suggest that individuals who are lonely, socially anxious, awkward, shy, or lacking in the social skills of charm and wit are also more able to form relationships over the Internet, as they may feel better able to express their true selves in this venue.[20] Virtual relationships forged on the basis of the "real me" may also develop faster and become stronger, deeper, and longer. Yet self-injurers' relationships have a dimension of convenience as well, and relationships quickly forged can be just as quickly abandoned, as we see from their transience. The careers of virtual relationships follow many of the same trajectories of their solid-world counterparts, with beginnings, shifts, withdrawals, comebacks, and terminations. But these transitions are easier, as people vanish in cyberspace and relationships may be casually or intentionally lost with little effort.

The character of the virtual self represents the strongest battleground between the modernists and postmodernists. In assessing the crisis of identity posed by the cyber self, we have to consider whether the selves of these cyber self-injurers are stable and coherent or flexible, fragmented, evolving, and mutable. They incorporate an ironic juxtaposition, simultaneously hyperembodied by the physical grounding of their self-injurious behavior yet disembodied by the virtual medium. Although people have always had masks and played roles, as Goffman (1959) pointed out, their connection to real-life families, friends, communities, and jobs kept this variance constrained. The opportunity for fabrication, fragmentation, and multiplicity in virtual self-presentation transcends what has been previously imaginable in the solid world. Yet virtual selves, like virtual communities, are shaped by the type of medium in which they are forged and through which they are communicated.

The opportunity for flexible self-construction exists even on the most passive Website, as people who post their diaries are free to embellish or self-censor, taking artistic or literary license (less so with their photographs). Most people considered the groups and bulletin boards the most authentic locations for self-presentation, as these are structured by their culture to be accepting and supportive. Although many acknowledged that they expected others to "bend," most denied doing so themselves. Misrepresentations and cycling through multiple selves seemed to be geared toward transitional self-discovery and growth, with people expressly voicing their interest in using the Internet to stage, to practice, and to achieve a "real me" self that they could ultimately transfer into the solid world. Stronger tales of deception emerged from the self-injury chat rooms, with people manipulating their presentations not only to enhance themselves but also to exploit others. Yet overall, nurturance and care for others was the dominant theme of these cyber self-injury venues.

Outside the virtual spaces in which these cyber self-injurers could construct themselves entirely and could "play" multiple characters in the dimensional detail found in cyber pubs and cafes, they clung to an essential core aspect of self-identification in their physical, embodied selves[21] and fell short of displaying fully fragmented selves. They bent but did not dissolve their cores, and each held on to some conception of their self as "real," even while they were displaying variations on that theme. Cyber self-injurers anchored their selves differently, depending on the medium they traversed, which usually varied with their degree of commitment to the solid versus the virtual world. Those with more satisfying outside lives used their cyber communities and relationships as an outlet to express the part of themselves that the solid world found unacceptable; those with fewer fulfillments in the outside world anchored themselves in these virtual realities. Their selves thus flexed along a sliding scale, neither fully traditional nor fully postmodern.

Stigma

The social stigma of self-injury has evolved and changed over the course of our research. Over time, more people learned about self-injury, and the general sentiment has shifted. Friends and family members lessened their overreactions when the subject arose. As self-injury became trendy, the way people defined it shifted from its being the practice of mentally ill or suicidal individuals to its being associated with troubled adolescents and people seeking a cry for help or seen as a deviant coping strategy. Individuals who self-injured were encouraged to think that greater public knowledge about their behavior might result in their becoming more accepted by society. Yet self-injury has and is likely to always retain some deviant stigma.

We might categorize four subpopulations of self-injury practitioners, whose stigma and level of support may be slightly different. First, the solid-world loners who have no cyber connections, described in chapter 6, engage in self-injury solitarily, lacking the help and support of others in their daily lives. To the extent that self-injury has become socially recognized as a broader phenomenon, it helps these practitioners realize that they are not alone, that they may not be "crazy," and assists them in partially legitimating and normalizing their behavior.

Second are those who self-injure faddishly, in less hidden ways. These people may be supported by peers or in limited ways by a solid-world, media-enhanced subculture that normalizes self-injury as a behavior that is trendy and fashionable. To the extent that these practitioners connect to and perform their acts within the scene of a musically related or alternative youth social movement, their stigma is diminished.

The third group comprises those who seek online support, who must have access to a computer and the Internet. Included here are both adolescents (starting at around 12 or 13) and a longer-term or later-starting population of adults who post blogs or journals, read and contribute to threads of conversations on message boards, belong to self-injury-related email groups, or participate in self-injury chat rooms. These people may have a wide range of cyber supporters who benefit them by being always available, portable, disposable, compartmentalized, intimate, and composed of peers. These features make cyber supporters more valuable to them than people in the solid world and diminish their stigma to themselves, especially within this social world.

Last is the less well-known group of structurally disadvantaged people or those who lack control over their lives, who engage their behavior as loners, individually, but may increasingly recognize it among others near them in similar situations and be supported by solid-world peers who share their difficulties. If a broader prevalence of self-injury is occurring among this population, it is likely to be known by other structurally disadvantaged people and given the somewhat reduced stigma of acceptance.

Sin, Sickness, and Selected

In chapter 8 we discussed the empirical foundations of the three perspectives on defining deviance that we referred to as the three S's: sin, sickness, and selected. During the Middle Ages and many earlier times when religious paradigms about the world prevailed, deviance from the norm was attributed to religious disorders or humors and viewed as sinful. Nonnormative attitudes, beliefs, and conditions were attributed to blessedly spiritual or satanic influences, and exorcisms were performed to cure people.[22] Deviants were burned at the stake. Religious leaders were the arbiters of official morality and were called on to make judgments and administer sanctions. Even today, some people adhere to this perspective, not only in societies that are officially religious in their governance but also within religious pockets of secular societies and among those who just believe in a morally absolutist definition of deviance as wrong.[23] The deviant or afflicted, in the eyes of these people, are strongly condemned and often viewed as contagious. They lack the moral regulation over their body that has increasingly become a public health imperative.[24]

One way of interpreting deviance in this perspective is to view people as intentionally sinful: they display moral weakness, they make wrong choices, they are wicked individuals engaged in violations of religious morality, or they have cast God out of their hearts and chosen the path of wickedness over righteousness. The other way is to view people as unintentionally sinful: they are innocents possessed by the devil or some evil spirit, forced to act immorally against their will. This latter interpretation is generally held by only the most religious adherents, with more people taking the former view and considering deviants intentionally sinful. Most deviant behaviors, from prostitution to gambling to drug use, can be viewed through the lens of sinfulness: these people are doing something wrong, they are making bad choices, they are violating our sense of what is morally appropriate. A harsh stigma accompanies the definition of deviance as sinful. It signifies individuals' deliberate movement onto a path of evil, a rejection of goodness and holiness, or a characterological flaw. It passes judgment on both the act and the actors as immoral, wrong, and bad. Yet it holds out the possibility of redemption for those who eschew their bad behavior and reembrace the path of righteousness.

Beginning in the first half of the twentieth century, the medicalization (or sickness) model emerged as a strong competing perspective for explaining deviance. Peter Conrad and Joseph Schneider (1980) have suggested that the process of medicalization begins when a behavior or condition defined as deviant is "prospected" by people with medical interests to see if they can gain rewards by pulling it under the therapeutic rubric.[25] Physicians and psychiatrists claimed that homosexuality, alcoholism/drug addiction, sexual misbehavior, mental illness, and many other deviant behaviors were rooted in people's psychiatric problems, mental "wiring," genetic abnormalities, inherited predispositions, and biochemical characteristics.[26] Psychiatrists sought to claim ownership over the diagnosis of these forms of deviance with the *Diagnostic and Statistical Manual of Mental Disorders* (DSM) so that they could administer inpatient or outpatient therapy and be reimbursed by insurance companies. Turf wars sprang up, with psychiatrists attempting to exert domain claims over a variety of behaviors that were previously conceived as biological or sociological, in order to receive research grants for further study, to diagnose patients, and then to treat them. "Anything you put in that book [the DSM], any little change you make, has huge implications not only for psychiatry but for pharmaceutical marketing, research, for the legal system, for who's considered to be normal or not, for who's considered disabled," said Dr. Michael First, a professor of psychiatry at Columbia University who edited the fourth edition of the DSM. "And it has huge implications for stigma," Dr. First continued, "because the more disorders you put in, the more people get labels, and the higher the risk that some get inappropriate treatment."[27]

For example, clumsy children (especially boys) were diagnosed with "dyspraxia," or "clumsy child syndrome," and told they would need the support of their families and qualified professionals to succeed in school. The most irritable and aggressive among them even received the misdiagnosis of "bipolar" and, as Benedict Carey (2010) notes, were "given powerful antipsychotic drugs, which have serious side effects, including metabolic changes." People who were boorish, disrespectful of authority, rude, or lacking in etiquette, psychiatrists suggested, might suffer from an "impulse control disorder." Those who spent too many hours on their computers might consider having themselves diagnosed with "Internet addiction disorder." Overly aggressive drivers might suffer clinically from "road rage." The next edition of the DSM (the DSM-V) is set to include a new category on "relational disorders" that identifies sickness in groups of individuals and their relationships, such as couples who constantly quarrel, parents and children who clash, and troubled relationships between siblings, defining these all as mental illness.[28] This specifically encroaches into the sociological domain, attempting to pathologize and psychiatrize these behaviors.

The recovery movement, with its coterie of self-help (often 12-step) pro-grams, educators, and public health organizations, further expanded the reach of this paradigm to include other behaviors in addition to self-injury, such as addictions, eating disorders, child abuse, child hyperactivity, com-pulsive gambling, and interpersonal violence. Doctors and drug companies leapt into the business, manufacturing and prescribing an array of medica-tions to "manage" or "cure" people. As a result, we are now the most legally medicated society in world history.[29]

The success of this medicalization movement, fueled by the prestige of science and the lure of the "easy fix" (a pill), drew huge areas of attitudes, behaviors, and conditions into its sphere, so that society no longer tolerates people being too sad, depressed, rebellious, rambunctious, or fidgety, eating too much or too little, or having too little or too much sex. One strong allure of the medicalization perspective has been its destigmatization of some devi-ance, since people who were seen as sick or acting on biological predisposi-tions or inherited "differences" were seen not as making immoral choices but as doing things "beyond their control." Behaviors that people found intensely satisfying were recast as "addictions" and explained as endorphin and dopa-mine cravings or withdrawals. This made such individuals less stigmatized by mainstream society, albeit not quite viewed as "normal" or "healthy." Rather than making a poor moral choice, they were sick and had a disease that should be treated rather than condemned. If they were sick, they could not be held intentionally responsible for their acts.

At the same time, some people thought that the medicalization move-ment had become overly pervasive, absorbing too great a swath of social life within its grasp. Some participants in these medicalized behaviors reached out to reclaim the rhetoric of *selection* over their attitudes, behaviors, and conditions, arguing that these were the result of voluntary choice. They, and the researchers who studied them, found groups of people who rejected the medicalized interpretation of such behaviors as homosexuality, gam-bling, eating disorders, and drug use. Participants chaffed at the control that "experts" held over them, their diagnoses, their treatments, and their medi-cation. Rejecting their label as actors who reacted pathologically through the compulsion of impulse, they cast their behaviors as intentionally selected, as forms of recreation, lifestyle choices, and coping strategies. Our research documents the strengthening of this view, as we increasingly observed peo-ple self-injuring instrumentally, weighing their reasons for when, how, and whether to do it. Self-injury is now a learned behavior, as people find out about it either indirectly, from their general cultural knowledge, directly from friends, or through media sources. In this learning process, they are socialized by their associates about ways to form shared perceptions, interpretations, anticipations, and evaluations of their behavior and ways to plan and to project lines of action.

But the stakes are high in the moral struggle over the definition of self-injury. Many contemporary self-injurers have several goals. First, they seek the destigmatization of their ongoing behavior. Unable to successfully reject their deviant labels individually, they recognize that they can best shed the label by engaging in a social "stigma contest" (to compare their deviance favorably against other stigmatized groups).[30] It will take their joint efforts to ameliorate their collective "spoiled identities"[31] to any degree. Second, in striving to redefine their behavior, they seek to free themselves from the control of the institutional experts of the psycho-medical establishment. Eschewing treatment signifies their resistance to becoming the technical objects of these experts.[32] They assert themselves as people exercising conscious decision-making and choice rather than acting on the compulsion of impulse. To be seen as ill is to be derogated; to be seen as self-healing is normal. Third, they seek to enable others to come forward with their behavior so that they, too, can discover that they are neither alone nor crazy. Thus, they want to carve out a space in society where they can assert their own understanding of self-injury as common, normalized, and voluntary. In so doing, they seek to fight their powerlessness and to reclaim control of their selves.

Moral Passage

The concept of *moral passage,* or the destigmatization of a behavior, was first articulated by Joseph Gusfield (1967) in his discussion of the American temperance movement, looking at the way society changed its view of drinking. Several models of moral passage have been articulated by sociologists since that time. For instance, in our analysis of the legitimation of child marijuana smokers during the countercultural years of the 1970s, we proposed a sequential model of social change.[33] Behaviors that are new to society, we suggested, may travel through different slices of the population, beginning with outsiders and moving toward the center. We traced this process of diffusion and legitimation, in which behaviors that originate as associated among stigmatized outgroups progressively move to ingroup deviants who identify with those stigmatized outgroups, to avant-garde ingroup members, to normal ingroup members, and finally to sacred groups (such as children). As the practice transfers from a marginalized to a more central population, the stigma associated with it fades, and it becomes more accepted. Ryan Matthews and Watts Wacker (2002) have proposed another model, suggesting that many ideas and products now considered acceptable, even popular, entered society from the fringe. Deviance thus serves the positive function, they argue, of providing a font of new ideas that start at the Fringe and become progressively more accepted as they move to the Edge, then to the Realm of the Cool, then to the Next Big Thing, and finally to Social Convention.

One of our goals in this research is to assess the extent of self-injury's moral passage by documenting its progress through different groups and statuses in society. Although it has not been accepted as the next great thing or as social convention, it certainly has evolved from being a symptom of mental illness practiced by suicidal individuals to becoming a visible, albeit not accepted, mode of expression for disaffected or disempowered youth and a coping mechanism for adults.

Influence Factors

We propose six structural factors that may lead to variance in the way emerging types of behaviors are morally accepted. First is social *awareness* of its existence. When something is hidden and unknown, unexamined by the media,[34] and unrecognized by the people who encounter it, it is likely to be highly stigmatized. People are often fearful of what they do not know. New behaviors and ideas, as noted earlier, are often relegated to the margins of social acceptability.

Second is the *spread* of the practice. When something is encapsulated into the domain of extremely small groups, it is much easier to stigmatize, reject, and condemn. Few people are known to do it, the weight of numbers goes against it, the public gains a glimpse of it only rarely, if ever, and it is often unknown and largely misunderstood. When the numbers of participants grow and members are able to organize and to fight to redefine the social meaning of their behavior, its social connotations may change.

Its *harmfulness* to others and themselves comes third. Most important is the health and welfare of others, as society seeks to prevent and ameliorate harm to nonparticipants and to itself as a whole. We are next, to a lesser degree, concerned if something is harmful to the individuals involved. Our concerns over physical, sexual, financial, verbal, and moral public harm are most easily justifiable. After that, we judge acts based on their effect on the welfare of individual practitioners. Here we tread a delicate line, balancing the right to life, liberty, and the pursuit of happiness against our concerns for social safety, public health, and morality. It is difficult to judge, for various issues, whether people have the right to engage in certain practices because they, as individuals, are inviolate or whether the public has the right or even the mandate to step in to protect itself. Violence of most types is condemned, for example, whether it is sexual, physical, or verbal. The torture of animals has become increasingly criminalized.[35] Talking on the phone or texting while driving, although originally considered hugely beneficial (i.e., car phones were once the Next Big Thing), has become socially shunned as "distracted driving" and increasingly banned legally.

Violation of professional commitments constitutes a fourth element that we propose as influencing the moral passage of a given behavior. People are much freer to commit various acts on their own free time, to themselves and others, when they are not at work, engaged in important practices, or responsible for the health and safety of others. When people breach the ethical mandates of their occupational or social roles, whether in the workplace or the family, they are more likely to be considered transgressing against society's norms. Such role violations add additional stigma to behaviors, driving them further into deviance.

Fifth, the *conformity* of the motivations underlying both the goals (values) driving a behavior and people's means (norms) of achieving them are likely to affect its degree of social acceptance. Alex Heckert and Druann Heckert (2004) have outlined a continuum of deviant types from hyperconformity to nonconformity that may affect the way people evaluate things positively or negatively. When people pursue deviant means in search of hyperconformity, such as through cheating, excessive plastic surgery, white-collar crime, or eating disorders, others understand their goals, even if they do not agree with their methods; it is easier to find others with similar outlooks. They enter the realm of the privileged by losing weight, earning money, or getting ahead. But when the behavior moves individuals away from conforming means and goals, such as rape or terrorism, the pool of potential sympathizers shrinks, and participants are condemned.

Finally, the *social power* of the participants must always be considered when calculating a behavior's moral assessment. The degree of power involves demographic factors such as social class, race/ethnicity, gender, age, social status, education, and the like. The rich and middle class have more power than the poor or working classes; whites have more power and status than nonwhites; men have more power than women; middle-aged people have more power than youth (who may even be seen as dangerous) or the elderly; people occupying or connected to respectable positions, religions, professions, and traditions have greater power than their counterparts; and the well educated can influence society and command more respect and attention than the uneducated. Behaviors associated with more powerful groups may thus more easily be evaluated as acceptable.

Comparisons

In addition to these influence factors, assessments of self-injury's moral passage may be aided by comparing and contrasting it with other deviant practices that are known and have been accepted to varying degrees. Some of these include drug use, eating disorders, tattooing/piercing, various kinds of addictions, sexually transmitted diseases, and suicide. Self-injury is more legitimated than some of these but less than others.

On the more accepted end of this scale lie some drugs, such as marijuana and various pharmaceuticals. Marijuana has now been approved for medical use in many states and decriminalized in others, and many pharmaceuticals, even antidepressants and antihyperactivity drugs, which used to have a mental-illness stigma associated with them,[36] are now widely prescribed, even for children.[37] Tattooing and piercing fall here as well. At one time these had a lower-class association, but when they became popular and widely practiced in the 1990s, they spread from low-status groups such as the poor and sailors to trendy youth and finally to the established middle class. These practices have gone fairly mainstream, attaining a solid measure of moral recognition and acceptance.[38]

A broad middle category includes anorexia and bulimia, sexually transmitted diseases, and addictions. Eating disorders were described by many of the people in our research as running a decade or so ahead of self-injury in social awareness and practice, and our participants expressed the hope that their behavior would someday follow the moral voyage of these other diseases and behaviors.[39] Anorexia is more concealable and less active (lack of eating as opposed to purging) than bulimia, which bears the greater shame. Originally the province of adolescent, white, middle- and upper-class, American women, eating disorders have spread to other age, racial/ethnic, social class, gender, and international populations, especially among upwardly mobile groups. Many addictions, such as drugs, sex, gambling, codependence, overspending, mental health, and chronic workaholism, which are morally condemned by society, are supported by face-to-face groups of fellow participants, who reinforce each other's efforts to cease this behavior and to deal with the social shame. Yet sexually transmitted diseases, like self-injury, cannot assemble support groups in the solid world, having to rely on the Internet to bring people together. And although sexually transmitted diseases have spread among uncoupled youth of all classes and races, they still carry the dual stigma of sexual promiscuity and contagion.[40] In the educational curriculum of most high school health classes, they, like self-injury, are included as dangers.

Least accepted of all is suicide, the ultimate self-harm, which tears a hole in the social fabric of families, friendships, and society.

Self-injury can be located somewhere toward the bottom of the middle portion of this continuum. It is less understood and established than eating disorders are, and it sometimes falls within the parameters of addiction for both its physiologically and psychologically reinforcing qualities and its progression of habituation. The six factors we have proposed now help us to place and understand the moral location of self-injury.

Aiding the moral passage of self-injury is its *awareness,* the rise of which we have charted, positioning it now as fairly well-known, with media coverage about it commonplace. In addition, it violates no *professional commitments* and even may aid people in carrying out some of their occupational and social roles, if it is successfully hidden and controlled.

Other factors restrain or have mixed effects on self-injury's moral passage. We have argued for its rising *spread* beyond the mentally disordered to known groups such as typical adolescents, those in subcultures regarding it as trendy, troubled youth and adults, and populations structurally disadvantaged or lacking control over their lives. The extent of its practice remains hard to gauge, but its broadened prevalence has so far invoked somewhat greater normalization without causing the uproar of a moral panic.

Although self-injury hurts and disfigures participants, the *harm* it causes to others is ephemeral but often vivid. As we observed, however, reactions to it may vary by participants' gender and gender-role enactments. For this perception of social damage to change, self-injury would have to become considered more voluntary (less addictive), temporary (a phase), and reparable (scars can fade to insignificance) and less maladaptive (a recognized coping strategy).

The *conformity* of self-injury is complex because it incorporates both prosocial (hyperconformist) and antisocial (nonconformist) elements. For the latter, fueled by negative experiences and emotions, self-injury represents people's destruction of their own bodies and appearance. At the same time, it represents individuals' sometimes calculated, other times desperate, need to feel better and often, ironically, to look normal. Many self-injurers desire to fit in to society, yet they use means that others would consider excessive to achieve this goal. This combination fuses them into the mode of deviant innovators,[41] since practitioners hold to the shared cultural goal of appearing normal yet use innovative and extremely nonlegitimate means to attain it.[42]

Finally, the demographics of self-injury have broadened, influencing its reception in interesting ways. Although it has a long, somewhat varied history, self-injury surfaced in its current incarnation not in fringe groups but within a socially weakened group, the mentally disordered. It then spread to people who resembled the profile for people with eating disorders: young, white women of the middle and upper classes. These individuals lacked power but engendered respect. Self-injury is now extending further into the groups we have discussed. This increasingly includes men as well as women, people successfully fulfilling occupational roles as well as those relying on disability, and members of all racial/ethnic groups and social classes. To the extent that this profile becomes socially recognized, it predicts that self-injury may be ripe for greater moral passage.

Three possible contrasting models can be hypothesized for the future of self-injury. First, it may be a passing fad, rising up as we have seen only to fade from the public practice and awareness it currently holds. In this scenario, it might breeze through like some drugs have done in popularity, commanding significant attention and interest for a time, only to reach a peak and decline in its practice. To the extent that the public becomes "scared" about its consequences, people may lose their fascination with it and turn away from its practice. This trajectory is possible, although it is not likely, since self-injury has not displayed the dramatic and rapid rise that short-term fads of this nature often follow. Second, it may become mainstreamed and relatively destigmatized like pharmaceutical drugs, cosmetic surgery, and tattoos/piercings. This is possible as well, although the power of the psycho-medical establishment and the vested interests of its various agents (definition, treatment, hospitalization, medicalization) exert a pull that holds self-injury more closely to the pathological realm. Finally, it may attain a lasting although stigmatized position in society, similar to eating disorders. Given the structural and demographic parallels between self-injury and eating disorders discussed earlier, this is a plausible outcome. But only the future will reveal the path it takes.

Notes

1. Out of respect for our subjects, throughout this book we have left people's spoken or written (Internet or other means of communication) uncorrected, unchanged from their original form. This is in line with what has been prescribed as part of the postmodern turn in ethnography, where giving participants' voice, in their own vernacular, is a hallmark of the epistemology (see Denzin and Lincoln, 2000, and Lather, 2001). However, all names used in this book are pseudonyms.

2. These typically required a minimum 30-day visit at a cost of $1,000 per day.

3. Conboy, Medina, and Stanbury, 1997; Cregan, 2006; Featherstone, Hepworth, and Turner, 1991; Howson, 2005; Shilling, 2003; Turner, 1984; Waskul and Vannini, 2006.

4. Foucault, 1979.

5. Synott, 1993.

6. Waskul and van der Riet, 2002.

7. Martinson, 1998. See also Briere and Gil, 1998; Langbehn and Pfohl, 1993; Nock et al., 2006.

8. Favazza and Conterio (1989), Gratz (2001), Herpertz (1995), and Whitlock, Eckenrode, and Silverman (2006) have also suggested that multiple methods of self-injuring are the most common.

9. In a 2006 study of a nontreatment sample, Whitlock, Eckenrode, and Silverman (2006) found scratching the most common form of self-injury.

10. As recently as the second half of the twentieth century, Pope John XXIII and Pope John Paul II practiced self-flagellation for religious purposes (Pope John XXIII, 1999; Yallop, 2007).

11. Favazza, 1987, 1998.

12. Favazza 1987, 1998; Jacobs 2000.

13. Asch, 1971; Clendenin and Murphy, 1971; Graff and Mallin, 1967; Gruenbaum and Klerman, 1967; Rosenthal et al., 1972; and Weissman, 1975.

14. Morgan, 1979; Pao, 1969; Pattison and Kahan, 1983; and Waisman, 1965.

15. Some popular treatments that came to public attention at around this time included films such as *Girl Interrupted, Nightmare on Elm Street III,* and *Secretary,* television shows with episodes on cutting such as *ER,* documentary treatments on the Learning Channel, popular songs such as "Hurt" by Nine Inch Nails, "Crawling" by Linkin Park, and "Last Resort" by Papa Roach.

16. See self-injury.net, "Famous Self-Injurers," www.self-injury.net/doyousi/famous.htm.

17. Egan, 1997.

18. Kalb, 1998; Thompson and Hickey, 1998.

19. For purposes of clarity, we more commonly refer to the face-to-face world as the *solid* world, as opposed to the *real* world, since some people we encountered during this research felt that the cyber world was more real than the physical, embodied world.

NOTES TO CHAPTER 2

1. Andover et al., 2005; Klonsky, Oltmanns, and Turkheimer, 2003.

2. Brumberg, 1988; Favaro and Santonastaso, 1998; Favazza, 1987, 1998; Favazza, DeRosear, and Conterio, 1989; and Whitlock, Powers, and Eckenrode, 2006.

3. Joiner, 2005.

4. Andover et al., 2005; Bowen and John, 2001; Coons and Milstein, 1990; Favazza, DeRosear, and Conterio, 1989; Greenspan and Samuel, 1989; Klonsky, Oltmanns, and Turkheimer, 2003; Miller and Bashkin, 1974; Morey and Zanarini, 2000; Pfohl, 1991; Pitman, 1990; Ross and Heath, 2002; Schaffer, Carroll, and Abramowitz, 1982; and Virkkunen, 1976.

5. Favazza and Conterio, 1989; Herpertz, 1995; Nock et al., 2006.

6. For a fuller discussion of the history, motivations, subcultures, and social meanings associated with tattooing, piercing, and scarifying, see DeMello, 1993, 2000; Fakir, 1996; K. Irwin, 2001; Sanders, 1989; and Vale and Juno, 1989.

7. Cavanaugh, 2002; Favazza, 1989; Favazza and Conterio, 1989; Gratz, Conrad, and Roemer, 2002; Kiselica and Zila, 2001; Noll et al., 2003; Tantam and Whittaker, 1992; van der Kolk, 1996; van der Kolk, Perry, and Herman, 1991.

8. Graff and Mallin, 1967; Rosenthal et al., 1972; Solomon and Farrand, 1996; Suyemoto and MacDonald, 1995.

9. Graff and Mallin, 1967; Rosenthal et al., 1972.

10. Klonsky, Oltmanns, and Turkheimer, 2003; Lundh, Karim, and Quilisch, 2007; Pinto and Whisman, 1996.

11. Bowen and John, 2001.

12. Favazza, 1989, 1998; Favazza and Rosenthal, 1993.

13. Callahan, 1996.

14. Greenspan and Samuel, 1989; Kennerley, 1996; Linehan, 1993; Pitman, 1990; van der Kolk, 1996.

15. Dipboye, Fromkin, and Wiback, 1975; Felson, 1980; and Hatfield and Sprecher, 1986.

16. Dion, Berscheid, and Walster, 1972.

17. Andreoni and Petroni, 2008; Aronson, 1999; Biddle and Hammermesh, 1998; and Jones et al., 1984.

18. Byrne, 1971; Dion, Berscheid, and Walster, 1972; Hesse-Biber, 1996; and Lennon, Lillethun, and Buckland, 1999.

19. De Beauvoir, 1989; Foucault, 1990; and Probyn, 1993.

20. Foucault, 1979.

21. Bartkey, 1997; Butler, 1990; Rosenfield, 1982; Ussher, 1992.

22. See Hawkes, Senn, and Thorn, 2004; and Rosenthal, 1986. In fact, the first decade of the twenty-first century has seen an increase in women removing their tattoos (see Armstrong et al., 2008).

23. Ellis, 2002; Ussher, 1992.

24. Bhardwaj, 2001; Fitzroy, 1999.

25. Jeffreys, 2000, p. 410. See also Jeffreys, 2005.

26. Barnes, 1985; Bartkey, 1997; Bordo, 1997.

27. Riley (2002) makes the argument that Jeffreys's critique fails women by suggesting that power should be understood as a top-down oppressive mechanism rather than a complex set of interactions and relationships. She explores these issues in the realm of body art. Guy and Banim (2000) challenge this view in the world of fashion as well, looking at power as both a top-down and a bottom-up process in looking at women's experiences of clothes, appearance, identity, and social structures. Burstow (1992), a feminist therapist and commentator, admits to seeing self-mutilation as serving a useful function for women.

28. Kitchin, 1998.

29. A. Shapiro, 1999.

30. Dowd, 1991.

31. Gergen, 1991.

32. Lifton, 1993; Martin, 1994.

33. Harré, 2001; Vollmer, 2005.

34. Tseëlon, 1992.

35. Goffman, 1959, 1974; Jameson 1984.

36. Lacan, 1968.

37. Dowd, 1991; Gergen, 1991; Jameson, 1984.

38. Connors, 2001; D'Onofrio, 2007; Farber, 2000; Fox and Hawton, 2004; Harrison, 1995; Hawton, Rodham, and Evans, 2006; Klonsky and Muehlenkamp, 2007; Milia, 2000; Morgan, 1979; Plante, 2007; Selekman, 2006; Simeon and Hollander, 2001; Spandler and Warner, 2007; V. Turner, 2002; Turp, 2003; B. Walsh, 2008; Walsh and Rosen, 1988.

39. Alderman, 1997; Clark and Henslin, 2007; Hollander, 2008; Levenkron, 1998; Pembroke, 1994; L. Shapiro, 2008; Smith, Cox, and Saradjian, 1998; Strong, 1998; Welch, 2004; Williams, 1997.

40. Clarke, 1999; Connors and Trautmann, 1994; Conterio and Lader, 1998; Kern, 2007; Ng, 1998; Phillips, 2006; Vega, 2007; and Winkler, 2003.

41. Favazza, 1989; Favazza and Conterio, 1988; Hodgson, 2004; Kiselica and Zila, 2001; Suyemoto and MacDonald, 1995.

42. For a further explanation, see Favazza, 1998; Kiselica and Zila, 2001; and Ross and Heath, 2002.

43. Hodgson, 2004.

44. Briere and Gil, 1998; Gratz, Conrad, and Roemer, 2002; Klonsky, Oltmanns, and Turkheimer, 2003; Suyemoto and MacDonald, 1995; Tyler et al., 2003; and Whitlock, Eckenrode, and Silverman, 2006, suggest that these numbers may be evening.

45. Holderness, Brooks-Gunn, and Warren, 1994; Kiselica and Zila, 2001.

46. Gratz, 2006; Guertin et al., 2001; Maden, Chamberlain, and Gunn, 2000; Ross and Heath, 2002.

47. See Briere and Gil, 1998.

48. The amount of self-inflicted injuries appearing in official emergency-room statistics is difficult to gauge because self-injury is clumped together with self-poisoning, the latter often a genuine suicide attempt (Hawton and Catalan, 1987; Sharkey, 2003). By 2005, in an American study, McCraig and Burt estimated that of 438,000 emergency-room admits nationally due to self-inflicted injury, nonpoisoning accounted for 119,454 cases.

49. Briere and Gil (1998) ventured an estimate of 4 percent self-injury in the general adult population, and the Priory Group (2005) speculated that 20 percent of all British adolescents engaged in self-injury.

50. Briere and Gil, 1998; Klonsky, Oltmanns, and Turkheimer, 2003.

51. Laye-Gindhu and Schonert-Reichl, 2005; Ross and Heath, 2002.

52. Lloyd-Richardson et al., 2007.

53. Gratz, 2001; Heath et al., 2008; Muehlenkamp, Swanson, and Brausch, 2005; Whitlock, Eckenrode, and Silverman, 2006.

54. For the incidence of self-injury in lesbian circles, see Addington, 2004; and Venning, 2004.

55. For a greater discussion of male homosocial bonding, see Bird, 1996; Gallmeier, 1998; Messner, 1987, 1992, 2002; and Raphael, 1988.

56. For a further explanation, see L. Coleman, 1987, 2004; and Swift 2006.

57. For discussions of self-injury's spread to a college population, see Gratz, Conrad, and Roemer, 2002; and Whitlock, Eckenrode, and Silverman, 2006.

58. Martinson, 1998.

59. For a further explanation, see Dusty Miller, 1994.

60. For a discussion of self-injury among Hispanic youth, see Croyle, 2007. For a discussion of the racial and gendered diffusion of self-injury, see also Muehlenkamp, Yates, and Alberts, 2004.

61. For a discussion of the spread of self-harm among troubled community adolescents, see Laye-Gindhu and Schonert-Reichl, 2005.

62. Tyler et al. (2003) have suggested that self-injury is prevalent among homeless street youth due to their childhood family abuse, their participation in deviant subsistence strategies, their street experiences, and their frequency of victimization. The researchers proposed that these youth use self-injury to regulate the overwhelming emotions they experience due to their stressful life events, with some using it to calm themselves, others turning to it for self-punishment, and others desiring the infliction of pain. In the researchers' sample, they found that 69 percent of the people they encountered had self-injured at least once, with no significant differences noted between men and women. Of their population, only 12 percent had ever received medical attention.

63. For specific discussions of self-injury among prison populations, see Babiker and Arnold, 1997; Blaauw et al., 2002; Fagan et al., 2010; Haycock, 1989; HM Prison Service, 2001; Kruttschnitt and Vuolo, 2007; and Smith and Kaminski, 2010. Lloyd (1990) offers an extensive review of the literature on deliberate self-injury and self-mutilation in British prisons. Penn et al. (2003) and Matsumoto et al. (2005) discuss the prevalence of self-injury among juvenile delinquents. Matsumoto et al. (2005) found that in the juvenile detention facility they studied in Japan, 16 percent of the inmates had cut, and 36 percent had burned themselves at least once, with the burners using additional types of body customizations as well. In reviewing a history of self-injury in prisons, Smith and Kaminski (2010) suggest that this behavior commonly results from people's difficulty in adjusting to the correctional environment. They found the prevalence of self-injury in prison the highest during the early years of people's incarceration.

64. For a survey of nearly 2,000 military recruits, see Klonsky, Oltmanns, and Turkheimer, 2003, which found that about 1 of every 25 members of this large group of relatively high-functioning nonclinical subjects reported a history of self-harm. The authors noted that these self-harmers' peers viewed them as having strange and intense emotions

and a heightened sensitivity to interpersonal rejection. For further evaluation of self-injury in the military and among military recruits, see also Anestis et al., 2009; and A. Jones, 1986.

65. For a further explanation, see Dokoupil, 2008.

NOTES TO CHAPTER 3

1. In Adler and Adler (2000, p. 8) we first introduced the idea that people can be labeled deviant as the result of what we called "the ABCs of deviance: their *attitudes, behaviors,* or *conditions.*" We used this mnemonic device to help students get beyond looking at deviance as falling merely within the behavioral realm, by encouraging them to see deviance as also lodged in deviant attitudes (alternative attitudes or belief systems) and conditions (both ascribed and achieved; by both appearance and social role or status).

2. Adler, 1985.

3. For further discussion of the problematic nature of doing research in this and other research we have done, see Adler and Adler, 2003.

4. Adler and Adler, 2009b; Atkinson and Delamont, 2003; Charmaz, 2006, 2008; and Strauss, 1987.

5. Adler and Adler, 2007, 2008.

6. This methodology in qualitative research has come to be known as "snowball" sampling (Biernacki and Waldorf, 1981).

7. Farrell and Petersen, 2010.

8. Fontana, 2002; Hine, 2000; Mann and Stewart, 2000.

9. Baym, 1995; Walther, 1992, 1996.

10. See Chen, Hall, and Johns, 2003; Correll, 1995; King, 1996; Kozinets, 2010; Mann and Stewart, 2000; Waskul, 2003, 2004; Waskul and Douglass, 1996.

11. One newspaper article (Berson, 2009) described *snark* as an Internet slang term referring to "a blithely hurtful and mean-spirited airing of petty cavils and resentments."

12. Cavazos, 1994; Frankel and Siang, 1999; Liu, 1999; Waskul and Douglass, 1996.

13. Rodham, Gavin, and Miles (2007) argued that given this view of open accessibility, they did not consider it necessary for them to contact or seek consent from the site managers of the self-harm message board or the individuals posting or responding to it that they studied. They followed the standards of the British Psychological Society's (2007) ethical code of conduct by ensuring that the anonymity of the site and the individuals who posted and/or responded to messages was maintained.

14. Capurro and Pingel, 2002; Elgesem, 2002; Frankel and Siang, 1999; King, 1996; Waskul and Douglass, 1996.

15. Allen, 1996; Reid, 1996; Waskul and Douglass, 1996.

NOTES TO CHAPTER 4

1. In fact, the number of Americans taking antidepressants doubled in a decade, from 13.3 million in 1996 to 27 million in 2005 (see Begley, 2010).

2. The question of whether media begets violence, especially among youth, has long been a controversial topic in the social sciences, with most psychologists unequivocally claiming that such a correlation is a foregone conclusion, while others are not so certain about this direct causality (see Anderson et al., 2003).

1. See Iscoe and Williams, 2006; and Adler and Adler, 1998.

2. The neurotransmitter dopamine causes the positive effects of drugs (alcohol, cocaine, ecstasy, methamphetamine, etc.), as well as the positive effects of a variety of other activities noted by self-injurers such as exercise and sex. Dopamine is the chemical messenger to the reward centers of the brain, promoting the sensation of pleasure, which comes on in an initial rush (see Kuhn et al., 2003).

3. See PBS.org, "Diana's 1995 BBC Interview," http://www.pbs.org/wgbh/pages/front-line/shows/royals/interviews/bbc.html.

4. Morton, 1992.

5. Warin, 2002, 2004.

6. Once dopamine levels in the bloodstream stop rising and begin falling, the dopamine rush dissipates (see Kuhn et al., 2003).

NOTES TO CHAPTER 6

1. Cressey, 1971.

2. Scully and Marolla, 1984; Stevens, 1999.

3. Winick, 1961; Dabney and Hollinger, 1999.

4. Lemert, 1962.

5. Henslin, 1972.

6. Lowery and Wetli, 1982; O'Halloran and Dietz, 1993; Turvey, 2009.

7. Gordon, 1990; McLorg and Taub, 1987; Way, 1995.

8. Athens, 1997.

9. Polsky, 1967.

10. Sheffield, 1989.

11. Goodlin, 2008; Potterat et al., 1998.

12. Snow and Anderson, 1993.

13. Beck and Rosenbaum, 1994; Biernacki, 1988; Goode, 2005.

14. Petrunik and Shearing, 1983; Rochford, 1983.

15. Herman, 1993.

16. Ekins, 1997.

17. Karp, 1996, 2006.

18. See Stevens, 1999; and Scully and Marolla, 1984.

19. Wagner and Rehfuss (2008) have suggested that a conservative Christian upbringing may be connected to feelings of unworthiness, fostering self-injury.

20. See Cromwell and Thurman, 2003.

21. See Coleman, 1961; Eckert, 1989; and Eder, 1995.

22. Favazza (1998) has also noted that some self-injurers do not feel the pain from their body mutilation.

23. K. Irwin, 2001.

24. Goffman, 1963.

25. Solomon and Farrand (1996) also reported a case in which a young woman chose self-injury as an alternative to suicide, considering the former preferable.

1. See McKenna and Green, 2002.
2. For further discussion of these types of groups, see McKenna and Green, 2002; and Whitlock, Powers, and Eckenrode, 2006.
3. Hindmarsh, Heath, and Fraser, 2006.
4. McKenna and Green, 2002.
5. McKenna and Green, 2002.
6. Whitlock, Powers, and Eckenrode, 2006.
7. For a discussion of pro-ED (eating disorder) communities and movements, see Force, 2005; Tierney, 2008; Vannini, McMahon, and McCright, 2005. For Websites dedicated to the pro-ED movement, see http://www.eating-disorder.org/prosites and http://www.anad.org/proanorexia.htm.
8. Kitsuse (1980) defines "tertiary deviance" as characterizing those who engage in deviance embracement. These are people who decide that their deviance is not a bad thing. Some identify strongly enough with their deviance that they fight to change and redefine the way society views their deviance so that they can shed the "deviant" label altogether; they seek to change society, not themselves. This can only be accomplished by organized groups and social movements.
9. Whitlock, Powers, and Eckenrode, 2006.
10. Goffman, 1963.
11. Deshotels and Forsyth, 2007.

NOTES TO CHAPTER 8

1. We first introduced the term to the literature on deviance of "the three categories of S's: *sin, sick, and selected*" in Adler and Adler, 2009a, 13.
2. Frankel and Siang, 1999.
3. Mitra (1997) has observed that a defining characteristic of the Internet as a medium is its ephemerality. Internet communities, postings, texts, references, Websites, communities, MUDs, MOOs, and bulletin boards appear and disappear. Some people in the self-injury community even complained about this.

NOTES TO CHAPTER 9

1. Turkle (1995) suggests that the speed with which virtual relationships evolve is caused by the isolation surrounding people's communications with each other. This is especially true for one-on-one interaction, which is possible in virtual spaces and in IMs that people initiate once they meet each other in other virtual venues.
2. McKenna and Bargh, 1998.
3. Akdeniz, 2002; Gyorgy, 2002; and Postmes et al., 2001.
4. Kendall (2002) has noted a disjuncture between how seriously people take online relationships, noting that some regard people they meet online as "pretty close friends," while others claim not to do so.
5. Bargh, McKenna, and Fitzsimons (2002) have also made this assertion in relation to self-harm message boards, as have Adams, Rodham, and Gavin (2005), and Hurley,

Sullivan, and McCarthy (2007) share this view based on the online support groups for victims of domestic violence. Ralph Turner (1976) discussed aspects of the real self and its grounding in social institutions versus impulses, and differentiated (1978) the way the individual's core self may be distinguished from among the various selves that are invoked by different audiences and social roles. Here, however, we use the members' term "real me" to convey their sense of their core, transsituational self, as opposed to a persona they invoke for the purpose of specific cyber presentation.

6. Baudrillard, 1983.

7. On the danger of Internet fraud, especially with regard to identity theft, cyber sex, false and fraudulent self-presentations, and creative authorship of the self, see Jewkes and Sharp (2003).

8. Bruckman and Resnick, 1995; Correll, 1995; Kendall, 2002; Mnookin, 1996; Turkle, 1995.

9. Thu Nguyen and Alexander, 1996.

10. Shaw (1997) has discussed how gay men occasionally misrepresented themselves in a gay chat room, but he noted that while some were there to "play," most were there in sincerity.

11. Kendall, 2002.

12. For a discussion of the authenticity of self-presentation in virtual self-injury groups, attributing it, in large part, to the anonymity and deindividuation found there, see also McKenna and Bargh, 1998, and Postmes et al., 2001.

13. The concept of disposable friendships becomes increasingly important as people spend more time on social networking sites. On one site, a thread explored whether social networking promotes more disposable relationships, with some people suggesting that inconvenient friends can simply be "defriended" and loved ones replaced with others who make thoughtful comments on one's photos. This trend is highlighted by people who break up with their partners through texting or networking sites.

14. This sentiment is similar to what many people expressed during both face-to-face and telephone interviews, when they noted that the separation between this research conversation and their everyday interactions enhanced the intimacy and rapport, rather than diminishing it.

15. Goffman (1963) discussed the process of "selective disclosure," in which people with potentially "discreditable" stigma (such as self-injurers) decide whether, and to whom, they will avow, or reveal their deviance, if at all.

16. Kitsuse, 1980.

17. Kendall, 2002; McKenna and Bargh, 1998; Thu Nguyen and Alexander, 1996; Turkle, 1995.

18. Kitchin, 1998; McKenna and Green, 2002; Turkle, 1995.

19. Turkle, 1995.

20. J. Carey, 1993.

21. S. Jones, 1997.

22. McLuhan, 1962.

23. Meyrowitz (1985) has asserted that information transmitted by electronic media is much more similar to face-to-face interaction than that conveyed by books or letters.

24. Kawakami, 1993.

25. Rodham, Gavin, and Miles, 2007; Whitlock, Powers, and Eckenrode, 2006.

1. On clustering, see L. Coleman, 1987.

2. On copycatting, see L. Coleman, 2004. On the contagiousness of self-injury among adolescents, see Taiminen et al., 1998, and on the contagion effect, see Davidson et al., 1989; Rosen and Walsh, 1989; and Walsh and Rosen, 1985.

3. Grossman, 2002.

4. "Women in L.A. Punk," 2004.

5. See Amorphous, 2009; Scatheweb, 2008; Wilkins, 2008.

6. Wilkins, 2008.

7. The school shootings at Columbine in 1999, at Red Lake High School in 2005, and at Dawson College outside of Montreal in 2006 raised public concern over the Goth scene and gave it a dark connotation, associating it with highly public violence.

8. Dekel, 2008; Greenwald, 2003; gURL, 2007; Dan Miller, 2003; and 3 News, 2006.

9. Greenwald, 2003; Sands, 2006; and J. Walsh, 2007.

10. On the way homeless youth verbally denigrate and "defensively other" homeless people who they perceive as more lower-statused than themselves, such as homosexuals and homeless street people, see Roschelle and Kaufman, 2004. Also see Kowalewski's (1988) discussion of how healthy gay men distanced themselves from gay men with AIDS and Blinde and Taub's (1992) discussion of heterosexual female athletes distancing themselves from lesbian athletes. All these groups regarded those who were doubly stigmatized among them as causing an additional stain on the reputation of them all.

11. Prus and Grills (2003) have discussed people's hesitations to pursue lines of action due to general cautions, earlier personal experiences, and concerns about the viewpoints and reactions of others.

12. Several waves of attention to vampires beginning in the 1970s changed the image of vampires from creepy and scary goblins to sexually alluring hipsters. Anne Rice's *Vampire Chronicles* series of books, beginning in the 1970s and exploding by the 1980s and '90s, was followed by the television hit *Buffy the Vampire Slayer,* which ran from 1997 to 2003. Stephanie Meyer's sexually suggestive but chaste vampires became a huge rage, from her *Twilight* books, published between 2005 and 2009, followed by the hugely successful movie franchise. HBO's *True Blood* exploded in 2008, casting vampires as highly lascivious and sexual. Vampires then hit mainstream television with a host of further series, including CW's *The Vampire Diaries* and ABC's vampire soap opera *The Gates.* These led to a heightened interest in blood and its many uses. *Blood play,* which is slightly different and which is practiced by "sanguinarians," is the act of using blood in sexual or fetish situations. For further information on this behavior, see "Blood Play," n.d.; Lorca and Hughes, 1997; Parks, 2000; and Yarkona, n.d.

13. For a discussion of pro-ED communities and movements, see Force, 2005; and Vannini, McMahon, and McCright, 2005. For Websites dedicated to the pro-ED movement, see http://www.eating-disorder.org/prosites and http://www.anad.org/proanorexia.htm.

14. Anorexics and bulimics use these message boards, chat rooms, and communities (such as http://ana.makeupyourmind.nu/, http://thinvision.conforums.com/, www.plagueangel.net/grotto, Shrine to ANA, Tricks of the Trade, Thinspiration, and others) to share diet tips and poetry, as well as to vent about their problems, related to their eating disorder or not. Close friendships sometimes developed between the people on

a message board, who would exchange phone numbers or even meet in person. What might be most disturbing about these sites to outsiders is the vast archives of "trigger" pictures they contained. For a discussion of how feminists ought to respond to these sites, see Pollack, 2003.

15. Pollack (2003) notes that the search engine Yahoo!, in the summer of 2001, under pressure from the National Association of Anorexia Nervosa and Associated Disorders (ANAD), removed pro-ED sites from its Webspace.

16. This perspective is similar to, but not the same as, Sykes and Matza's (1957) "denial of injury" and Cromwell and Thurman's (2003) "justification by comparison." Unlike in those cases, our self-injurers never alleged that without the outlet of self-harming they might turn their frustration, anger, or sadness against others. This "only harming myself" account thus represents a perspective that has never been discussed in the literature, as people were suggesting that they were not only avoiding harming others but that what they were doing should be viewed more positively than other acts by comparison.

17. What Goffman (1963) referred to as "minstrelization."

NOTES TO CHAPTER 11

1. Becker, 1963; Coombs, 1981; Faupel, 1991; Fiddle, 1976; Goffman, 1959, 1963; Rubington, 1967.

2. On the "compressed career," see Gallmeier, 1987.

3. This is similar to the way heroin addicts matured out of their drug-using careers, as discussed by Faupel, 1991; Ray, 1961; Waldorf, 1983; and Winick, 1962.

4. In fact, some researchers have suggested that people with eating disorders also move into using alcohol and drugs. See Beary, Lacey, and Merry, 1986; Holderness, Brooks-Gunn, and Warren, 1994; Hudson et al., 1987, and Jones, Cheshire, and Moorhouse, 1985.

5. This pattern contrasts with Patti's research on high-level drug traffickers (Adler, 1992): those who started the behavior later, and had a wider base of life experiences, had an easier time quitting.

6. Shover, 1985.

7. Several scholars have discussed the process of career exits and the pathways these take; see, for example, Adler, 1992; Adler and Adler, 1983, 2012; Anspach, 1979; Becker, 1963; Brown, 1991; Ebaugh, 1988; Faupel, 1991; Harris, 1973; J. Irwin, 1970; Livingston, 1974; Lofland, 1969; Luckenbill and Best, 1981; Meisenhelder, 1977; Petersilia, 1980; Ray, 1961; Sharp and Hope, 2001; Stebbins, 1971.

8. On overcoming drug addiction without treatment, see Granfield and Cloud, 1999.

9. On the effects of deviants' former activities on their subsequent lives, see Adler, 1992; Chambliss, 1984; Shover, 1985; Snodgrass, 1982; and Steffensmeier and Ulmer, 2005.

NOTES TO CHAPTER 12

1. McCrea, 1983.
2. Bordo, 1997.
3. Sanders, 2006.
4. Foucault, 1979.
5. Bartky, 1997.

6. Bordo (1997) discusses this self-mastery aspect of the behavior as empowering anorexic women to engage in a range of privileged values and possibilities that Western culture has traditionally coded as "male" and rarely made available to women.

7. Crawshaw, 2007; Lupton, 1995.

8. For a discussion of how vocabularies of motive, or accounts, can be divided into these two categories, excuses and justifications, see Scott and Lyman, 1968.

9. K. Irwin, 2000; and Sanders, 1989.

10. Schutz, 1967.

11. Tillich, 1959.

12. Putnam, 2000.

13. Cerulo, 1997; Foster, 1997.

14. Bellah et al., 1985.

15. In Tierney's (2008) discussion of pro-anorexia Websites, she suggests that these viral networks provide people information, resistances to dominant discourses of anorexia, and social support.

16. McLaughlin, Osborne, and Ellison, 1997; Zhao, 2003.

17. McKenna and Green, 2002.

18. For a discussion of how attractive people are assumed to be smarter, more personable, and preferential to those who look worse, see Dion, Berscheid, and Walster, 1972.

19. McKenna and Green, 2002. Uslander (2000) has also suggested that communication in cyber communities transcends identifiers such as appearance, gender, age, class, and race.

20. McKenna, Green, and Gleason, 2002.

21. Weigert and Gecas, 2005.

22. Cregan, 2006.

23. Hendershott, 2002.

24. Crawshaw, 2007; Lupton, 1995.

25. See also Foucault's (1975) discussion of the shift in the treatment of the mentally ill from spiritual rehabilitation to their detention in medicalized mental asylums and other institutions.

26. In an interview with Edward Shorter, a historian of psychiatry who has been critical of the *Diagnostic and Statistical Manual of Mental Disorders* (DSM), Benedict Carey (2010) documents Shorter's assertion that "the scientific status of the main diseases in previous editions of the D.S.M.—the keystones of the vault of psychiatry—is fragile."

27. Quoted in ibid.

28. Denton, 2007; Kirn, 2002.

29. Barber, 2008.

30. Schur, 1980.

31. Goffman, 1963.

32. Granfield and Cloud, 1999; Gusfield, 1985.

33. Adler and Adler, 1978.

34. Jenkins (2009) has also discussed why the rise of Internet pornography as a moral panic has been restrained by the public's lack of awareness of its existence, due to the technical difficulties associated with accessing it, the media's inability to convey visual images of it because of moral restrictions, its preemption by other causes and interest groups, and its general invisibility as a social problem.

35. Irvine, 2003, 2004.

36. For a discussion of the destigmatization of psychiatric or antipsychotic medications, see Karp, 2006.

37. For discussions of the broadening of prescription medications such as Ritalin and Adderall to treat ADD and ADHD in children and the recognition within the psycho-medical profession of the overprescription of psychiatric medications, see Carey, 2010; and Leo, 2002.

38. See Katherine Irwin's (2001) discussion of the rise of hip and trendy tattoos as a middle-class style movement.

39. For a further explanation of the moral passage associated with eating disorders, see Vogler, 1993; and Way, 1995.

40. Nack, 2008.

41. Merton, 1938.

42. See also Hodgson, 2004.

References

Adams, Joanna, Karen Rodham, and Jeff Gavin. 2005. "Investigating the 'Self' in Deliberate Self-Harm." *Qualitative Health Research* 15:1293–1309.

Addington, Deborah. 2004. "Playing with Fire." Pp. 136–39 in *On Our Backs: Guide to Lesbian Sex,* edited by Diana Cage. Los Angeles: Alyson Books.

Adler, Patricia A. 1992. "The 'Post' Phase of Deviant Careers: Reintegrating Drug Traffickers." *Deviant Behavior* 13:101–22.

———. 1985. *Wheeling and Dealing.* New York: Columbia University Press.

Adler, Patricia A., and Peter Adler, eds. 2012. *Constructions of Deviance: Social Power, Context, and Interaction.* 7th ed. Belmont, CA: Cengage Wadsworth.

———. 2009a. Introduction to *Constructions of Deviance: Social Power, Context, and Interaction,* 6th ed., edited by Adler and Adler. Belmont, CA: Thomson Wadsworth.

———. 2009b. "Using a Gestalt Perspective to Analyze Children's Worlds." Pp. 225–37 in *Ethnographies Revisited: The Stories behind the Story,* edited by Antony J. Puddephat, William Shaffir, and Steven W. Kleinknecht. New York: Routledge.

———. 2008. "Self-Injury." Pp. 633–34 in *Encyclopedia of Interpersonal Violence,* edited by Claire M. Renzetti and Jeffrey L. Edleson. Thousand Oaks, CA: Sage.

———. 2007. "Self-Harm." Pp. 50–51 in *International Encyclopedia of Men and Masculinities,* vol. 1, edited by Michael Flood, Judith Kegan Gardiner, Bob Pease, and Keith Pringle. London: Routledge.

———. 2003. "Do University Lawyers and the Police Define Research Values?" Pp. 34–42 in *Walking the Tightrope: Ethical Issues for Qualitative Researchers,* edited by Will C. van den Hoonaard. Toronto: University of Toronto Press.

———. 2000. Introduction to *Constructions of Deviance: Social Power, Context, and Interaction,* 3rd ed., edited by Adler and Adler. Belmont, CA: Wadsworth.

———. 1998. *Peer Power.* New Brunswick: Rutgers University Press.

———. 1983. "Shifts and Oscillations in Deviant Careers: The Case of Upper-Level Drug Dealers and Smugglers." *Social Problems* 31:195–207.

———. 1978. "Tinydopers: A Case Study of Deviant Socialization." *Symbolic Interaction* 1:90–105.

Akdeniz, Yaman. 2002. "Anonymity, Democracy, and Cyberspace." *Social Research* 69:223–37.

Alderman, Tracy. 1997. *The Scarred Soul: Understanding and Ending Self-Inflicted Violence.* Oakland, CA: New Harbinger.

Allen, Christina. 1996. "What's Wrong with the 'Golden Rule'? Conundrums of Conducting Ethical Research in Cyberspace." *Information Society* 12:175–87.

Amorphous. 2009. "Gothic and Goth Subculture—DarkIndependent.net." *Darkplanet.eu.* http://www.darkplanet.eu/Gothic-and-Goth-Subculture-35973.html.

Anderson, Craig A., Leonard Berkowitz, Edward Donnerstein, L. Rowell Huesmann, James D. Johnson, Daniel Linz, Neil M. Malamuth, and Ellen Wartella. 2003. "The Influence of Violence on Youth." *Psychological Science in the Public Interest* 4:81–110.

Andover, Margaret S., Carolyn M. Pepper, Karen A. Ryabchenko, Elizabeth G. Orrico, and Brandon E. Gibb. 2005. "Self-Mutilation and Symptoms of Depression, Anxiety, and Borderline Personality Disorder." *Suicide and Life-Threatening Behavior* 35:581–91.

Andreoni, James, and Ragan Petroni. 2008. "Beauty, Gender and Stereotypes: Evidence from Laboratory Experiments." *Journal of Economic Psychiatry* 29:73–93.

Anestis, Michael D. Craig J. Bryan, Michelle M. Cornette, and Thomas E. Joiner. 2009. "Understanding Suicidal Behavior in the Military: An Evaluation of Joiner's Interpersonal-Psychological Theory of Suicidal Behavior in Two Case Studies of Active Duty Post-deployers." *Free Library.* http://www.thefreelibrary.com/Understanding suicidal behavior in the military: an evaluation of...-a0193182089.

Anspach, Renee. 1979. "From Stigma to Identity Politics: Political Activism among the Physically Disabled and Former Mental Patients." *Social Science and Medicine* 13:765–73.

Armstrong, Myra L., Alden E. Roberts, Jerome R. Koch, Jana C. Saunders, Donna C. Owen, and R. Rox Anderson. 2008. "Motivation for Contemporary Tattoo Removal: A Shift in Identity." *Archives of Dermatology* 144:879–84.

Aronson, Elliot. 1999. *The Social Animal.* New York: Worth.

Asch, Solomon S. 1971. "Wrist Scratching as a Symptom of Anhedonia." *Psychoanalysis Quarterly* 40:630–37.

Athens, Lonnie. 1997. *Violent Criminal Acts and Actors Revisited.* Urbana: University of Illinois Press.

Atkinson, Paul, and Sara Delamont. 2003. "Analytic Perspectives." Pp. 285–311 in *Collecting and Interpreting Qualitative Materials,* edited by Norman Denzin and Yvonna Lincoln. Thousand Oaks, CA: Sage.

Babiker, Gloria, and Lois Arnold. 1997. *The Language of Injury: Comprehending Self-Mutilation.* Leicester, UK: British Psychological Society.

Barber, Charles. 2008. *Comfortably Numb: How Psychiatry Is Medicating a Nation.* New York: Pantheon.

Barnes, R. 1985. "Women and Self-Injury." *International Journal of Women's Studies* 8:465–75.

Bargh, John A., Katelyn Y. A. McKenna, and Grainne M. Fitzsimons. 2002. "Can You See the Real Me? Activation and Expression of the 'True Self' on the Internet." *Journal of Social Issues* 58:33–48.

Bartkey, Sandra Lee. 1997. "Foucault, Femininity, and the Modernization of Patriarchal Power." Pp. 129–54 in *Writing on the Body: Female Embodiment and Feminist Theory,* edited by Katie Conboy, Nadia Medina, and Sarah Stanbury. New York: Columbia University Press.

Baudrillard, Jean. 1983. *Simulations.* Translated by Paul Foss, Paul Patton, and Philip Beitchman. New York: Semiotext(e).

Baym, Nancy. 1995. "The Emergence of Community in Computer-Mediated Communication." Pp. 184–63 in *CyberSociety: Computer-Mediated Communication and Community,* edited by Steve Jones. Thousand Oaks, CA: Sage.

Beary, Michael D., J. Hubert Lacey, and Julius Merry. 1986. "Alcoholism and Eating Disorders in Women of Fertile Age." *British Journal of Addiction* 81:685–89.

Beck, Jerome, and Marsha Rosenbaum. 1994. *Pursuit of Ecstasy*. Albany: SUNY Press.

Becker, Howard S. 1963. *Outsiders*. New York: Free Press.

Begley, Sharon. 2010. "The Depressing News about Antidepressants." *Newsweek*, February 8, 35–41.

Bellah, Robert, Richard Madsen, William M. Sullivan, Ann Swidler, and Steven Tipton. 1985. *Habits of the Heart*. Berkeley: University of California Press.

Berson, Misha. 2009. "The Art of Snark." *Seattle Times*, March 1.

Best, Joel, and David F. Luckenbill. 1982. *Organizing Deviance*. Englewood Cliffs, NJ: Prentice-Hall.

Bhardwaj, Anita. 2001. "Growing Up Young, Asian and Female in Britain: A Report on Self-Harm and Suicide." *Feminist Review* 68:52–67.

Biddle, Jeff E., and Daniel S. Hammermesh. 1998. "Beauty, Productivity, and Discrimination: Lawyers' Looks and Lucre." *Journal of Labor Economics* 15:172–201.

Biernacki, Patrick A. 1988. *Pathways from Heroin Addiction: Recovery without Treatment*. Philadelphia: Temple University Press.

Biernacki, Patrick A., and Dan Waldorf. 1981. "Snowball Sampling." *Sociological Methods and Research* 10:141–63.

Bird, Sharon R. 1996. "Welcome to the Men's Club: Homosociality and the Maintenance of Hegemonic Masculinity." *Gender & Society* 10:120–32.

Blaauw, E., E. Arensman, V. Kraaij, F. W. Winkel and R. Bout. 2002. "Traumatic Life Events and Suicide Risk among Jail Inmates: The Influence of Types of Events, Time Periods." *Journal of Traumatic Stress* 15:9–16.

Blinde, Elaine M., and Diane E. Taub. 1992. "Homophobia and Women's Sport: The Disempowerment of Athletes." *Sociological Focus* 25:155–66.

"Blood Play." N.d. *Urban Dictionary*. www.urbandictionary.com/define. php?term=bloodplay.

Bordo, Susan. 1997. "The Body and the Reproduction of Femininity." Pp. 90–110 in *Writing on the Body: Female Embodiment and Feminist Theory*, edited by Katie Conboy, Nadia Medina, and Sarah Stanbury. New York: Columbia University Press.

Bowen, Arabella C. L., and Alexandra M. H. John. 2001. "Gender Differences in Presentation and Conceptualization of Adolescent Self-Injurious Behaviour: Implications for Therapeutic Practice." *Counselling Psychology Quarterly* 14:357–79.

Bray, Abigail. 1996. "The Anorexic Body: Reading Disorders." *Cultural Studies* 10:413–29.

Briere, John, and Eliana Gil. 1998. "Self-Mutilation in Clinical and General Population Samples: Prevalence, Correlates, and Functions." *American Journal of Orthopsychiatry* 68:609–20.

British Psychological Society. 2007. *Report of the Working Party on Conducting Research on the Internet: Guidelines for Ethical Practice in Psychological Research Online*. Leicester, UK: British Psychological Society.

Brown, J. David. 1991. "Preprofessional Socialization and Identity Transformation: The Case of the Professional Ex-." *Journal of Contemporary Ethnography* 20:157–78.

Bruckman, Amy, and Mitchel Resnick. 1995. "The MediaMOO Project: Constructionism and Professional Community." *Convergence* 1:94–109.

Brumberg, Joan J. 1988. *Fasting Girls: The Emergence of Anorexia Nervosa as a Modern Disease*. Cambridge: Harvard University Press.

Burstow, Bonnie. 1992. *Radical Feminist Therapy: Working in the Context of Violence*. Newbury Park, CA: Sage.

Butler, Judith. 1990. *Gender Trouble: Feminism and the Subversion of Identity*. New York: Routledge.

Byrne, Donn. 1971. *The Attraction Paradigm*. New York: Academic Press.

Callahan, John. 1996. "A Specific Therapeutic Approach to Suicide Risk in Borderline Clients." *Clinical Social Work Journal* 24:443–59.

Capurro, Rafael, and Christoph Pingel. 2002. "Ethical Issues of Online Communication Research." *Ethics and Information Technology* 4:189–94.

Carey, Benedict. 2010. "Revising Book on Disorders of the Mind." *New York Times,* February 10.

Carey, James W. 1993. "Everything That Rises Must Diverge: Notes on Communications, Technology and the Symbolic Construction of the Social." Pp. 171–84 in *Beyond Agendas,* edited by Phillip Gaunt. Westport, CT: Greenwood.

Cavanaugh, Robert M. 2002. "Self-Mutilation as a Manifestation of Sexual Abuse in Adolescent Girls." *Journal of Pediatric Adolescent Gynecology* 15:97–100.

Cavazos, Edward A. 1994. "Intellectual Property in Cyberspace: Copyright Law in a New World." Pp. 44–55 in *Cyberspace and the Law: Your Rights and Duties in the On-Line World,* edited by Edward Cavazos and Gavino Morin. Cambridge: MIT Press.

Cerulo, Karen A. 1997. "Reframing Sociological Concepts for a Brave New (Virtual?) World." *Sociological Inquiry* 67:48–58.

Chambliss, William J. 1984. *Harry King: A Professional Thief's Journey*. New York: Wiley.

Charmaz, Kathy. 2008. "Shifting the Grounds: Constructivist Grounded Theory Methods for the 21st Century." Pp. 127–93 in *Developing Grounded Theory: The Second Generation,* edited by Janice Morse, Janice M., Phyllis Noerager Stern, Juliet Corbin, Barbara Bowers, Kathy Charmaz, and Adele E. Clarke. Walnut Creek, CA: Left Coast.

———. 2006. *Constructing Grounded Theory: A Practical Guide through Qualitative Analysis*. Thousand Oaks, CA: Sage.

Chen, Shing-Ling, G. Jon Hall, and Mark D. Johns, eds. 2003. *Online Social Research: Methods, Issues, and Ethics*. New York: Peter Lang.

Clark, Jerusha, and Earl R. Henslin. 2007. *Inside a Cutter's Mind: Helping and Healing Those Who Self-Injure*. Colorado Springs, CO: NavPress.

Clarke, Alicia. 1999. *Coping with Self-Mutilation: A Helping Book for Teens Who Hurt Themselves*. New York: Rosen.

Clendenin, William W., and George E. Murphy. 1971. "Wrist Cutting: New Epidemiological Findings." *Archives of General Psychiatry* 25:465–69.

Coleman, James. 1961. *The Adolescent Society*. Glencoe, IL: Free Press.

Coleman, Loren. 2004. *The Copycat Effect*. New York: Paraview.

———. 1987. *Suicide Clusters*. New York: Faber and Faber.

Conboy, Katie, Nadia Medina, and Sarah Stanbury. 1997. "Introduction." Pp. 1–12 in *Writing on the Body,* edited by Katie Conboy, Nadia Medina, and Sarah Stanbury. New York: Columbia University Press.

Connors, Robin E. 2001. *Self Injury: Psychotherapy with People Who Engage in Self-Inflicted Violence*. Northvale, NJ: Jason Aronson.

Connors, Robin E., and Kristy Trautmann. 1994. *Understanding Self-Injury: A Workbook for Adults.* Pittsburgh: Pittsburgh Action Against Rape.

Conrad, Peter, and Joseph W. Schneider. 1980. *Deviance and Medicalization: From Badness to Sickness.* St. Louis: Mosby.

Conterio, Karen, and Wendy Lader. 1998. *Bodily Harm: The Breakthrough Healing Program for Self-Injurers.* New York: Hyperion.

Coombs, Robert H. 1981. "Drug Abuse as Career." *Journal of Drug Issues* 11:369–87.

Coons, Philip M., and Victor Milstein. 1990. "Self-Mutilation Associated with Dissociative Disorders." *Dissociation* 3:81–87.

Correll, Shelley. 1995. "The Lesbian Café." *Journal of Contemporary Ethnography* 24:270–98.

Crawshaw, Paul. 2007. "Governing the Healthy Male Citizen: Men, Masculinity and Popular Health in *Men's Health* Magazine." *Social Science and Medicine* 65:1606–18.

Cregan, Kate. 2006. *The Sociology of the Body.* Thousand Oaks, CA: Sage.

Cressey, Donald R. 1971. *Other People's Money: A Study in the Social Psychology of Embezzlement.* Belmont, CA: Wadsworth.

Cromwell, Paul, and Quint Thurman. 2003. "The Devil Made Me Do It: Use of Neutralizations by Shoplifters." *Deviant Behavior* 24:535–55.

Croyle, Kristin L. 2007. "Self-Harm Experiences among Hispanic and Non-Hispanic White Young Adults." *Hispanic Journal of Behavioral Science* 29:242–53.

Dabney, Dean A., and Richard C. Hollinger. 1999. "Illicit Prescription Drug Use among Pharmacists: Evidence of a Paradox of Familiarity." *Work and Occupations* 26:77–106.

Davidson, Lucy, Mark L. Rosenberg, James Mercy, Jack Franklin, and Jane Simmons. 1989. "An Epidemiologic Study of Risk Factors in Two Teenage Suicide Clusters." *Journal of the American Medical Association* 17:2689–92.

de Beauvoir, Simone. 1989. *The Second Sex.* Translated and edited by H. M. Parshley. New York: Knopf.

Dekel, Jonathan. 2008. "Emo—The Meaning of Life or Just of Emo!" *Incendiary Magazine,* February 1. http://www.incendiarymag.com/drupal/node/21.

DeMello, Margo. 2000. *Bodies of Inscription: A Cultural History of the Modern Tattoo Community.* Durham: Duke University Press.

———. 1993. "The Convict Body: Tattooing among Male American Prisoners." *Anthropology Today* 9:10–13.

Denton, Wayne H. 2007. "Issues for DSM-V: Relational Diagnosis: An Essential Component of Biopsychosocial Assessment." *American Journal of Psychiatry* 164:1146–47.

Denzin, Norman K., and Yvonna S. Lincoln. 2000. "The Seventh Moment: Out of the Past." Pp. 1025–46 in *Handbook of Qualitative Research,* 2nd ed., edited by Norman K. Denzin and Yvonna S. Lincoln. Thousand Oaks, CA: Sage.

Deshotels, Tina H., and Craig J. Forsyth. 2007. "Postmodern Masculinities and the Eunuch." *Deviant Behavior* 28:201–18.

Dion, Karen, Ellen Berscheid, and Elaine Walster. 1972. "What Is Beautiful Is Good." *Journal of Personality and Social Psychology* 24:285–90.

Dipboye, Robert L., Howard L. Fromkin, and Kent Wiback. 1975. "Relative Importance of Applicant Sex, Attractiveness, and Scholastic Standing in Evaluation of Job Applicant Resumes." *Journal of Applied Psychology* 60:39–43.

Dokoupil, Tony. 2008. "Anything Not to Go Back." *Newsweek,* June 16.

D'Onofrio, Amelio A. 2007. *Adolescent Self-Injury: A Comprehensive Guide for Counselors and Healthcare Professionals.* New York: Springer.

Dowd, James J. 1991. "Social Psychology in a Postmodern Age: A Discipline without a Subject." *American Sociologist* 22:188–209.

Ebaugh, Helen Fuchs. 1988. *Becoming an Ex.* Chicago: University of Chicago Press.

Eckert, Penelope. 1989. *Jocks and Burnouts.* New York: Teachers College Press.

Eder, Donna, with Catherine C. Evans and Stephen Parker. 1995. *School Talk.* New Brunswick: Rutgers University Press.

Egan, Jennifer. 1997. "The Thin Red Line." *New York Times Magazine,* July 27, pp. 21–35, 34, 40, 43–44, 48.

Ekins, Richard. 1997. *Male Femaling: A Grounded Theory Approach to Cross-Dressing and Sex-Changing.* New York: Routledge.

Elgesem, Dag. 2002. "What Is Special about the Ethical Issues in Online Research?" *Ethics and Information Technology* 4:195–203.

Ellis, Rosemary L. 2002. "A Feminist Qualitative Study of Female Self-Mutilation." Master's thesis, Virginia Polytechnic Institute and State University, Department of Sociology.

Fagan, Thomas J., Judith Cox, Steven J. Helfand, and Dean Aufderheide. 2010. "Self-Injurious Behavior in Correctional Settings." *Journal of Correctional Health Care* 16:48–66.

Fakir, Musafar. 1996. "Body Play: State of Grace or Sickness?" Pp. 325–34 in *Bodies under Siege: Self-Mutilation and Body Modification in Culture and Psychiatry,* edited by Armando Favazza. Baltimore: Johns Hopkins University Press.

Farber, Sharon K. 2000. *When the Body Is the Target: Self-Harm, Pain and Traumatic Attachments.* Northvale, NJ: Jason Aronson.

Farrell, Dan, and James C. Petersen. 2010. "The Growth of Internet Research Methods and the Reluctant Sociologist." *Sociological Inquiry* 80:114–25.

Faupel, Charles E. 1991. *Shooting Dope: Career Patterns of Hard-Core Heroin Users.* Gainesville: University Press of Florida.

Favaro, Angela, and Paolo Santonastaso. 1998. "Impulsive and Compulsive Self-Injurious Behavior in Bulimia Nervosa: Prevalence and Psychological Correlates." *Journal of Nervous and Mental Diseases* 186:157–65.

Favazza, Armando R. 1998. "The Coming of Age of Self-Mutilation." *Journal of Nervous and Mental Disease* 186:259–68.

———. 1989. "Why Patients Mutilate Themselves." *Hospital and Community Psychiatry* 40:137–45.

———. 1987. *Bodies under Siege: Self-Mutilation and Body Modification in Culture and Psychiatry.* Baltimore: Johns Hopkins University Press.

Favazza, Armando R., and Karen Conterio. 1989. "The Plight of Chronic Self-Mutilators." *Community Mental Health Journal* 24:22–30.

Favazza, Armando R., Lori DeRosear, and Karen Conterio. 1989. "Self-Mutilation and Eating Disorders." *Suicide and Life-Threatening Behavior* 19:352–61.

Favazza, Armando R., and Richard J. Rosenthal. 1993. "Diagnostic Issues in Self-Mutilation." *Hospital and Community Psychiatry* 44:134–41.

Featherstone, Mike, Mike Hepworth, and Bryan Turner. 1991. *The Body: Social Process and Cultural Theory.* Thousand Oaks, CA: Sage.

Felson, Richard B. 1980. "Physical Attractiveness, Grade and Teachers' Attributions of Ability." *Representative Research in Social Psychology* 11:64–71.

Fiddle, Seymour. 1976. "Sequences in Addiction." *Addictive Diseases* 2:553–68.

Fitzroy, Lee. 1999. "Mother/Daughter Incest: Making Sense of the Unthinkable." *Feminism & Psychology* 9:402–5.

Fontana, Andrea. 2002. "Postmodern Trends in Interviewing." Pp. 161–76 in *Handbook of Interview Research*, edited by Jaber F. Gubrium and James A. Holstein. Thousand Oaks, CA: Sage.

Force, William Ryan. 2005. "There Are No Victims Here: Determination versus Disorder in Pro-Anorexia." Paper presented at the Couch-Stone Symposium of the Society for the Study for Symbolic Interaction, Boulder, Colorado, February.

Foster, Derek. 1997. "Community and Identity in the Electronic Village." Pp. 23–27 in *Internet Culture*, edited by David Porter. New York: Routledge.

Foucault, Michel. 1990. *The History of Sexuality*. Translated by Robert Hurley. New York: Vintage.

———. 1979. *Discipline and Punish: The Birth of the Prison*. New York: Vintage.

———. 1975. *The Birth of the Clinic: An Archaeology of Medical Perception*. Translated by A. M. Sheridan Smith. New York: Random House.

Fox, Claudia, and Keith Hawton. 2004. *Deliberate Self-Harm in Adolescence*. London: Jessica Kingsley.

Frable, Deborrah E. S. 1993. "Being and Feeling Unique: Statistical Deviance and Psychological Marginality." *Journal of Personality* 61:85–110.

Frankel, Mark S., and Sanyin Siang. 1999. *Ethical and Legal Aspects of Human Subjects Research on the Internet*. Report of a workshop, June 10–11. Available online at http://www.aaas.org/ssp/dspp/sfrl/projects/intres/main.htm.

Gallmeier, Charles P. 1998. "In the Company of Men: Homosocial Bonding and the Symbolic Objectification of Women." Paper presented at the annual meeting of the North Central Sociological Association, Cleveland, Ohio, April.

———. 1987. "Dinosaurs and Prospects: Toward a Sociology of the Compressed Career." Pp. 95–103 in *Sociological Inquiry: A Humanistic Perspective*, 4th ed., edited by Kooros Mahmoudi, Bradley W. Parlin, and Marty E. Zusman. Dubuque, IA: Kendall-Hunt.

Gergen, Kenneth J. 1991. *The Saturated Self*. New York: Basic Books.

Goffman, Erving. 1974. *Frame Analysis*. New York: Harper and Row.

———. 1963. *Stigma: Notes on the Management of Spoiled Identity*. Englewood Cliffs, NJ: Prentice-Hall.

———. 1959. *The Presentation of Self in Everyday Life*. New York: Anchor.

Goode, Erich. 2005. *Drugs in American Society*. 6th ed. New York: McGraw Hill.

Goodlin, Wendi E. 2008. "Not Your Typical 'Pretty Woman': Factors Associated with Prostitution." Ph.D. diss., Bowling Green State University. Abstract in *Dissertation Abstracts International*, A: The Humanities and Social Sciences, vol. 69, no. 11, pp. 4539.

Gordon, Richard. 1990. *Anorexia and Bulimia: Anatomy of a Social Epidemic*. Cambridge, MA: Basil Blackwell.

Graff, Harold, and Richard Mallin. 1967. "The Syndrome of the Wrist Cutter." *American Journal of Psychiatry* 124:36–42.

Granfield, Robert, and William Cloud. 1999. *Coming Clean: Overcoming Treatment without Addiction*. New York: NYU Press.

Gratz, Kim L. 2006. "Risk Factors for Deliberate Self-Harm among Female College Students: The Role and Interaction of Childhood Maltreatment, Emotional Inexpressivity, and Affect Intensity/Reactivity." *American Journal of Orthopsychiatry* 76:238–50.

————. 2001. "Measurement of Deliberate Self-Harm: Preliminary Data on the Deliberate Self-Harm Inventory." *Journal of Psychopathology and Behavioral Assessment* 23:253–63.

Gratz, Kim L., Sheree D. Conrad, and Lizabeth Roemer. 2002. "Risk Factors for Deliberate Self-Harm among College Students." *American Journal of Orthopsychiatry* 72:128–40.

Greenspan, Gail C., and Steven E. Samuel. 1989. "Self-Cutting after Rape." *American Journal of Psychiatry* 146:789–90.

Greenwald, Andy. 2003. *Nothing Feels Good: Punk Rock, Teenagers, and Emo.* New York: St. Martin's Griffin.

Grossman, Perry. 2002. "Punk." *St. James Encyclopedia of Pop Culture,* January 29. Available online at http://findarticles.com/p/articles/mi_g1epc/is_tov/ai_2419101001/.

Gruenbaum, Henry V., and Gerald L. Klerman. 1967. "Wrist Slashing." *American Journal of Psychiatry* 124:527–34.

Guertin, Tracey, Elizabeth Lloyd-Richardson, Anthony Spirito, Diedre Donaldson, and Julie Boergers. 2001. "Self-Mutilative Behavior in Adolescents Who Attempt Suicide by Overdose." *Journal of the American Academy of Child and Adolescent Psychiatry* 40:1062–69.

gURL. N.d. "Label It . . . Emo." http://www.gurl.com/findout/label/pages/0,,673303,00. html.

Gusfield, Joseph. 1985. "Foreword." Pp. v–x in *Deviance and Medicalization: From Badness to Sickness,* 2nd ed., by Peter Conrad and Joseph W. Schneider. Columbus, OH: Merrill.

————. 1967. "Moral Passage: The Symbolic Process in Public Designations of Deviance." *Social Problems* 15:175–88.

Guy, Alison, and Maura Banim. 2000. "Personal Collections: Women's Clothing Use and Identity." *Journal of Gender Studies* 9:313–27.

Gyorgy, Peter. 2002. "The Tale of Cookies (Dr. Jekyll and Mr. Hyde)." *Social Research* 69:239–45.

Hanna, Refaat. 2000. *Suicide Associated Deaths and Hospitalization: Virginia 2000.* Center for Injury and Violence Prevention, Virginia Department of Health.

Harré, Rom. 2001. "Metaphysics and Narrative: Singularities and Multiplicities of the Self." Pp. 59–73 in *Narrative and Identity: Studies in Autobiography, Self and Culture,* edited by Jens Brockmeier and Donal Carbaugh. Amsterdam: John Benjamins.

Harris, Mervyn. 1973. *The Dilly Boys.* Rockville, MD: New Perspectives.

Harrison, Diane. 1995. *Vicious Circles: An Exploration of Women and Self-Harm in Society.* London: Good Practices in Mental Health.

Hatfield, Elaine, and Susan Sprecher. 1986. *Mirror, Mirror: The Importance of Looks in Everyday Life.* Albany: SUNY Press.

Hawkes, Diana, Charlene Y. Senn, and Chantal Thorn. 2004. "Factors That Influence Attitudes toward Women with Tattoos." *Sex Roles* 50:593–604.

Hawton, Keith, and Jose Catalan. 1987. *Attempted Suicide: A Practical Guide to Its Nature and Management.* Oxford: Oxford University Press.

Hawton, Keith, Karen Rodham, and Emma Evans. 2006. *By Their Own Young Hand: Deliberate Self-Harm and Suicidal Ideas in Adolescents.* London: Jessica Kingsley.

Haycock, Joel. 1989. "Manipulation and Suicide Attempts in Jails and Prisons." *Psychiatric Quarterly* 60:85–98.

Heath, Nancy L., Jessica R. Toste, Tatiana Nedecheva, and Alison Charlebois. 2008. "An Examination of Nonsuicidal Self-Injury among College Students." *Journal of Mental Health Counseling* 30:137–56.

Heckert, Alex, and Druann Heckert. 2004. "Using a New Typology of Deviance to Analyze Ten Common Norms of the United States Middle-Class." *Sociological Quarterly* 45:209–28.

Hendershott, Anne B. 2002. *The Politics of Deviance*. San Francisco: Encounter Books.

Henslin, James. 1972. "Studying Deviance in Four Settings: Researcher Experiences with Cabbies, Suicidees, Drug Users, and Abortionees." Pp. 35–70 in *Research on Deviance*, edited by Jack D. Douglas. New York: Random House.

Herman, Nancy J. 1993. "Return to Sender: Reintegrative Stigma-Management Strategies of Ex-Psychiatric Patients." *Journal of Contemporary Ethnography* 22:295–330.

Herpertz, Stephan. 1995. "Self-Injurious Behavior: Psychopathological and Nosological Characteristics in Subtypes of Self-Injurers." *Acta Psychiatrica Scandinavica* 91:57–68.

Hesse-Biber, Sharlene. 1996. *Am I Thin Enough Yet? The Cult of Thinness and the Commercialization of Identity*. New York: Oxford University Press.

Hindmarsh, Jon, Christian Heath, and Mike Fraser. 2006. "(Im)materiality, Virtual Reality and Interaction: Grounding the 'Virtual' in Studies of Technology of Action." *Sociological Review* 54:795–817.

Hine, Christine. 2000. *Virtual Ethnography*. London: Sage.

HM Prison Service. 2001. *Prevention of Suicide and Self-Harm in the Prison Service: An Internal Review*.

Hodgson, Sarah. 2004. "Cutting through the Silence: A Sociological Construction of Self-Injury." *Sociological Inquiry* 74:162–79.

Holderness, Claire C., Jeanne Brooks-Gunn, and Michelle P. Warren. 1994. "Comorbidity of Eating Disorders and Substance Abuse: Review of the Literature." *International Journal of Eating Disorders* 16:1–34.

Hollander, Michael R. 2008. *Helping Teens Who Cut*. New York: Guilford.

Homan, Roger. 1991. *The Ethics of Social Research*. London: Longman.

Howson, Alexandra. 2005. *Embodying Gender*. Thousand Oaks: CA. Sage.

Hudson, James I., Harrison G. Pope, Deborah Yurgelun-Todd, Jeffrey M. Jonas, and Frances R. Frankenburg. 1987. "A Controlled Study of Lifetime Prevalence of Affective and Other Psychiatric Disorders in Bulimic Outpatients." *American Journal of Psychiatry* 144:1283–87.

Hurley, Anna L., Paul Sullivan, and John McCarthy. 2007. "The Construction of Self in Online Support Groups for Victims of Domestic Violence." *British Journal of Social Psychology* 46:859–74.

Irvine, Leslie. 2004. *If You Tame Me: Understanding Our Connection with Animals*. Philadelphia: Temple University Press.

———. 2003. "The Problem of Unwanted Pets: A Case Study in How Institutions 'Think' about Clients' Needs." *Social Problems* 50:550–66.

Irwin, John. 1970. *The Felon*. Englewood Cliffs, NJ: Prentice-Hall.

Irwin, Katherine. 2001. "Legitimating the First Tattoo: Moral Passage through Informal Interaction." *Symbolic Interaction* 24:49–73.

———. 2000. "Negotiating the Tattoo." Pp. 469–79 in *Constructions of Deviance: Social Power, Context, and Interaction*, 3rd ed., edited by Patricia A. Adler and Peter Adler. Belmont, CA: Wadsworth.

Iscoe, Ira, and Martha S. Williams. 2006. "Experimental Variables Affecting the Conformity of Children." *Journal of Personality* 31:234–46.

Jacobs, Mary Jo. 2000. "Self-Injurious Behavior." *Paradigm* 22:12–13.

Jameson, Fredric. 1984. "Postmodernism, or the Cultural Logic of Late Capitalism." *New Left Review* 146:30–72.

Jeffreys, Sheila. 2005. *Beauty and Misogyny: Harmful Cultural Practices in the West*. New York: Routledge.

———. 2000. "'Body Art' and Social Status: Cutting, Tattooing and Piercing from a Feminist Perspective." *Feminism & Psychology* 10:409–29.

Jenkins, Philip. 2009. "Failure to Launch: Why Do Some Issues Fail to Detonate Moral Panics?" *British Journal of Criminology* 49:35–47.

———. 2001. *Beyond Tolerance: Child Pornography on the Internet*. New York: NYU Press.

Jewkes, Yvonne, and Keith Sharp. 2003. "Crime, Deviance and the Disembodied Self: Transcending the Dangers of Corporeality." Pp. 1–14 in *Dot.cons: Crime, Deviance, and Identity on the Internet*, edited by Yvonne Jewkes. Portland, OR: Willan.

Joiner, Thomas E. 2005. *Why People Die by Suicide*. Cambridge: Harvard University Press.

Jones, Ann. 1986. "Self-Mutilation in Prison: A Comparison of Mutilators and Non-mutilators." *Criminal Justice and Behavior* 13:286–96.

Jones, D. Alun, Neil Cheshire, and Helen Moorhouse. 1985. "Anorexia Nervosa Bulimia and Alcoholism: Association of Eating Disorder and Alcohol." *Journal of Psychiatry Research* 19:377–80.

Jones, Edward, Amerigo Farina, Albert Hastorf, Hazel Markus, Dale Miller, and Robert Scott. 1984. *Social Stigma: The Psychology of Marked Relationships*. New York: Freeman.

Jones, Steve G. 1997. "The Internet and Its Social Landscape." Pp. 5–35 in *Virtual Culture: Identity and Communication in Cybersociety*, edited by Steve Jones. Thousand Oaks, CA: Sage.

Kalb, Claudia. 1998. "An Armful of Agony: Treatment Options for Self-Mutilators." *Newsweek*, November 9, p. 82.

Kantrowitz, Barbara, and Karen Springen. 2005. "A Teen Health Gap." *Newsweek*, December 12, pp. 62–65.

Karp, David A. 2006. *Is It Me or My Meds?* Cambridge: Harvard University Press.

———. 1996. *Speaking of Sadness: Depression, Disconnection, and the Meanings of Illness*. New York: Oxford University Press.

Kawakami, Yoshiro. 1993. "ROM and RAM Which Support Computer Conferencing." *Modern Esprit*, January: 119–26.

Kendall, Lori. 2002. *Hanging Out in the Virtual Pub: Masculinities and Relationships Online*. Berkeley: University of California Press.

Kennerley, Helen. 1996. "Cognitive Therapy of Dissociative Symptoms Associated with Trauma." *British Journal of Clinical Psychology* 35:325–40.

Kern, Jan. 2007. *Scars That Wound, Scars That Heal: A Journey Out of Self Injury (Live Free)*. Cincinnati: Standard.

King, Storm A. 1996. "Researching Internet Communities: Proposed Ethical Guidelines for the Reporting of Results." *Information Society* 12:119–27.

Kirn, Walter. 2002. "Some Psychiatrists Want to Start Treating 'DSM-IV, Relational Disorders': Are They Nuts?" *Time*, September 6.

Kiselica, Mark S., and Laurie Zila. 2001. "Understanding and Counseling Self-Mutilation in Female Adolescents and Young Adults." *Journal of Counseling and Development* 79:46–52.

Kitchin, Rob. 1998. *Cyberspace*. New York: Wiley.

Kitsuse, John. 1980. "Coming Out All Over: Deviants and the Politics of Social Problems." *Social Problems* 28:1–13.

Klonsky E. David, and Deborah Muehlenkamp. 2007. "Self-Injury: A Research Review for the Practitioner." *Journal of Clinical Psychology: In Session* 63:1045–56.

Klonsky E. David, Thomas F. Oltmanns, and Eric Turkheimer. 2003. "Deliberate Self-Harm in a Non-clinical Population." *American Journal of Psychiatry* 160:1501–8.

Kowalewski, Mark R. 1988. "Double Stigma and Boundary Maintenance: How Gay Men Deal with AIDS." *Journal of Contemporary Ethnography* 17:211–28.

Kozinets, Robert V. 2010. *Netnography: Doing Ethnographic Research Online.* Thousand Oaks, CA: Sage.

Kruttschnitt, Candace, and Mike Vuolo. 2007. "The Cultural Context of Women Prisoners' Mental Health: A Comparison of Two Prison Systems." *Punishment & Society* 9:115–50.

Kuhn, Cynthia, Scott Swartzwelder, and Wilkie Wilson, with Leigh Heather Wilson and Jeremy Foster. 2003. *Buzzed: The Straight Facts about the Most Used and Abused Drugs from Alcohol to Ecstasy.* New York: Norton.

Lacan, Jacques. 1968. *The Language of the Self.* Translated with notes and commentary by Anthony Wilden. Baltimore: Johns Hopkins University Press.

Lack, Tony. 1995. "Consumer Society and Authenticity: The (Il)logic of Punk Practices." *Undercurrent* 3, October. The Library of Nothingness Collection, http://library.nothingness.org/articles/SI/en/display/86. Originally published at http://darkwing.uoregon.edu/~ucurrent/uc3/3-lack.html.

Langbehn, Douglas R., and Bruce Pfohl. 1993. "Clinical Correlates of Self-Mutilation among Psychiatric Inpatients." *Annals of Clinical Psychiatry* 5:45–51.

Lather, Patti. 2001. "Postmodernism, Post-structuralism, and Post(Critical) Ethnography: Of Ruins, Aporias, and Angels." Pp. 477–92 in *Handbook of Ethnography,* edited by Paul Atkinson, Amanda Coffey, Sara Delamont, John Lofland, and Lyn Lofland. Thousand Oaks, CA: Sage.

Laye-Gindhu, Aviva, and Kimberly A. Schonert-Reichl. 2005. "Nonsuicidal Self-Harm among Community Adolescents: Understanding the 'Whats' and 'Whys' of Self-Harm." *Journal of Youth and Adolescence* 34:447–57.

Lemert, Edwin. 1967. *Human Deviance, Social Problems, and Social Control.* Englewood Cliffs, NJ: Prentice-Hall.

———. 1962. "Paranoia and the Dynamics of Exclusion." *Sociometry* 25:2–25.

Lennon, Sharron J., Abby Lillethun, and Sandra S. Buckland. 1999. "Attitudes toward Social Comparison as a Function of Self-Esteem: Idealized Appearance and Body Image." *Family and Consumer Sciences Research Journal* 27:379–405.

Leo, Jonathan. 2002. "American Preschoolers on Ritalin." *Society* 39:52–60.

Levenkron, Steven. 1998. *Cutting: Understanding and Overcoming Self-Mutilation.* New York: Norton.

Lifton, Robert Jay. 1993. *The Protean Self: Human Resilience in an Age of Fragmentation.* New York: Basic Books.

Linehan, Marsha M. 1993. *Cognitive-Behavioral Treatment of Borderline Personality Disorder.* New York: Guilford.

Liu, Geoffrey Z. 1999. "Virtual Community Presence in Internet Relay Chatting." *Journal of Computer-Mediated Communication* 5(1). Available online at http://jcmc.indiana.edu/issues.html.

Livingston, Jay. 1974. *Compulsive Gamblers.* New York: Harper and Row.

Lloyd, Charles. 1990. *Suicide and Self-Injury in Prison: A Literature Review*. Great Britain Home Office, Research and Planning Unit, United Kingdom. London: Her Majesty's Stationery Office.

Lloyd-Richardson, Elizabeth, Nicholas Perrine, Lisa Dierker, and Mary L. Kelley. 2007. "Characteristics and Functions of Non-suicidal Self-Injury in a Community Sample of Adolescents." *Psychological Medicine* 37:1183–92.

Lofland, John. 1969. *Deviance and Identity*. Englewood Cliffs, NJ: Prentice-Hall.

Lorca, Federico García, and Ted Hughes. 1997. *Blood Wedding*. New York: Dramatists Play Service.

Lowery, Shearon A., and Charles V. Wetli. 1982. "Sexual Asphyxia: A Neglected Area of Study." *Deviant Behavior* 4:19–39.

Luckenbill, David, and Joel Best. 1981. "Careers in Deviance and Respectability: The Analogy's Limitations." *Social Problems* 29:197–206.

Lundh, Lars-Gunnar, Jessica Karim, and Eva Quilisch. 2007. "Deliberate Self-Harm in 15-Year-Old Adolescents: A Pilot Study with a Modified Version of the Deliberate Self-Harm Inventory." *Scandinavian Journal of Psychology* 48:33–41.

Lupton, Deborah. 1995. *The Imperative of Health: Public Health and the Regulated Body*. London: Sage.

Maden, Anthony, Sherelle Chamberlain, and John Gunn. 2000. "Deliberate Self-Harm in Sentenced Male Prisoners in England and Wales: Some Ethnic Factors." *Criminal Behavior in Mental Health* 10:199–204.

Mann, Chris, and Fiona Stewart. 2000. *Internet Communication and Qualitative Research: A Handbook for Researching Online*. London: Sage.

Martin, Emily. 1994. *Flexible Bodies: Tracking Immunity in American Culture from the Days of Polio to the Age of AIDS*. Boston: Beacon.

Martinson, Deb. 1998. "Self-Injury: You Are NOT the Only One." *Palace.net*. http://www.palace.net/~llama/psych/injury.html.

Matsumoto, Toshihiko, Akiko Yamaguchi, Yasuhiko Chiba, Takeshi Asami, Eizo Iseki, and Yoshio Hirayasu. 2005. "Self-Burning versus Self-Cutting: Patterns and Implications of Self-mutilation: A Preliminary Study of Differences between Self-Cutting and Self-Burning in a Japanese Juvenile Detention Center." *Psychiatry and Clinical Neurosciences* 59:62–69.

Matthews, Ryan, and Watts Wacker. 2002. *The Deviant's Advantage: How Fringe Ideas Create Mass Markets*. New York: Random House.

McCraig, Linda, and Catharine Burt. 2005. "National Hospital Ambulatory Medical Care Survey: 2003 Emergency Department Summary." *Advance Data from Vital and Health Statistics* 358. Huntsville, MD: National Center for Health Statistics.

McCrea, Frances B. 1983. "The Politics of Menopause: The 'Discovery' of a Deficiency Disease." *Social Problems* 31:111–23.

McKenna, Katelyn Y. A. and John A. Bargh. 1998. "Coming Out in the Age of the Internet: Identity 'Demarginalization' through Virtual Group Participation." *Journal of Personality and Social Psychology* 75:681–94.

McKenna, Katelyn Y. A., and Amie S. Green. 2002. "Virtual Group Dynamics." *Group Dynamics: Theory, Research and Practice* 6:116–27.

McKenna, Katelyn Y. A., Amie S. Green, and Marci E. J. Gleason. 2002. "Relationship Formation on the Internet: What's the Big Attraction?" *Journal of Social Issues* 58:9–31.

McLaughlin, Margaret L., Kerry K. Osborne, and Nicole B. Ellison. 1997. "Virtual Community in a Telepresence Environment." Pp. 146–68 in *Virtual Culture: Identity and Communication in Cybersociety,* edited by Steve Jones. Thousand Oaks, CA: Sage.

McLorg, Penelope A., and Diane E. Taub. 1987. "Anorexia and Bulimia: The Development of Deviant Identities." *Deviant Behavior* 8:177–89.

McLuhan, Marshall. 1962. *The Guttenberg Galaxy.* Toronto: University of Toronto Press.

Meisenhelder, Tom. 1977. "An Exploratory Study of Exiting from Criminal Careers." *Criminology* 15:319–34.

Melbin, Murray. 1978. "Night as Frontier." *American Sociological Review* 43:3–22.

Menninger, Karl. 1938. *Man against Himself.* New York: Harcourt Brace World.

Merton, Robert. 1938. "Social Structure and Anomie." *American Sociological Review* 3:672–82.

Messner, Michael A. 2002. *Taking the Field: Women, Men, and Sports.* Minneapolis: University of Minnesota Press.

———. 1992. *Power at Play: Sports and the Problem of Masculinity.* Boston: Beacon.

———. 1987. "The Meaning of Success: The Athletic Experience and the Development of Male Identity." Pp. 193–210 in *The Making of Masculinities,* edited by Harry Brod. Boston: Allen & Unwin.

Meyrowitz, Joshua. 1985. *No Sense of Place: The Impact of Electronic Media on Social Behavior.* New York: Oxford University Press.

Milia, Diana. 2000. *Self-Mutilation and Art Therapy: Violent Creation.* London: Jessica Kingsley.

Miller, Dan. 2003. "In Defense of Emo." *Knot Magazine,* October 2. http://www.knotmag.com/?article=885.

Miller, Dusty. 1994. *Women Who Hurt Themselves: A Book of Hope and Understanding.* New York: Basic Books.

Miller, Frank, and Edmund Bashkin. 1974. "Depersonalization and Self-Mutilation." *Psychoanalysis Quarterly* 43:638–49.

Mitra, Ananda. 1997. "Virtual Commonality: Looking for India on the Internet." Pp. 55–79 in *Virtual Culture: Identity and Communication in Cybersociety,* edited by Steve Jones. Thousand Oaks, CA: Sage.

Mnookin, Jennifer L. 1996. "Virtual(ly) Law: The Emergence of Law in LambdaMOO." *Journal of Computer-Mediated Communication* 2(1). Available online at http://jcmc.indiana.edu/issues.html.

Morey, Leslie C., and Mary C. Zanarini. 2000. "Borderline Personality: Traits and Disorder." *Journal of Abnormal Psychology* 109:733–37.

Morgan, Howard G. 1979. *Death Wishes? The Understanding and Management of Deliberate Self-Harm.* New York: Wiley.

Morton, Andrew. 1992. *Diana: The True Story in Her Own Words.* New York: Pocket.

Muehlenkamp, Jennifer J., Jenny D. Swanson, and Amy M. Brausch. 2005. "Self-Objectification, Risk Taking, and Self-Harm in College Women." *Psychology of Women Quarterly* 29:24–32.

Muehlenkamp, Jennifer J., William Yates, and Albert Alberts. 2004. "Gender and Racial Differences in Self-Injury." Paper presented at the annual American Association of Suicidology Conference, Miami, Florida.

Nack, Adina. 2008. *Damaged Goods? Women Living with Incurable Sexually Transmitted Disease.* Philadelphia: Temple University Press.

Ng, Gina. 1998. *Everything You Need to Know about Self-Mutilation: A Helping Book for Teens Who Hurt Themselves*. New York: Rosen.

Nock, Matthew K., Thomas E. Joiner, K. H. Gordon, E. Lloyd-Richardson, and Mitchell J. Prinstein. 2006. "Nonsuicidal Self-Injury among Adolescents: Diagnostic Correlates and Relation to Suicide Attempts." *Psychiatry Research* 144:65–72.

Noll, Jennie G., Lisa A. Horowitz, George A. Bonanno, Penelope K. Trickett, and Frank W. Putnam. 2003. "Revictimization and Self-Harm in Females Who Experienced Childhood Sexual Abuse." *Journal of Interpersonal Violence* 18:1452–71.

O'Halloran, Ronald L., and Park Elliott Dietz. 1993. "Autoerotic Fatalities with Power Hydraulics." *Journal of Forensic Sciences* 38:359–64.

Paccagnella, Luciano. 1997. "Getting the Seats of Your Pants Dirty: Strategies for Ethnographic Research on Virtual Communities." *Journal of Computer-Mediated Communication* 3.

Pao, N.-P. 1969. "The Syndrome of Deliberate Self-Cutting." *British Journal of Medical Psychology* 42:195–206.

Parks, Suzan-Lori. 2000. *In the Blood*. New York: Dramatists Play Service.

Pattison, E. Mansell, and Joel Kahan. 1983. "The Deliberate Self-Harm Syndrome." *American Journal of Psychiatry* 140:867–72.

Pembroke, Louise R. 1994. *Self-Harm: Perspectives from Personal Experience*. London: Survivors Speak Out.

Penn, Joseph V., Christianne L. Esposito, Leah E. Schaeffer, Gregory K. Fritz, and Anthony Spirito. 2003. "Suicide Attempts and Self-Mutilative Behavior in a Juvenile Correctional Facility." *Journal of the American Academy of Child and Adolescent Psychiatry* 4:762–69.

Petersilia, Joan. 1980. "Criminal Career Research: A Review of Recent Evidence." Pp. 321–79 in *Crime and Justice: An Annual Review of Research*, vol. 2, edited by Norval Morris and Michael Tonry. Chicago: University of Chicago Press.

Petrunik Michael, and Clifford Shearing. 1983. "Fragile Facades: Stuttering and the Strategic Manipulation of Awareness." *Social Problems* 31:125–38.

Pfohl, Bruce. 1991. "Histrionic Personality Disorder." *Journal of Personality Disorders* 5:150–65.

Phillips, Alysa. 2006. *Stranger in My Skin*. Minneapolis: Word Warriors.

Pinto, Aureen, and Mark A. Whisman. 1996. "Negative Affect and Cognitive Biases in Suicidal and Nonsuicidal Hospitalized Adolescents." *Journal of the American Academy of Child and Adolescent Psychiatry* 35:158–65.

Pitman, Roger K. 1990. "Self-Mutilation in Combat Related Post-traumatic Stress Disorder." *American Journal of Psychiatry* 147:123–24.

Plante, Lori G. 2007. *Bleeding to Ease the Pain: Cutting, Self-Injury, and the Adolescent Search for Self*. Westport, CT: Praeger.

Pollack. Deborah. 2003. "Pro-Eating Disorder Websites: What Should Be the Feminist Response?" *Feminism & Psychology* 13:246–51.

Polsky, Ned. 1967. *Hustlers, Beats, and Others*. Chicago: Aldine.

Pope John XXIII. 1999. *Journal of a Soul: The Autobiography of Pope John XXIII*. New York: Random House.

Postmes, Tom, Russell Spears, Khaled Sakhel, and Daphne de Groot. 2001. "Social Influence in Computer-Mediated Communication: The Effect of Anonymity on Group Behavior." *Personality and Social Psychology Bulletin* 27:1243–54.

Potterat, John J., Richard B. Rothenberg, Stephen Q. Muth, William W. Darrow, and Lynanne Phillips-Plummer. 1998. "Pathways to Prostitution: The Chronology of Sexual and Drug Abuse Milestones." *Journal of Sex Research* 35:333–40.

Priory Group. 2005. *Adolescent Angst*. Surrey, UK: Priory Group.

Probyn, Elspeth. 1993. "This Body Which Is Not One: Speaking an Embodied Self." *Hypatia* 6:111–24.

Prus, Robert, and Scott Grills. 2003. *The Deviant Mystique: Involvements, Realities, and Regulation*. Westport, CT: Praeger.

Putnam, Robert D. 2000. *Bowling Alone: The Collapse and Revival of American Community*. New York: Simon and Schuster.

Quinn, James F., and Craig J. Forsyth. 2005. "Describing Sexual Behavior in the Era of the Internet: A Typology for Empirical Research." *Deviant Behavior* 26:191–207.

Raphael, Ray. 1988. *The Men from the Boys: Rites of Passage in Male America*. Lincoln: University of Nebraska Press.

Ray, Marsh B. 1961. "The Cycle of Abstinence and Relapse among Heroin Addicts." *Social Problems* 9:132–40.

Reid, Elizabeth. 1996. "Informed Consent in the Study of On-Line Communities: A Reflection on the Effects of Computer-Mediated Social Research." *Information Society* 12:169–74.

Rheingold, Howard. 1993. *The Virtual Community: Homesteading on the Electronic Frontier*. Reading, MA: Addison-Wesley.

Riley, Sarah. 2002. "A Feminist Construction of Body Art as a Response to Jeffreys." *Feminism & Psychology* 12:540–45.

Rochford, E. Burke. 1983. "Stutterers' Practices: Folk Remedies and Therapeutic Intervention." *Journal of Communication Disorders* 16:373–84.

Rodham, Karen, Jeff Gavin, and Meriel Miles. 2007. "I Hear, I Listen and I Care: A Qualitative Investigation into the Function of a Self-Harm Message Board." *Suicide and Life-Threatening Behavior* 37:422–30.

Roschelle, Anne R., and Peter Kaufman. 2004. "Fitting In and Fighting Back: Homeless Kids' Stigma Management Strategies." *Symbolic Interaction* 27:23–46.

Rosen Paul M., and Barent M. Walsh. 1989. "Patterns of Contagion in Self-Mutilation Epidemics." *American Journal of Psychiatry* 146:656–58.

Rosenfield, Sarah. 1982. "Sex Roles and Societal Reactions to Mental Illness: The Labelling of 'Deviant' Deviance." *Journal of Health and Social Behavior* 23:18–24.

Rosenthal, Richard J. 1986. "Media Violence, Anti-social Behavior, and the Social Consequences of Small Effects." *Journal of Social Issues* 42:141–54.

Rosenthal, Richard J., Carl Rinzler, Rita Walsh, and Edmund Klausner. 1972. "Wrist-Cutting Syndrome." *American Journal of Psychiatry* 128:1363–68.

Ross, Shana, and Nancy Heath. 2002. "A Study of the Frequency of Self-Mutilation in a Community Sample of Adolescents." *Journal of Youth and Adolescence* 31:67–77.

Rubington, Earl. 1967. "Drug Addiction as a Deviant Career." *International Journal of the Addictions* 2:3–20.

Sanders, Clinton. 2006. "Viewing the Body: An Overview, Exploration and Extension." Pp. 279–94 in *Body/Embodiment*, edited by Dennis Waskul and Phillip Vannini. Burlington, VT: Ashgate.

———. 1989. *Customizing the Body: The Art and Culture of Tattooing.* Philadelphia: Temple University Press.

Sands, Sarah. 2006. "EMO Cult Warning for Parents." *Daily Mail,* August 16. http://www.dailymail.co.uk/pages/live/articles/news/news.html?in_article_id=400953&in_page_id=1770.

Scatheweb. 2008. "A Brief Guide to Goth." www.scathe.demon.co.uk/fastgoth.htm.

Schaffer, Charles B., Jacqueline Carroll, and Stephen I. Abramowitz. 1982. "Self-Mutilation and the Borderline Personality." *Journal of Nervous Mental Disorders* 170:468–73.

Schur, Edwin M. 1980. *The Politics of Deviance: Stigma Contests and the Uses of Power.* Englewood Cliffs, NJ: Prentice-Hall.

Schutz, Alfred. 1967. *The Phenomenology of the Social World.* Evanston, IL: Northwestern University Press.

Scott, Marvin B., and Stanford Lyman. 1968. "Accounts." *American Sociological Review* 33:46–62.

Scully, Diana, and Joseph Marolla. 1984. "Convicted Rapists' Vocabulary of Motive: Excuses and Justifications." *Social Problems* 31:530–44.

Selekman, Matthew D. 2006. *Working with Self-Harming Adolescents: A Collaborative, Strengths-Based Therapy Approach.* New York: Norton.

Shapiro, Andrew. 1999. "The Net That Binds." *Nation,* June 21, pp. 11–12.

Shapiro, Lawrence E. 2008. *Stopping the Pain: A Workbook for Teens Who Self-Injure.* Oakland, CA: Instant Help Books.

Sharkey, Valerie. 2003. "Self-Wounding: A Literature Review." *Mental Health Practice* 6:35–37.

Sharp, Susan F., and Trina L. Hope. 2001. "The Professional Revisited: Cessation or Continuation of a Deviant Career?" *Journal of Contemporary Ethnography* 27:678–703.

Shaw, David F. 1997. "Gay Men and Computer Communication: A Discourse of Sex and Identity in Cyberspace." Pp. 133–45 in *Virtual Culture: Identity and Communication in Cybersociety,* edited by Steve Jones. Thousand Oaks, CA: Sage.

Sheffield, Carole J. 1989. "The Invisible Intruder: Women's Experiences of Obscene Phone Calls." *Gender & Society* 3:483–88.

Shilling, Chris. 2003. *The Body and Social Theory.* 2nd ed. Thousand Oaks, CA. Sage.

Shover, Neil. 1985. *Aging Criminals.* Newbury Park, CA: Sage.

Simeon, Daphne, and Eric Hollander, eds. 2001. *Self-Injurious Behaviors: Assessment and Treatment.* Washington, DC: American Psychiatric Press.

Smith, Gerrilyn, Dee Cox, and Jacqui Saradjian. 1998. *Women and Self-Harm.* London: Women's Press.

Smith, Hayden, and Robert J. Kaminski. 2010. "Inmate Self-Injurious Behaviors: Distinguishing Characteristics within a Retrospective Study." *Criminal Justice and Behavior* 37:81–96.

Snodgrass, Jon. 1982. *The Jack-Roller at Seventy: A Fifty-Year Follow-Up.* Lexington, MA: Lexington Books.

Snow, David A., and Leon Anderson. 1993. *Down on Their Luck: A Study of Homeless Street People.* Berkeley: University of California Press.

Solomon, Yvette, and Julie Farrand. 1996. "Why Don't You Do It Properly? Young Women Who Self-Injure." *Journal of Adolescence* 19:111–19.

Spandler, Helen, and Sam Warner, eds. 2007. *Beyond Fear and Control: Working with Young People Who Self-Harm.* Ross-on-Wye, UK: PCCS Books.

Stebbins, Robert A. 1971. *Commitment to Deviance*. Westport, CT: Greenwood.

Steffensmeier, Darrell J., and Jeffery T. Ulmer. 2005. *Confessions of a Dying Thief*. New Brunswick, NJ: Transaction.

Stevens, Dennis J. 1999. *Inside the Mind of a Serial Rapist*. San Francisco: Austin & Winfield.

Strauss, Anselm L. 1987. *Qualitative Analysis for Social Scientists*. New York: Cambridge University Press.

Strong, Marilee. 1998. *A Bright Red Scream: Self-Mutilation and the Language of Pain*. New York: Viking Penguin.

Suyemoto, Karen L., and Marian L. MacDonald. 1995. "Self-Cutting in Female Adolescents." *Psychotherapy* 32:162–71.

Swift, E. M. 2006. "What Went Wrong in Winthrop?" *Sports Illustrated,* January 9, pp. 60–65.

Sykes, Gresham, and David Matza. 1957. "Techniques of Neutralization: A Theory of Delinquency." *American Sociological Review* 22:664–70.

Synott, Anthony. 1993. *The Body Social*. New York: Routledge.

Taiminen, Tero J., Kristiina Kallio-Soukainen, Hannele Nokso-Koivisto, Anne Kaljonen, and Hans Helenius. 1998. "Contagion of Deliberate Self-Harm among Adolescents." *Journal of the American Academy of Child and Adolescent Psychiatry* 37:211.

Tantam, Digby, and James K. Whittaker. 1992. "Personality Disorder and Self-Wounding." *British Journal of Psychiatry* 161:451–64.

Thompson, William E., and Joseph V. Hickey. 1998. "What the Cutters Feel." *Time,* November 9, p. 93.

3News. 2006. "Emos—Why the Long Fringe?" http://www.3news.co.nz/Emos---why-the-long-fringe-2006/tabid/1321/articleID/143078/Default.aspx.

Thu Nguyen, Dan, and Jon Alexander. 1996. "The Coming of Cyberspace and the End of Polity." Pp. 99–124 in *Cultures of the Internet: Virtual Spaces, Real Histories and Living Bodies,* edited by Robert M. Shields. London: Sage.

Tierney, Stephanie. 2008. "Creating Communities in Cyberspace: Pro-Anorexia Web Sites and Social Capital." *Journal of Psychiatric & Mental Health Nursing* 15:340–43.

Tillich, Paul. 1959. *Theology of Culture*. Edited by Robert C. Kimball. New York: Oxford University Press.

Tseëlon, Efrat. 1992. "Is the Postmodern Self Sincere? Goffman, Impression Management, and the Postmodern Self." *Theory, Culture, and Society* 9:115–28.

Turkle, Sherry. 1995. *Life on the Screen: Identity in the Age of the Internet*. New York: Simon & Schuster.

Turner, Bryan. 1984. *The Body and Social Theory*. Thousand Oaks, CA: Sage.

Turner, Ralph H. 1978. "The Role and the Person." *American Journal of Sociology* 84:1–23.

———. 1976. "The Real Self: From Institution to Impulse." *American Journal of Sociology* 81:989–1016.

Turner, V. J. 2002. *Secret Scars: Uncovering and Understanding the Addiction of Self-Injury*. Center City, MN: Hazelden.

Turp, Maggie. 2003. *Hidden Self-Harm: Narratives from Psychotherapy*. London: Jessica Kingsley.

Turvey, Brent. 2009. "Autoerotic Sexual Asphyxia." Pp. 451–62 in *Constructions of Deviance,* 6th ed., edited by Patricia A. Adler and Peter Adler. Belmont, CA: Wadsworth.

Tyler, Kimberly A., Les B. Whitbeck, Dan R. Hoyt, and Kurt D. Johnson. 2003. "Self-Mutilation and Homeless Youth: The Role of Family Abuse, Street Experiences, and Mental Disorders." *Journal of Research on Adolescence* 13:457–74.

Uslander, E. M. 2000. "Social Capital and the Net." *Communications of the ACM* 43:60–64.

Ussher, Jane M. 1992. *Women's Madness: Misogyny or Mental Illness?* Amherst: University of Massachusetts Press.

Vale, V., and Andrea Juno. 1989. *Modern Primitives*. San Francisco: Re/Search.

van der Kolk, Bessel A. 1996. "The Complexity of Adaptation to Trauma: Self-Regulation, Stimulus Discrimination, and Characterological Development." Pp. 182–213 in *Traumatic Stress: The Effects of Overwhelming Experience on Mind, Body, and Society,* edited by Bessel A. van der Kolk, Alexander C. McFarlane, and Lars Weisaeth. New York: Guilford.

van der Kolk, Bessel A., J. Christopher Perry, and Judith Lewis Herman. 1991. "Childhood Origins of Self-Destructive Behavior." *American Journal of Psychiatry* 148:1665–71.

Vannini, Phillip, Martha McMahon, and Aaron McCright. 2005. "Not a Pretty Site: Gendered Bodies, Endangered Selves, and Eating (Dis)orders." Paper presented at the Couch-Stone Symposium of the Society for the Study of Symbolic Interaction, Boulder, Colorado, February.

Vega, Vanessa. 2007. *Comes the Darkness, Comes the Light: A Memoir of Cutting, Healing, and Hope*. New York: American Management Association.

Venning, Rachel. 2004. "The Art of Cutting." Pp. 133–35 in *On Our Backs: Guide to Lesbian Sex,* edited by Diana Cage. Los Angeles: Alyson Books.

Virkkunen, Matti. 1976. "Self-Mutilation in Antisocial Personality Disorder." *Acta Psychiatrica Scandinavica* 54:347–52.

Vogler, Robin Jane Marie. 1993. *The Medicalization of Eating: Social Control in an Eating Disorders Clinic*. Greenwich, CT: JAI.

Vollmer, Fred. 2005. "The Narrative Self." *Journal for the Theory of Social Behavior* 35:189–205.

Wagner, Joyce, and Mark Rehfuss. 2008. "Self-Injury, Sexual Self-Concept and a Conservative Christian Upbringing: An Exploratory Study of Three Young Women's Perspectives." *Journal of Mental Health Counseling* 3:173–88.

Waisman, Morris. 1965. "Pickers, Pluckers and Impostors: A Panorama of Cutaneous Self-Mutilation." *Postgraduate Medicine* 38:620–30.

Waldorf, Dan. 1983. *Careers in Dope*. Englewood Cliffs, NJ: Prentice-Hall.

Walsh, Barent W. 2008. *Treating Self-Injury: A Practical Guide*. New York: Guilford.

Walsh, Barent W., and Paul M. Rosen. 1988. *Self-Mutilation: Theory, Research and Treatment*. New York: Guilford.

———. 1985. "Self-Mutilation and Contagion: An Empirical List." *American Journal of Psychiatry* 142:119–20.

Walsh, Jeremy. 2007. "Bayside Takes Manhattan." *Queens Time Ledger,* October 18. http://www.yournabe.com/articles/2007/10/18/import/20071018-archive6.txt.

Walther, Joseph B. 1996. "Computer-Mediated Communication: Impersonal, Interpersonal, and Hyperpersonal Interaction." *Communication Research* 23:3–43.

———. 1992. "Interpersonal Effects in Computer-Mediated Interaction: A Relational Perspective." *Communication Research* 19:52–90.

Warin, Megan. 2004. "Primitivising Anorexia: The Irresistible Spectacle of Not Eating." *Australian Journal of Anthropology* 15:95–104.

———. 2002. "Becoming and Unbecoming: Abject Relations in Anorexia." Ph.D. diss., University of Adelaide, Department of Anthropology and Social Inquiry.

Waskul, Dennis, ed. 2004. *Net.seXXX: Readings on Sex, Pornography, and the Internet.* New York: Peter Lang.

———. 2003. *Self-Games and Body-Play: Personhood in Online Chat and Cybersex.* New York: Peter Lang.

Waskul, Dennis, and Mark Douglass. 1996. "Considering the Electronic Participant: Some Polemical Observations on the Ethics of On-Line Research." *Information Society* 12:129–39.

Waskul, Dennis and Pamela van der Riet. 2002. "The Abject Embodiment of Cancer Patients: Dignity, Selfhood, and the Grotesque Body." *Symbolic Interaction* 25:487–513.

Waskul, Dennis and Phillip Vannini. 2006. "Introduction: The Body in Symbolic Interactionism." Pp. 1–18 in *Body/Embodiment,* edited by Dennis D. Waskul and Phillip Vannini. Burlington, VT: Ashgate.

Way, Karen. 1995. "Never Too Rich . . . or Too Thin: The Role of Stigma in the Social Construction of Anorexia Nervosa." Pp. 91–113 in *Eating Agendas: Food and Nutrition as Social Problems,* edited by Donna Maurer and Jeffery Sobal. Hawthorne, NY: Aldine de Gruyter.

Weigert, Andrew J., and Viktor Gecas. 2005. "Symbolic Interactionist Reflections on Erikson, Identity, and Postmodernism." *Identity: An International Journal of Theory and Research* 5:161–74.

Weissman, Myrna M. 1975. "Wrist Cutting: Relationship between Clinical Observations and Epidemiological Finds." *Archives of General Psychiatry* 32:1166–71.

Welch, Edward T. 2004. *Self-Injury: When Pain Feels Good.* Phillipsburg, NJ: P&R.

Whitlock, Janis, John Eckenrode, and Daniel Silverman. 2006. "Self-Injurious Behaviors in a College Population." *Pediatrics* 117:1939–48.

Whitlock, Janis, Jane L. Powers, and John Eckenrode. 2006. "The Virtual Cutting Edge: The Internet and Adolescent Self-Injury." *Developmental Psychology* 40:7–17.

Wilkins, Amy C. 2008. *Wannabes, Goths, and Christians: The Boundaries of Sex, Style, and Status.* Chicago: University of Chicago Press.

Williams, Mark. 1997. *Cry of Pain: Understanding Suicide and Self-Harm.* Harmondsworth, UK: Penguin.

Winick, Charles. 1962. "Maturing Out of Narcotic Addiction." *Bulletin on Narcotics* 14:1–7.

———. 1961. "Physician Narcotic Addicts." *Social Problems* 9:174–86.

Winkler, Kathleen. 2003. *Cutting and Self-Mutilation: When Teens Injure Themselves.* Berkeley Heights, NJ: Enslow.

"Women in L.A. Punk: Archived Interview with Ms. Dinah Cancer." 2004. *Alicebag.com,* November. http://www.alicebag.com/dinahcancerinterview.html.

Yallop, David. 2007. *The Power and the Glory: Inside the Dark Heart of Pope John Paul II's Vatican.* New York: Carroll & Graf.

Yarkona, Am-Chau. N.d. "Blood Play." *Glass Onion.* http://glassonion.populli.org/archive/7/bloodplay.shtml.

Zhao, Shanyang. 2003. "Toward a Taxonomy of Copresence." *Presence: Teleoperators and Virtual Environments* 12:445–55.

Index

Addiction, 62, 64, 78, 94, 97, 99, 103, 110, 120, 132, 134, 135–36, 138, 163, 165, 182, 186, 196, 210, 211, 215, 216, 228n3, 228n9

Alternative youth subcultures, 2, 16, 17, 30–31, 57, 63, 75, 83, 169–72, 175, 199, 208; stigma and, 208, 216, 222n62, 227n7

Body, 4–5, 203–5, 229n6; concealment, 69, 80, 105, 204; damage to, 88–89; decorations on, 82, 111; locations on, 63, 82–83, 99, 105, 121; practices of, 26; scars, 72, 84, 98, 100, 105, 155, 158–59, 180, 186, 197, 216

Bone-breaking, 9–10, 56

Branding, 8, 56, 62, 71

Bruising, 10–11

Burning, 7–8; 62, 63, 64, 71, 89

Coping strategy, 1, 3, 15, 59,65, 79, 96, 99, 120, 123, 137, 142, 173, 178–79, 182, 186, 187, 188, 192, 194, 200, 208, 211, 213, 216; suggestions for, 115

Cry for help, 2, 73–74, 100, 128–29, 208

Cyberspace, 205–7; acquiring knowledge through 108–10; advice from, 90; and community, 3, 114, 116–27, 132–37, 139–43, 205–7; birth of era of, 17–19; chat rooms, 113–14, 148–50, 208; deviant subcultures in, 123, 208; effect on self-injury, 163–66; flame wars in, 148; intimacy in, 144–45; message boards, 44–45, 51, 111–14, 208; regulation of groups in, 120–21; relationships in, 144–66; research via, 41–51; roles in, 128–32; romantic relations in, 148–50; support groups in, 74, 112–13, 120–25, 208; transience in, 139–43,

150–51, 159–61, 208, 225n3, 226n13; trust and misrepresentation in, 147–50, 226n7; types of participation in, 110–14; versus solid world, 146–47, 151–63, 206, 208, 220n19

Diagnostic and Statistical Manual of Mental Disorders, 22–23, 210, 229n26

Eating disorders, 18, 76, 103, 106, 125, 215, 216, 217, 227n13, 227n14, 228n15, 228n4, 229n6, 229n15, 230n39

Emo, 2, 169–72, 181

Emotions, 23, 25, 28, 30, 33, 35, 38, 40, 53, 57, 59, 67–73, 75, 77–78, 84, 85, 86, 87–88, 89–90, 96, 99, 102, 105–6, 109, 123, 128, 135, 136, 137, 140, 141, 147, 151, 155, 158, 159, 168, 170, 171, 173, 178, 181, 182, 186, 187, 188, 190, 191, 192, 193, 194, 197, 204, 216, 222n62, 222n64

Endorphin/dopamine rush, 72, 74, 75, 76, 78, 87, 224n2, 224n6

Favazza, A., 23, 200, 219n8, 219n11, 219n12, 220n5, 220n7, 220n12, 224n22

Feminist perspective, model of self-injury, 4, 25–27, 200–203, 221n27, 227–28n14

Goth, 2, 11, 19, 57, 58, 63, 75, 79, 85, 86, 88, 96, 117, 158, 169–72, 181, 183, 227n7

Homosocial bonding, 13

Institutional review, 39, 42, 223n13

Isolation, 94–95, 97–99, 127, 154–59, 163, 208

Jeffreys, S. 26–27, 201, 221n27

Panopticon, 5, 202, 204
Picking, 11–12, 109
Postmodern perspective: model of self-injury, 27–28, 206–7; view of self, 27–28
Psycho-medical perspective: causes, 24–25; disease model of, 134–36, 186, 216; disorders, 23–24, 53–54, 67, 70 71, 74, 75, 80, 87, 89, 118, 124, 155, 210; effects, 25; medications, 54, 68, 104, 185, 187, 194, 210, 215, 223n1, 230n36, 230n37; model of self-injury, 22–25; psychiatric wards, 59–60, 92–93, 124, 229n25; rejection of, 212; therapists, 68, 100, 117, 194, 210

Rebellion, 31, 55, 57, 62, 65, 96, 97, 201, 204
Religion, 14, 31, 96, 97, 105, 133–34, 201, 209, 224n19

Scratching, 12–13; 88, 116, 129
Self-injurers: age and, 33–35, 116–18, 129–32, 160, 183, 186, 187, 193–94, 208, 214, 217, 222n61, 222n62; careers of, 64–65; gender and, 2, 13, 35–36, 68–69, 70, 75, 82–83, 106, 158–59, 201–3, 214, 216, 217; hospitalization of, 91–93, 97, 100, 102, 117, 185; identification as, 137–39; in the military, 17–18, 37, 200, 222–23n64; in prisons, 17, 222n63; race and social class of, 17, 36–7, 201, 208, 214, 215, 217, 222n60
Self-injury: adolescent stress and, 31–33; aging out of, 34–35; as a fad, 2, 18–19, 31, 183, 208, 216, 217; awareness of, 15–17, 38, 59, 109–10, 208, 213, 216; being discovered, 90; celebrities and, 15, 16, 30, 74, 76, 169, 170, 219n15, 219n16; control and, 76; family conflict and, 69, 70, 74,

80, 83, 185; focus on blood and, 31, 59, 61, 83, 85, 86–87, 88, 116, 175, 227n12; history of, 14–17; implements for, 7, 13, 58, 62, 68, 83–85, 125; location for performing, 81–83; managing, 188–90; media and, 7, 33, 57–59, 61, 62, 76, 201, 205, 216; motivations for, 32, 53–55, 66–73, 77–78; onset of, 55–60, 64–65, 181–82; planning and, 172–75; positive orientation toward, 120–25, 137–39, 164–65, 176–80, 187–88, 225n7, 227n13; preparation for, 85–86; prevalence of, 3, 6, 19, 29–30, 33–37, 221n44, 221n48, 222n49, 222n54, 222n57, 222n60; 222n62, 222n63, 222n64; 227n7; progression of, 60–65, 79, 96, 188–90; quitting, 165–66, 182–86, 190–96, 228n3, 228n5, 228n5, 228n6, 228n7, 228n8; rationalizations for, 73–78, 95–97, 228n16; relation to alcohol and drugs, 185, 228n3, 228n4; revealing of, 153; sexual assault and, 68, 111, 112–13; social contagion of, 3, 59–60, 81, 100, 106, 167–72, 217, 227n2; social participation and, 175–76; terms for, 3–4, 14; timing of, 78–81; types of, 1, 5–14, 77, 114
Stigma, 2, 115, 133–37, 204, 207–17; and shame, 103; concealable locations and, 126; disclosure, 226n15; of disease, 134–36, 209–10; doubly stigmatized groups, 227n10; of mental illness, 90, 101, 117, 208, 215, 229n25; moral passage and, 212–217; rejection of, 158–59, 179, 180, 212; of sin, 133–34, 209, 229n25; of suicidality, 101, 208; of voluntary choice, 136–37, 210, 212, 216
Suicide: attempts at, 64, 87, 97, 112; inclination against, 1, 72–73, 97, 104, 224n25; inclination toward, 24, 72–73, 104, 130

About the Authors

PATRICIA A. ADLER is Professor of Sociology at the University of Colorado. PETER ADLER is Professor of Sociology at the University of Denver. They are the coauthors and coeditors of numerous books, including *Momentum, Wheeling and Dealing, Membership Roles in Field Research, Backboard & Blackboards, Peer Power, Paradise Laborers, Constructions of Deviance,* and *Sociological Odyssey.*